LOOKIT!
COMEDY & MAYHEM
VOL. # 1

a CHEESE RELATED MISHAP AND OTHER STORIES

by **Ray Friesen**

Don't Eat Any Bugs Productions · California

LOOKIT! COMEDY & MAYHEM VOL. 1

Table of Contents

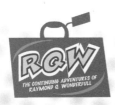

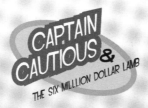

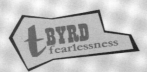

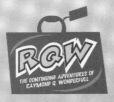

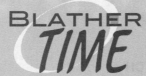

Introduction

Hi! I'm Ray. I'm responsible for all this nonsense. I started my cartooning career at age 12, and here I am, a certain number of years later (hint: somewhere between 4 & 6) hoping you'll enjoy this volume of my wordage and drawage.

I have to warn you that there's quite a lot of silliness, but it's all of the highest caliber. Also, my stories tend to be character-driven. Oh, sure, there's a plot, but it comes and goes. Don't be overly concerned.

I can truly be proud to say that this is genuinely an "All Ages Humor" book. I can say this because at least two people have read it, and they're definitely not the same age.

So, while you're enjoying the comedy and mayhem, make sure you pay attention, as there'll be a short quiz at the end.

Sincerely,

Ray Friesen

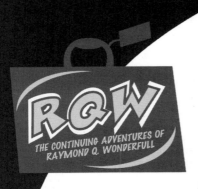

RQW
THE CONTINUING ADVENTURES OF RAYMOND Q. WONDERFULL

a CHEESE RELATED MISHAP

PART 1: WHO ARE ALL THESE PEOPLE?

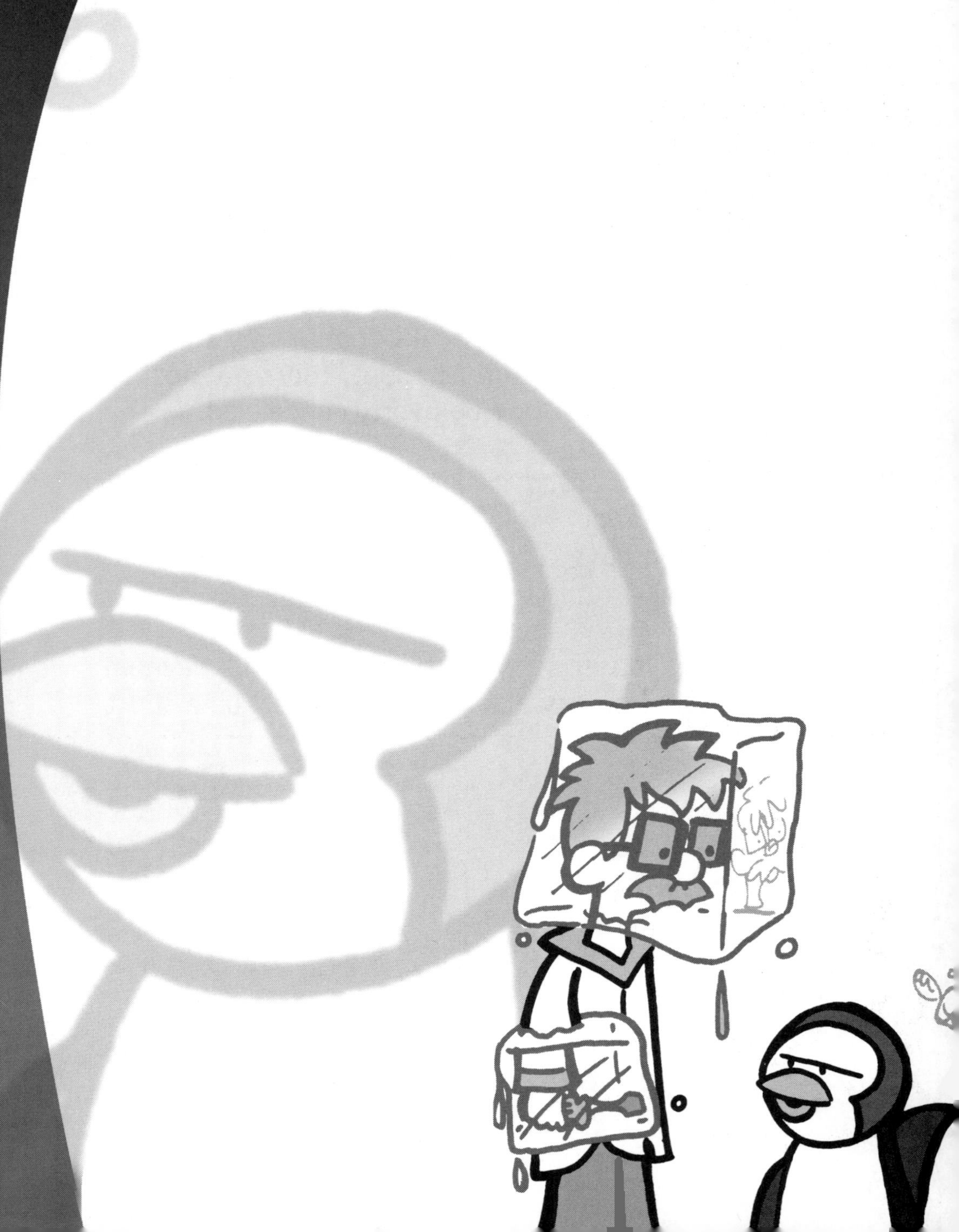

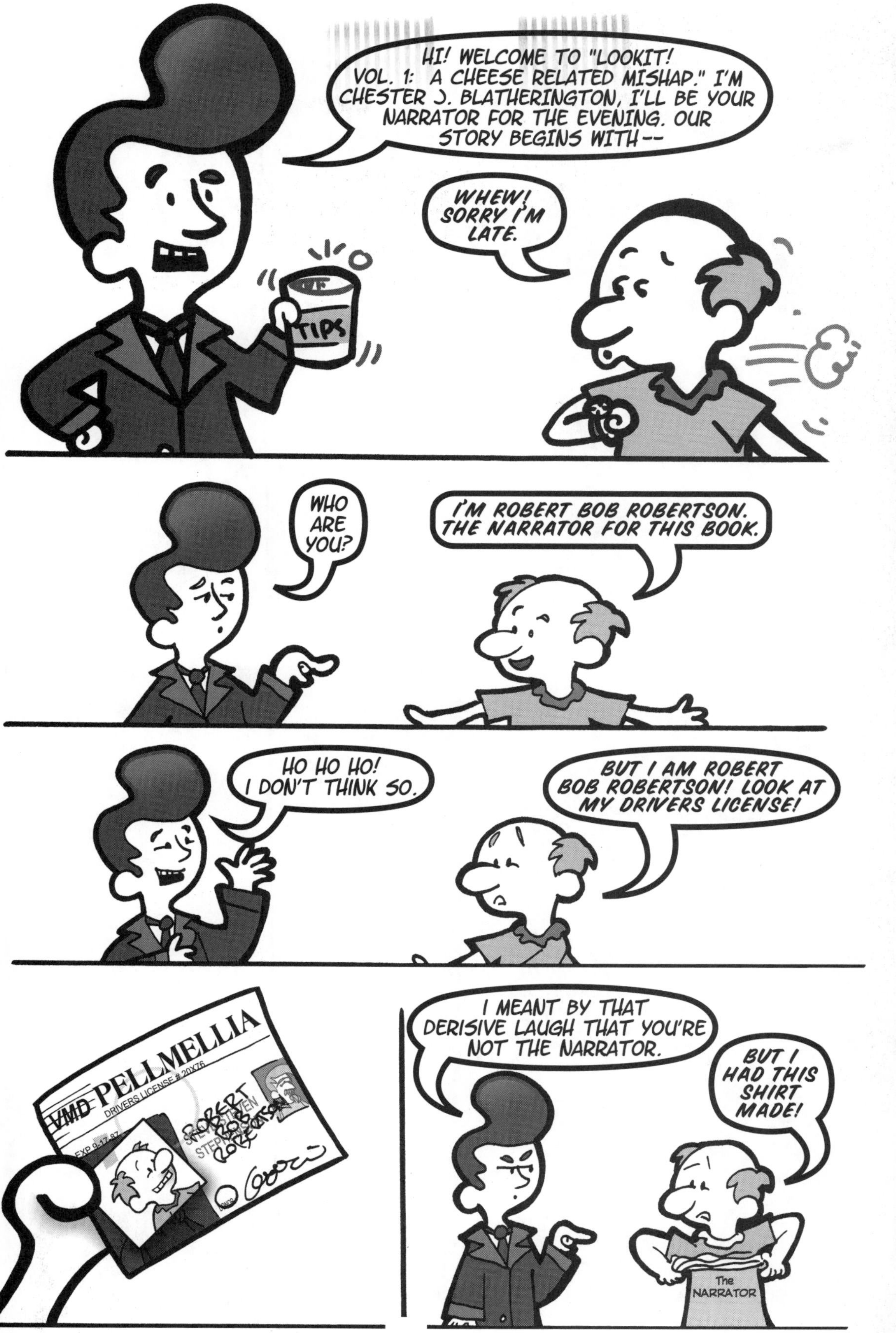
HI! WELCOME TO "LOOKIT! VOL. 1: A CHEESE RELATED MISHAP." I'M CHESTER J. BLATHERINGTON, I'LL BE YOUR NARRATOR FOR THE EVENING. OUR STORY BEGINS WITH--
TIPS
WHEW! SORRY I'M LATE.
WHO ARE YOU?
I'M ROBERT BOB ROBERTSON. THE NARRATOR FOR THIS BOOK.
HO HO HO! I DON'T THINK SO.
BUT I AM ROBERT BOB ROBERTSON! LOOK AT MY DRIVERS LICENSE!
VMD PELLMELLIA
DRIVERS LICENSE # 20X76
ROBERT BOB ROBERTSON
I MEANT BY THAT DERISIVE LAUGH THAT YOU'RE NOT THE NARRATOR.
BUT I HAD THIS SHIRT MADE!
The NARRATOR

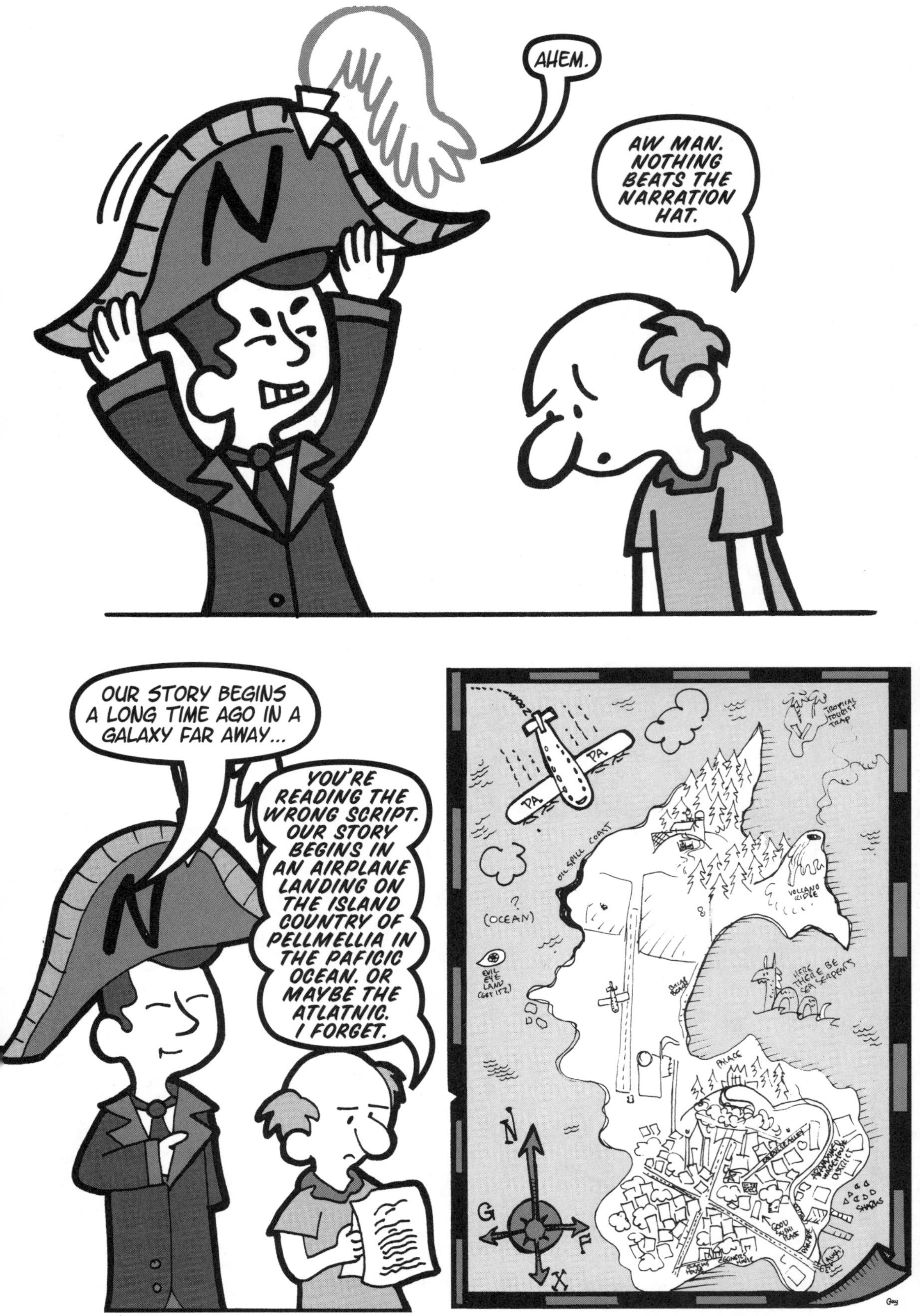
AHEM.
AW MAN. NOTHING BEATS THE NARRATION HAT.
N
OUR STORY BEGINS A LONG TIME AGO IN A GALAXY FAR AWAY...
YOU'RE READING THE WRONG SCRIPT. OUR STORY BEGINS IN AN AIRPLANE LANDING ON THE ISLAND COUNTRY OF PELLMELLIA IN THE PAFICIC OCEAN. OR MAYBE THE ATLATNIC. I FORGET.
N
PA.
PA.
TROPICAL TOURIST TRAP
OIL SPILL COAST
(OCEAN)
EVIL EYE LAND
HERE THERE BE SEA SERPENTS
PALACE
SHARKS
N
G
F
X

NOW, ON WITH THE STORY!

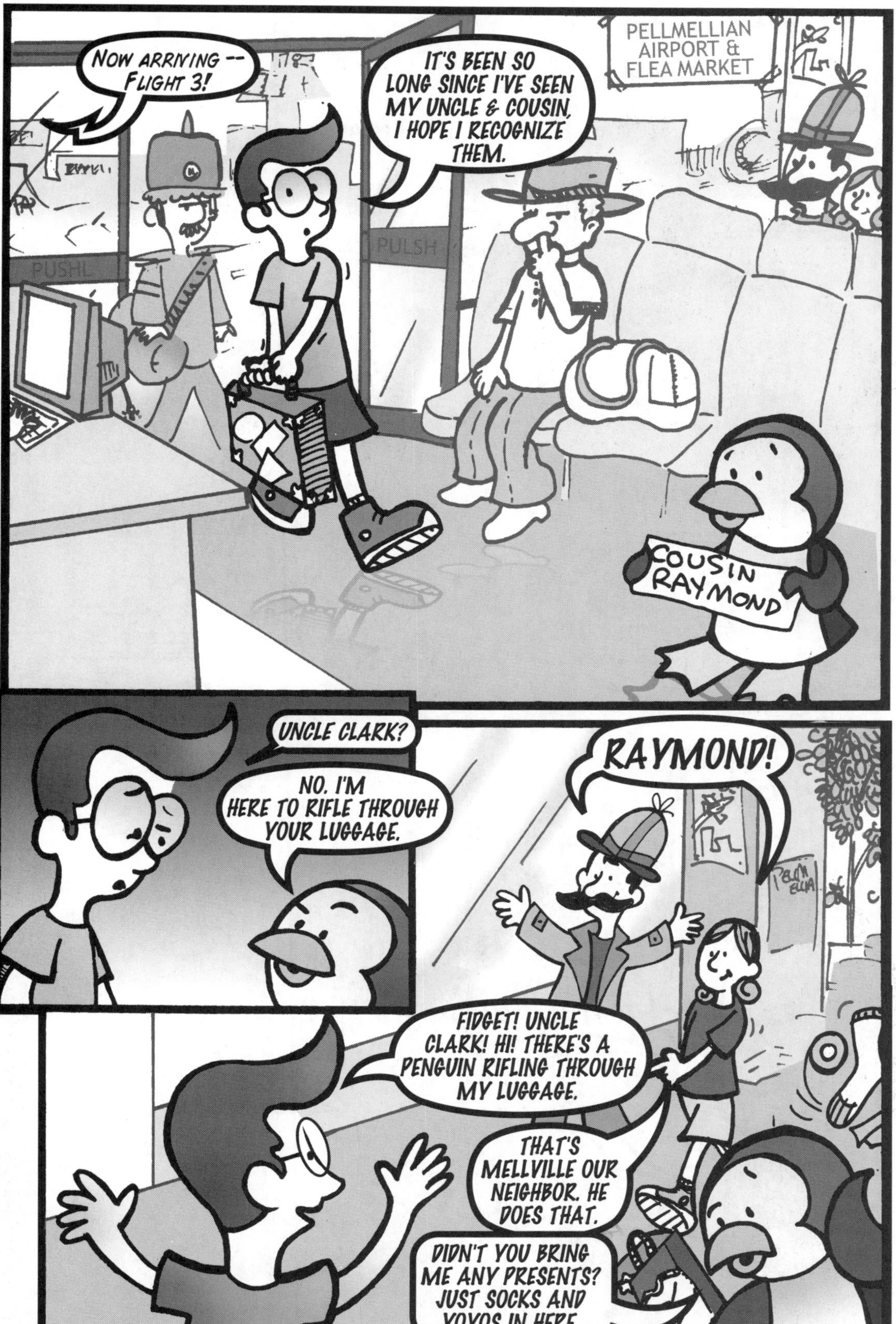
PELLMELLIAN AIRPORT & FLEA MARKET
NOW ARRIVING -- FLIGHT 3!
IT'S BEEN SO LONG SINCE I'VE SEEN MY UNCLE & COUSIN, I HOPE I RECOGNIZE THEM.
PUSH
PUSH
COUSIN RAYMOND
UNCLE CLARK?
NO. I'M HERE TO RIFLE THROUGH YOUR LUGGAGE.
RAYMOND!
FIDGET! UNCLE CLARK! HI! THERE'S A PENGUIN RIFLING THROUGH MY LUGGAGE.
THAT'S MELLVILLE OUR NEIGHBOR. HE DOES THAT.
DIDN'T YOU BRING ME ANY PRESENTS? JUST SOCKS AND YOYOS IN HERE.

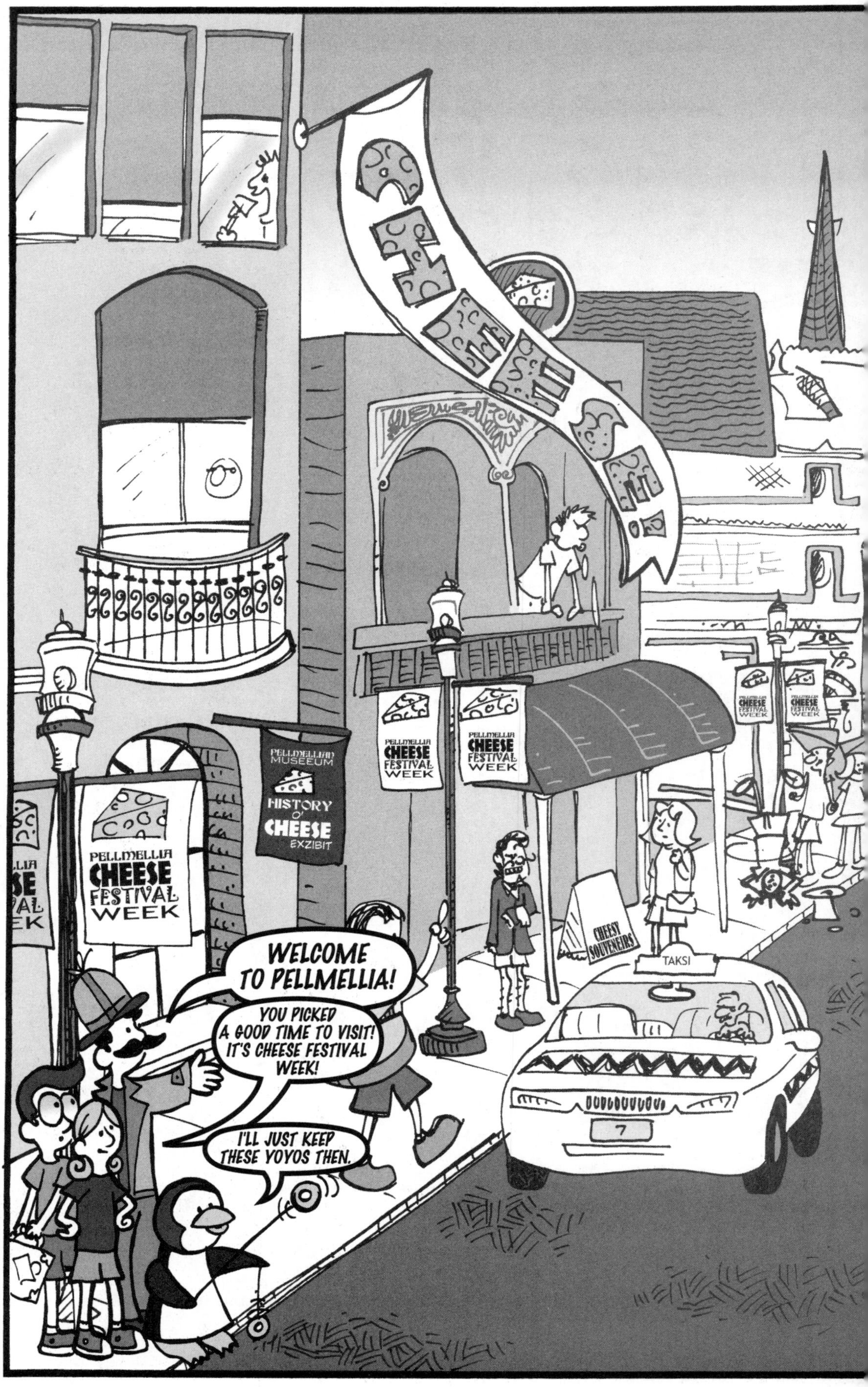
PELLMELLIAN MUSEUM
HISTORY O' CHEESE EXZIBIT
PELLMELLIA CHEESE FESTIVAL WEEK
CHEESY SOUVENEIRS
TAKSI
7
WELCOME TO PELLMELLIA!
YOU PICKED A GOOD TIME TO VISIT! IT'S CHEESE FESTIVAL WEEK!
I'LL JUST KEEP THESE YOYOS THEN.

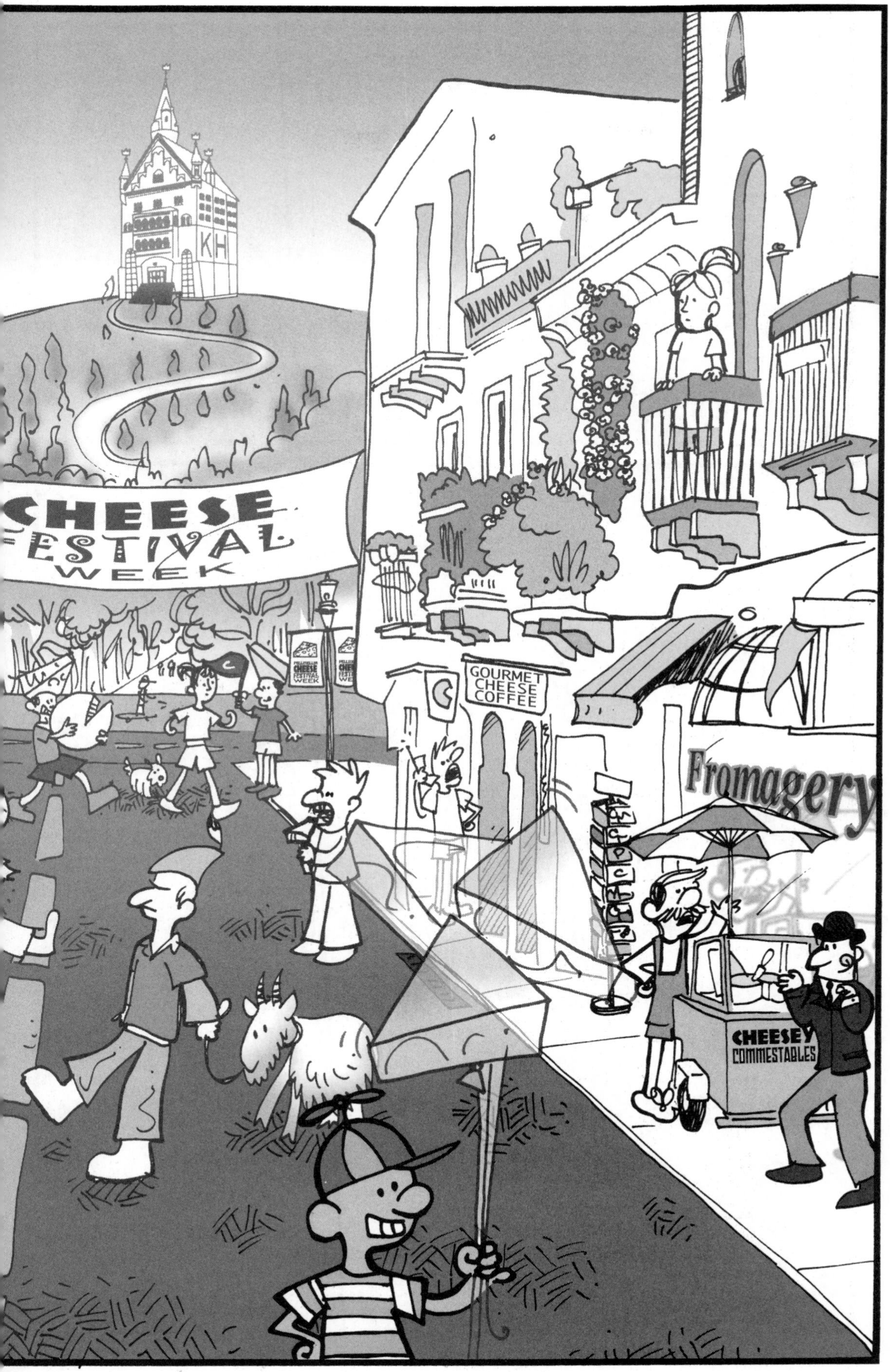
CHEESE
FESTIVAL
WEEK
CHEESE
FESTIVAL
WEEK
GOURMET
CHEESE
COFFEE
Fromagery
CHEESEY
COMMESTABLES

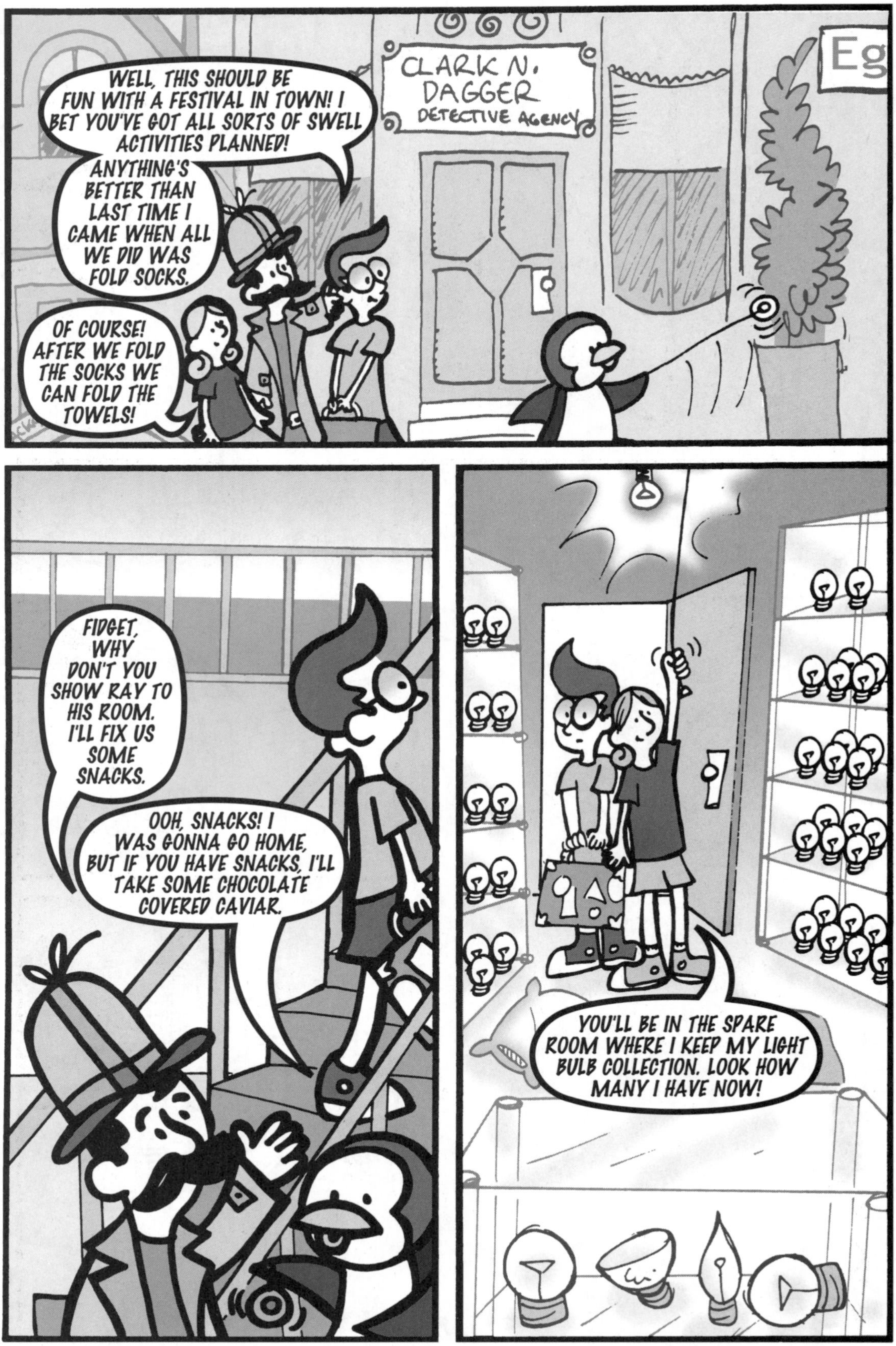
CLARK N. DAGGER DETECTIVE AGENCY
WELL, THIS SHOULD BE FUN WITH A FESTIVAL IN TOWN! I BET YOU'VE GOT ALL SORTS OF SWELL ACTIVITIES PLANNED!
ANYTHING'S BETTER THAN LAST TIME I CAME WHEN ALL WE DID WAS FOLD SOCKS.
OF COURSE! AFTER WE FOLD THE SOCKS WE CAN FOLD THE TOWELS!
FIDGET, WHY DON'T YOU SHOW RAY TO HIS ROOM. I'LL FIX US SOME SNACKS.
OOH, SNACKS! I WAS GONNA GO HOME, BUT IF YOU HAVE SNACKS, I'LL TAKE SOME CHOCOLATE COVERED CAVIAR.
YOU'LL BE IN THE SPARE ROOM WHERE I KEEP MY LIGHT BULB COLLECTION. LOOK HOW MANY I HAVE NOW!

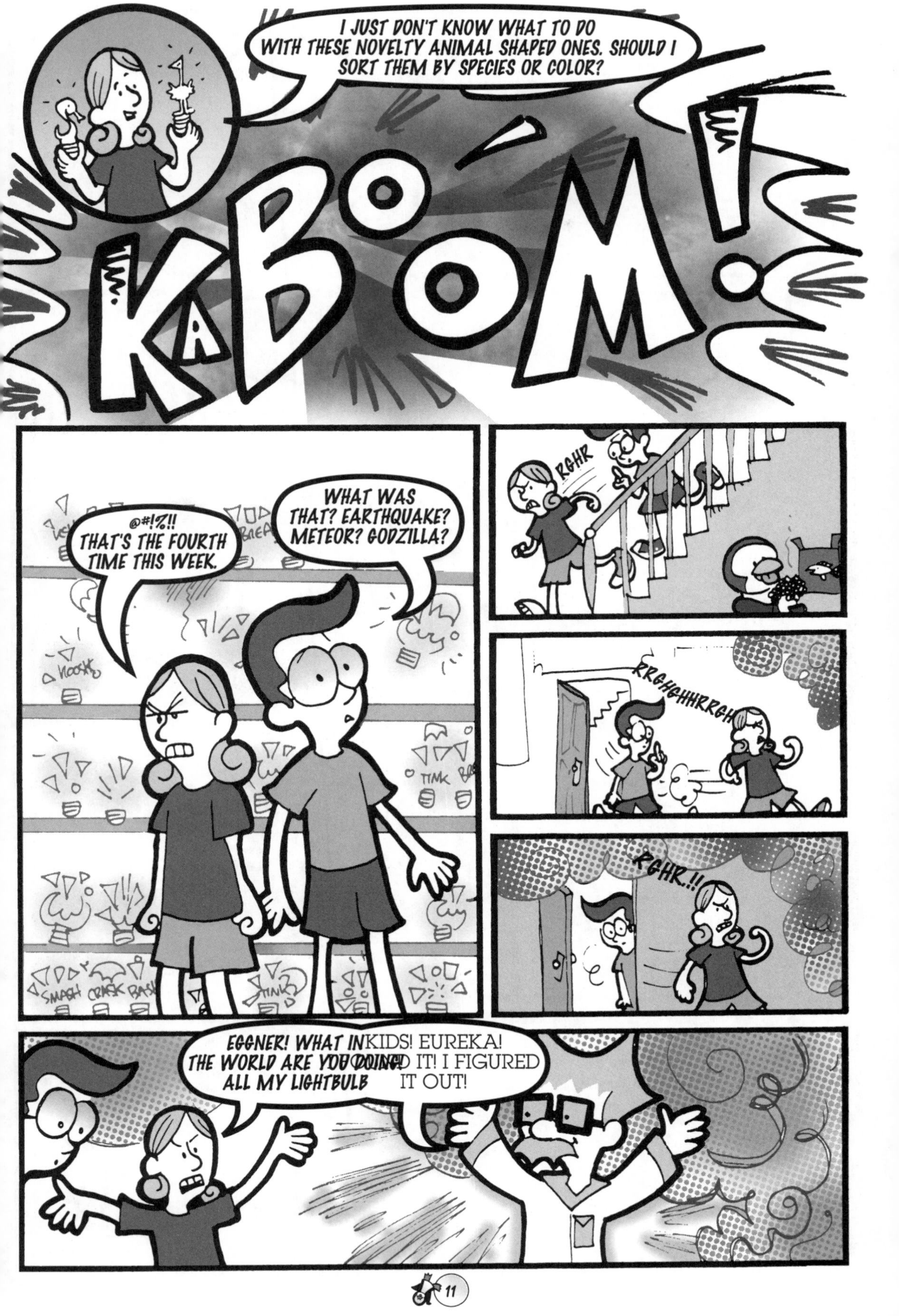
I JUST DON'T KNOW WHAT TO DO WITH THESE NOVELTY ANIMAL SHAPED ONES. SHOULD I SORT THEM BY SPECIES OR COLOR?
KABOOM!
@#!%!! THAT'S THE FOURTH TIME THIS WEEK.
WHAT WAS THAT? EARTHQUAKE? METEOR? GODZILLA?
RGHR
RRGHGHHRRGH
RGHR.!!
EGGNER! WHAT IN THE WORLD ARE YOU DOING! ALL MY LIGHTBULB
KIDS! EUREKA! D IT! I FIGURED IT OUT!

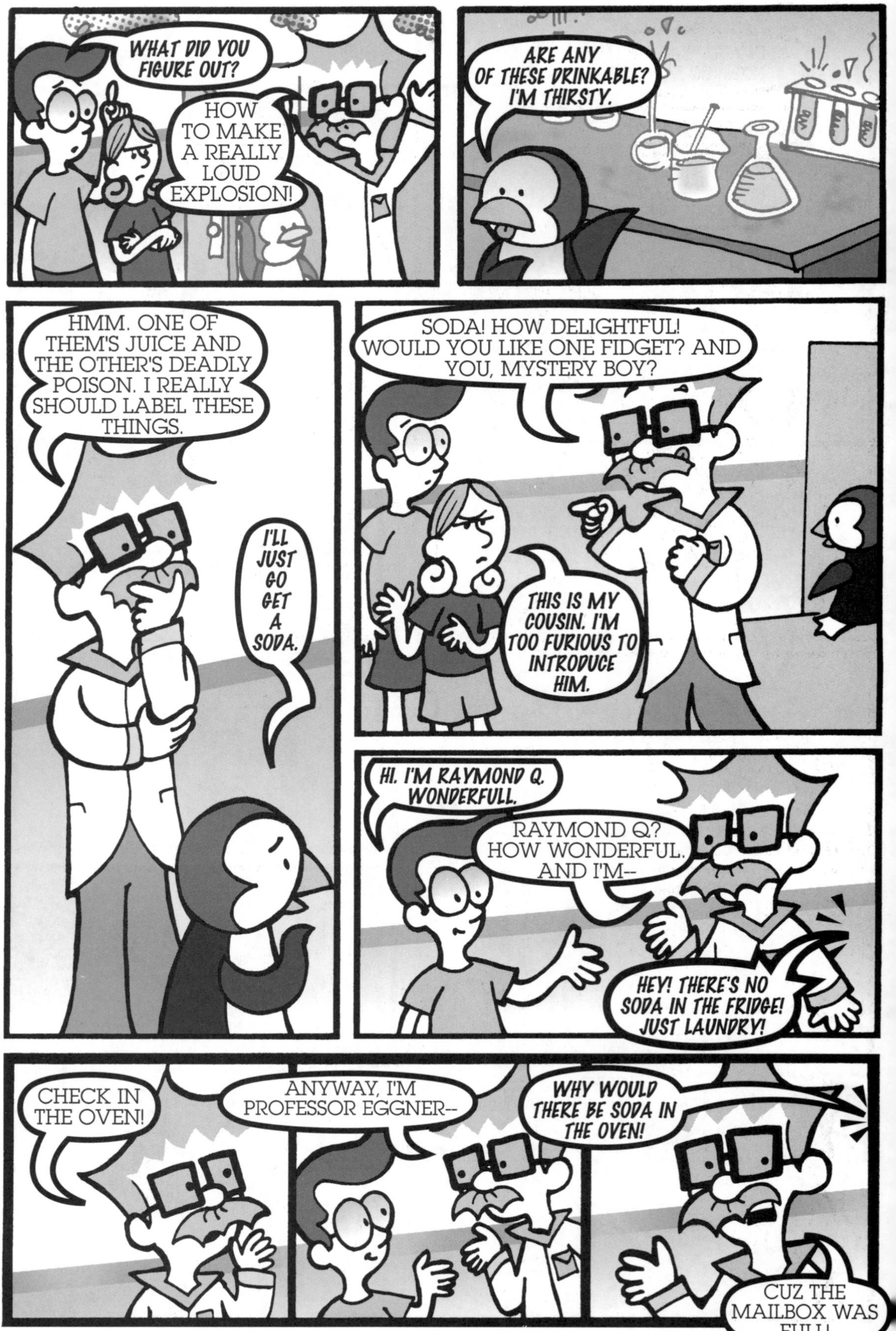
WHAT DID YOU FIGURE OUT?
HOW TO MAKE A REALLY LOUD EXPLOSION!
ARE ANY OF THESE DRINKABLE? I'M THIRSTY.
HMM. ONE OF THEM'S JUICE AND THE OTHER'S DEADLY POISON. I REALLY SHOULD LABEL THESE THINGS.
I'LL JUST GO GET A SODA.
SODA! HOW DELIGHTFUL! WOULD YOU LIKE ONE FIDGET? AND YOU, MYSTERY BOY?
THIS IS MY COUSIN. I'M TOO FURIOUS TO INTRODUCE HIM.
HI. I'M RAYMOND Q. WONDERFULL.
RAYMOND Q? HOW WONDERFUL. AND I'M--
HEY! THERE'S NO SODA IN THE FRIDGE! JUST LAUNDRY!
CHECK IN THE OVEN!
ANYWAY, I'M PROFESSOR EGGNER--
WHY WOULD THERE BE SODA IN THE OVEN!
CUZ THE MAILBOX WAS FULL!

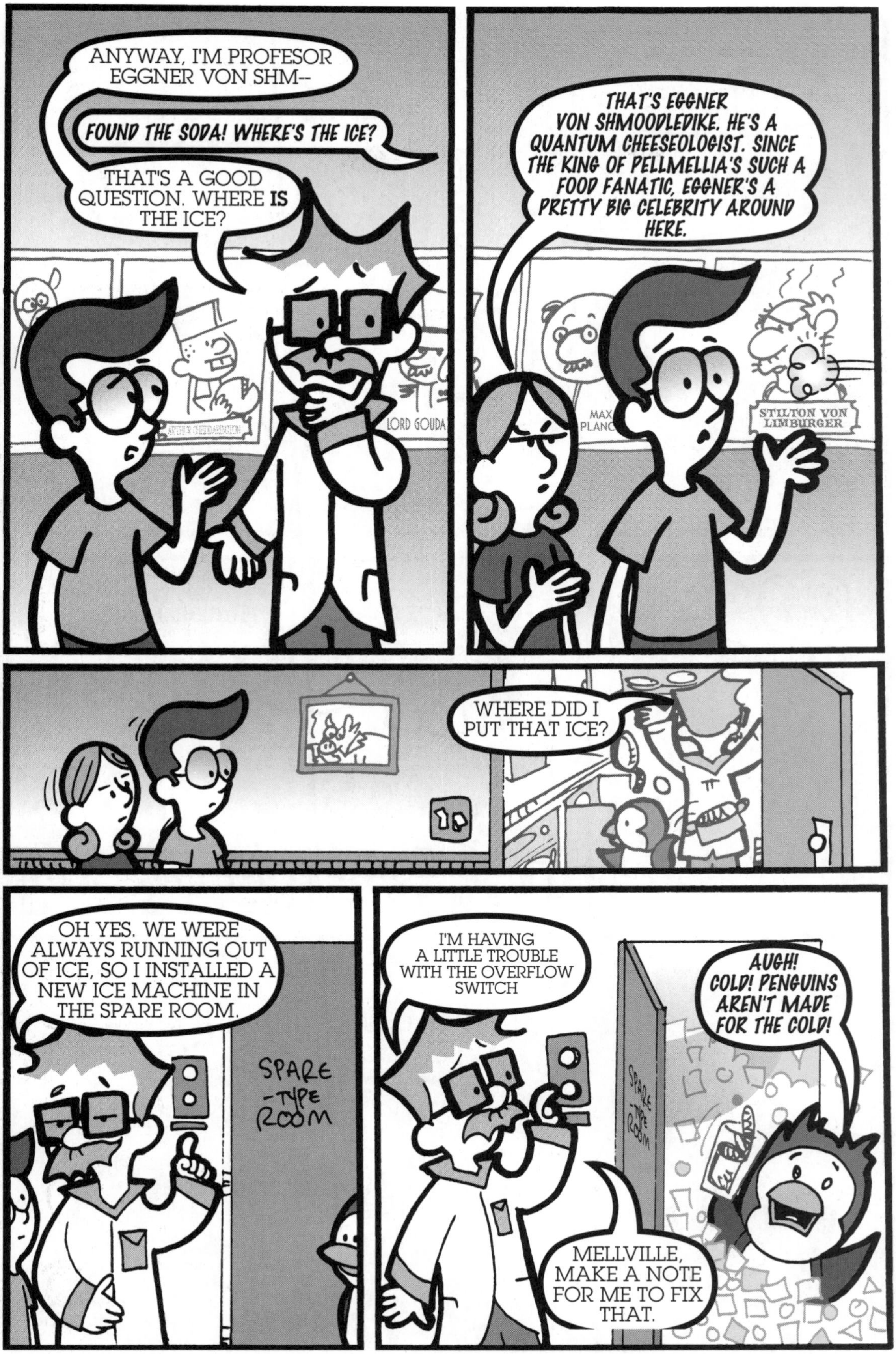
ANYWAY, I'M PROFESOR EGGNER VON SHM--
FOUND THE SODA! WHERE'S THE ICE?
THAT'S A GOOD QUESTION. WHERE **IS** THE ICE?
LORD GOUDA
THAT'S EGGNER VON SHMOODLEDIKE. HE'S A QUANTUM CHEESEOLOGIST. SINCE THE KING OF PELLMELLIA'S SUCH A FOOD FANATIC, EGGNER'S A PRETTY BIG CELEBRITY AROUND HERE.
MAX PLANC
STILTON VON LIMBURGER
WHERE DID I PUT THAT ICE?
OH YES. WE WERE ALWAYS RUNNING OUT OF ICE, SO I INSTALLED A NEW ICE MACHINE IN THE SPARE ROOM.
SPARE -TYPE ROOM
I'M HAVING A LITTLE TROUBLE WITH THE OVERFLOW SWITCH
AUGH! COLD! PENGUINS AREN'T MADE FOR THE COLD!
SPARE -TYPE ROOM
MELLVILLE, MAKE A NOTE FOR ME TO FIX THAT.

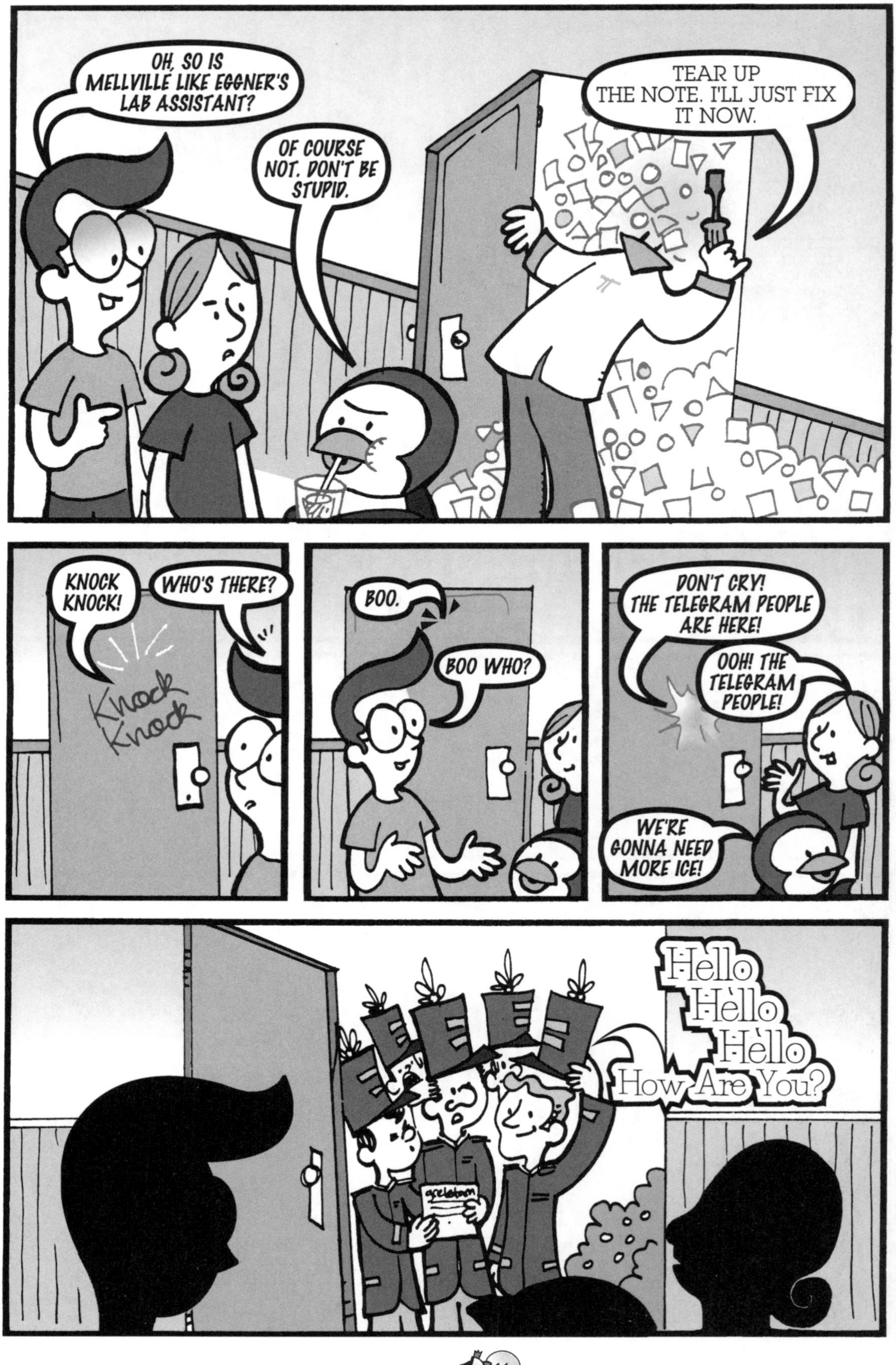
OH, SO IS MELLVILLE LIKE EGGNER'S LAB ASSISTANT?
OF COURSE NOT. DON'T BE STUPID.
TEAR UP THE NOTE. I'LL JUST FIX IT NOW.
KNOCK KNOCK!
WHO'S THERE?
Knock Knock
BOO.
BOO WHO?
DON'T CRY! THE TELEGRAM PEOPLE ARE HERE!
OOH! THE TELEGRAM PEOPLE!
WE'RE GONNA NEED MORE ICE!
Hello Hello Hello How Are You?

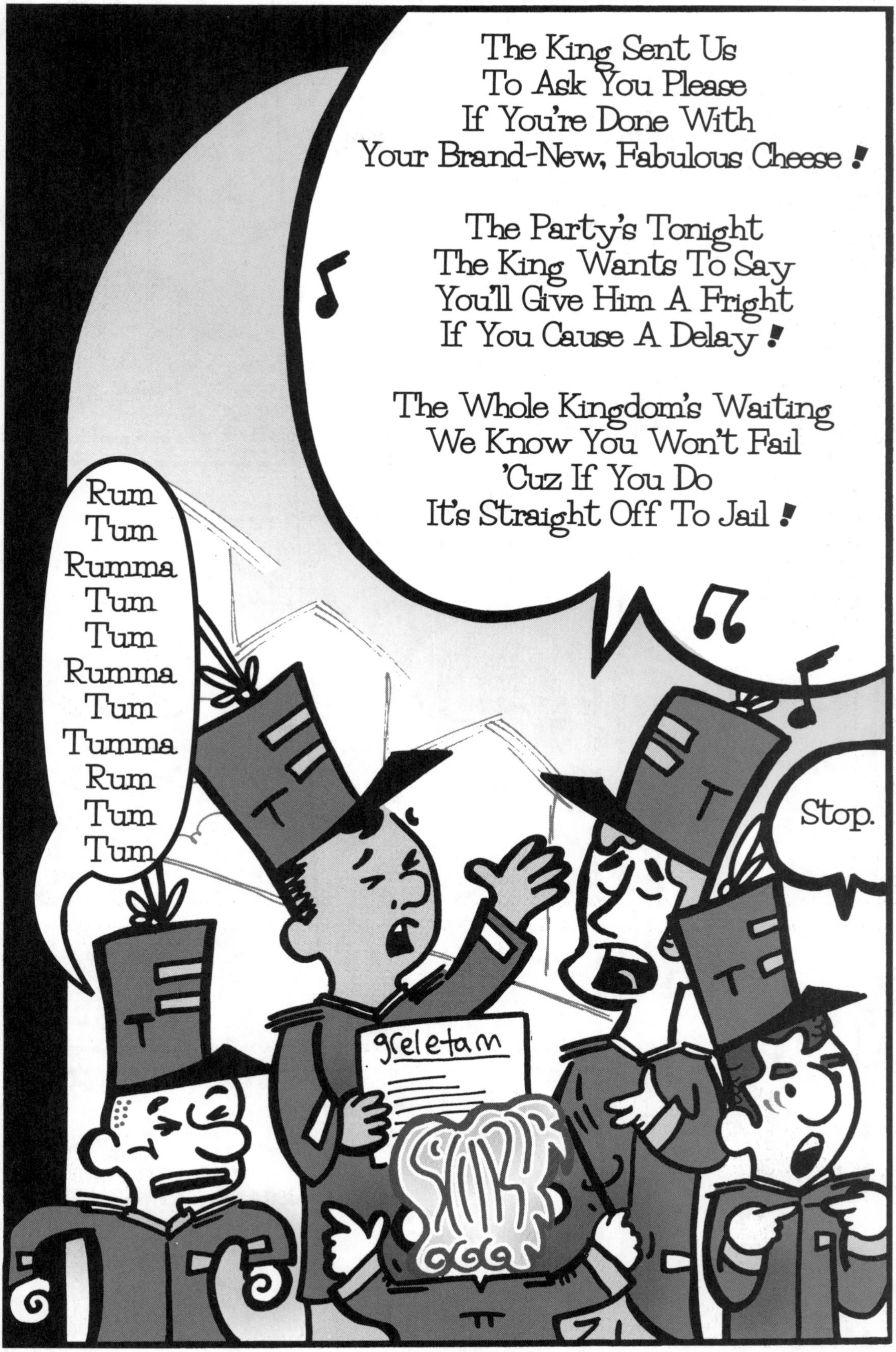
The King Sent Us To Ask You Please If You're Done With Your Brand-New, Fabulous Cheese!
The Party's Tonight The King Wants To Say You'll Give Him A Fright If You Cause A Delay!
The Whole Kingdom's Waiting We Know You Won't Fail 'Cuz If You Do It's Straight Off To Jail!
Rum Tum Rumma Tum Tum Rumma Tum Tumma Rum Tum Tum
Stop.
greletam

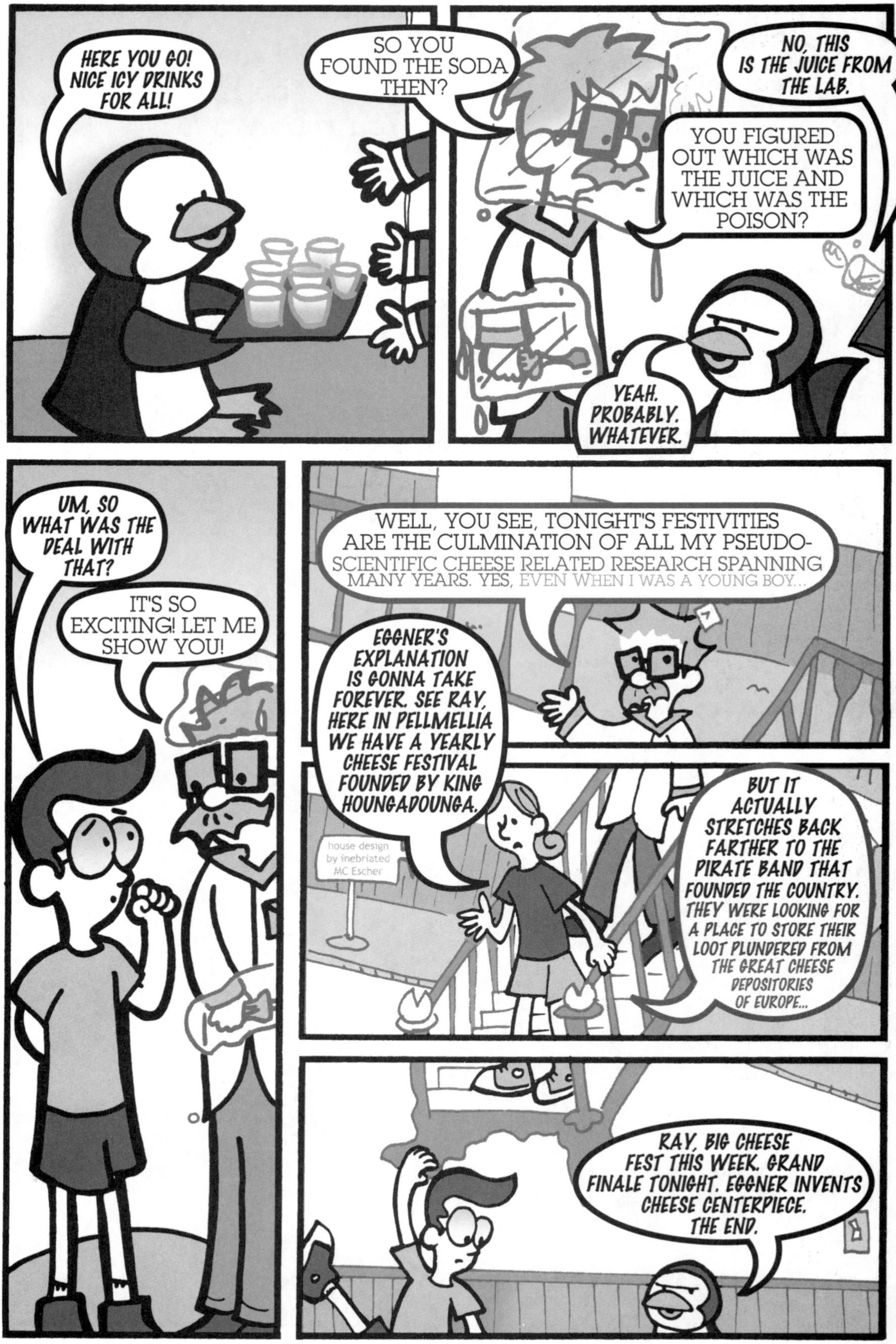
HERE YOU GO! NICE ICY DRINKS FOR ALL!
SO YOU FOUND THE SODA THEN?
NO, THIS IS THE JUICE FROM THE LAB.
YOU FIGURED OUT WHICH WAS THE JUICE AND WHICH WAS THE POISON?
YEAH. PROBABLY. WHATEVER.
UM, SO WHAT WAS THE DEAL WITH THAT?
IT'S SO EXCITING! LET ME SHOW YOU!
WELL, YOU SEE, TONIGHT'S FESTIVITIES ARE THE CULMINATION OF ALL MY PSEUDO-SCIENTIFIC CHEESE RELATED RESEARCH SPANNING MANY YEARS. YES, EVEN WHEN I WAS A YOUNG BOY...
EGGNER'S EXPLANATION IS GONNA TAKE FOREVER. SEE RAY, HERE IN PELLMELLIA WE HAVE A YEARLY CHEESE FESTIVAL FOUNDED BY KING HOUNGADOUNGA.
house design by inebriated MC Escher
BUT IT ACTUALLY STRETCHES BACK FARTHER TO THE PIRATE BAND THAT FOUNDED THE COUNTRY. THEY WERE LOOKING FOR A PLACE TO STORE THEIR LOOT PLUNDERED FROM THE GREAT CHEESE DEPOSITORIES OF EUROPE...
RAY, BIG CHEESE FEST THIS WEEK. GRAND FINALE TONIGHT. EGGNER INVENTS CHEESE CENTERPIECE. THE END.

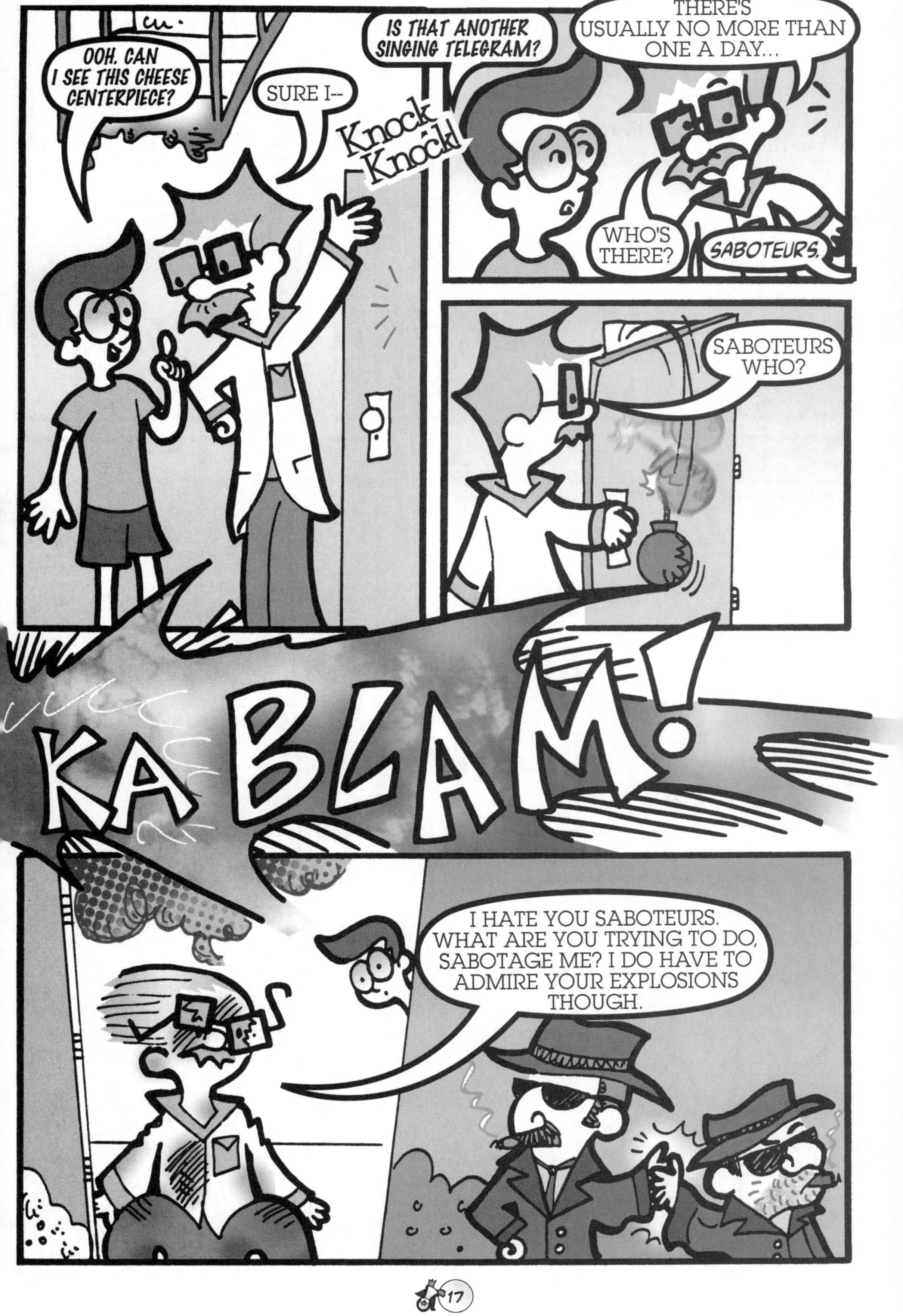

OOH. CAN I SEE THIS CHEESE CENTERPIECE?
SURE I--
Knock Knock!
IS THAT ANOTHER SINGING TELEGRAM?
THERE'S USUALLY NO MORE THAN ONE A DAY...
WHO'S THERE?
SABOTEURS.
SABOTEURS WHO?
KABLAM!
I HATE YOU SABOTEURS. WHAT ARE YOU TRYING TO DO, SABOTAGE ME? I DO HAVE TO ADMIRE YOUR EXPLOSIONS THOUGH.

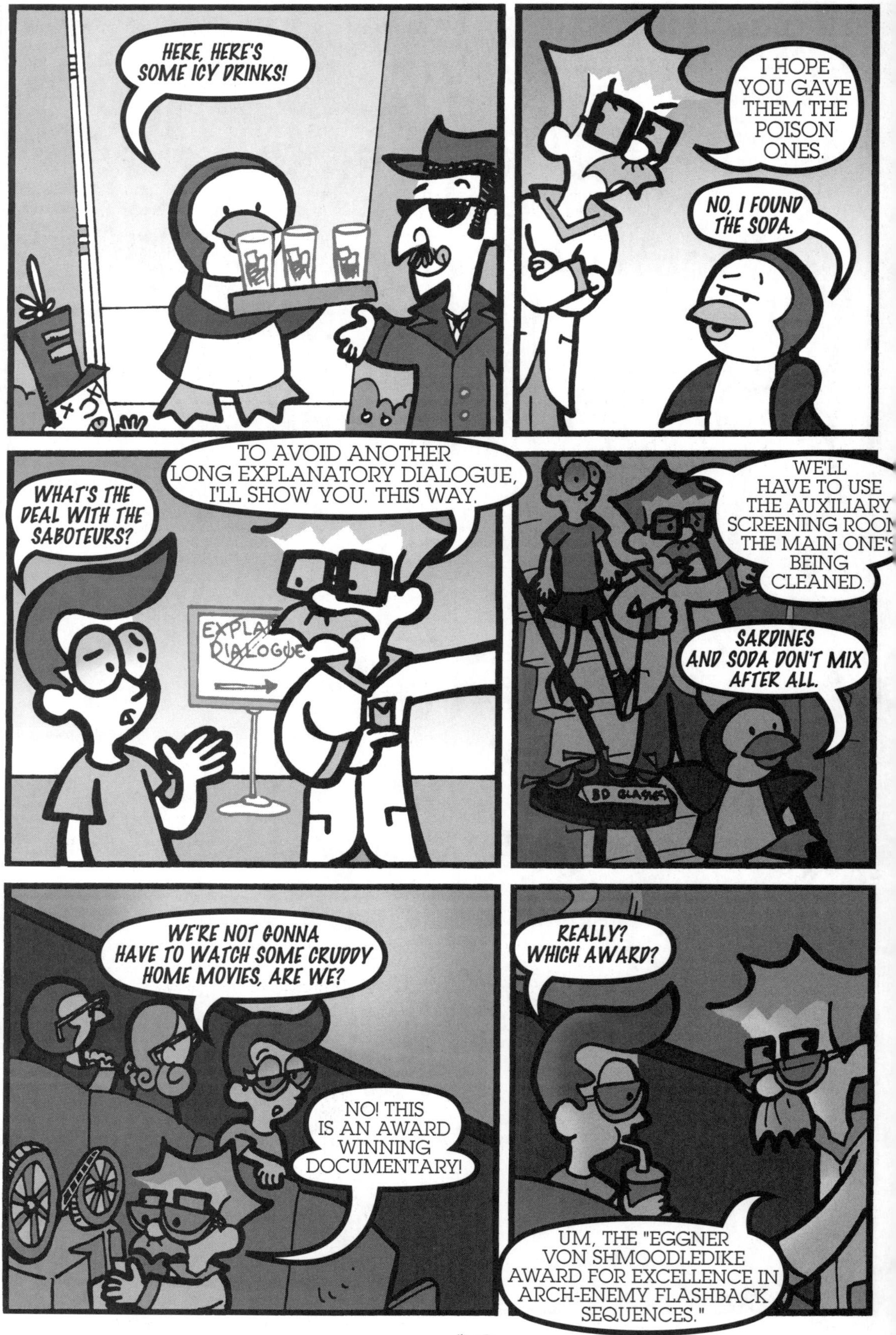

HERE, HERE'S SOME ICY DRINKS!
I HOPE YOU GAVE THEM THE POISON ONES.
NO, I FOUND THE SODA.
WHAT'S THE DEAL WITH THE SABOTEURS?
TO AVOID ANOTHER LONG EXPLANATORY DIALOGUE, I'LL SHOW YOU. THIS WAY.
WE'LL HAVE TO USE THE AUXILIARY SCREENING ROO
THE MAIN ONE'
BEING CLEANED.
SARDINES AND SODA DON'T MIX AFTER ALL.
WE'RE NOT GONNA HAVE TO WATCH SOME CRUDDY HOME MOVIES, ARE WE?
NO! THIS IS AN AWARD WINNING DOCUMENTARY!
REALLY? WHICH AWARD?
UM, THE "EGGNER VON SHMOODLEDIKE AWARD FOR EXCELLENCE IN ARCH-ENEMY FLASHBACK SEQUENCES."

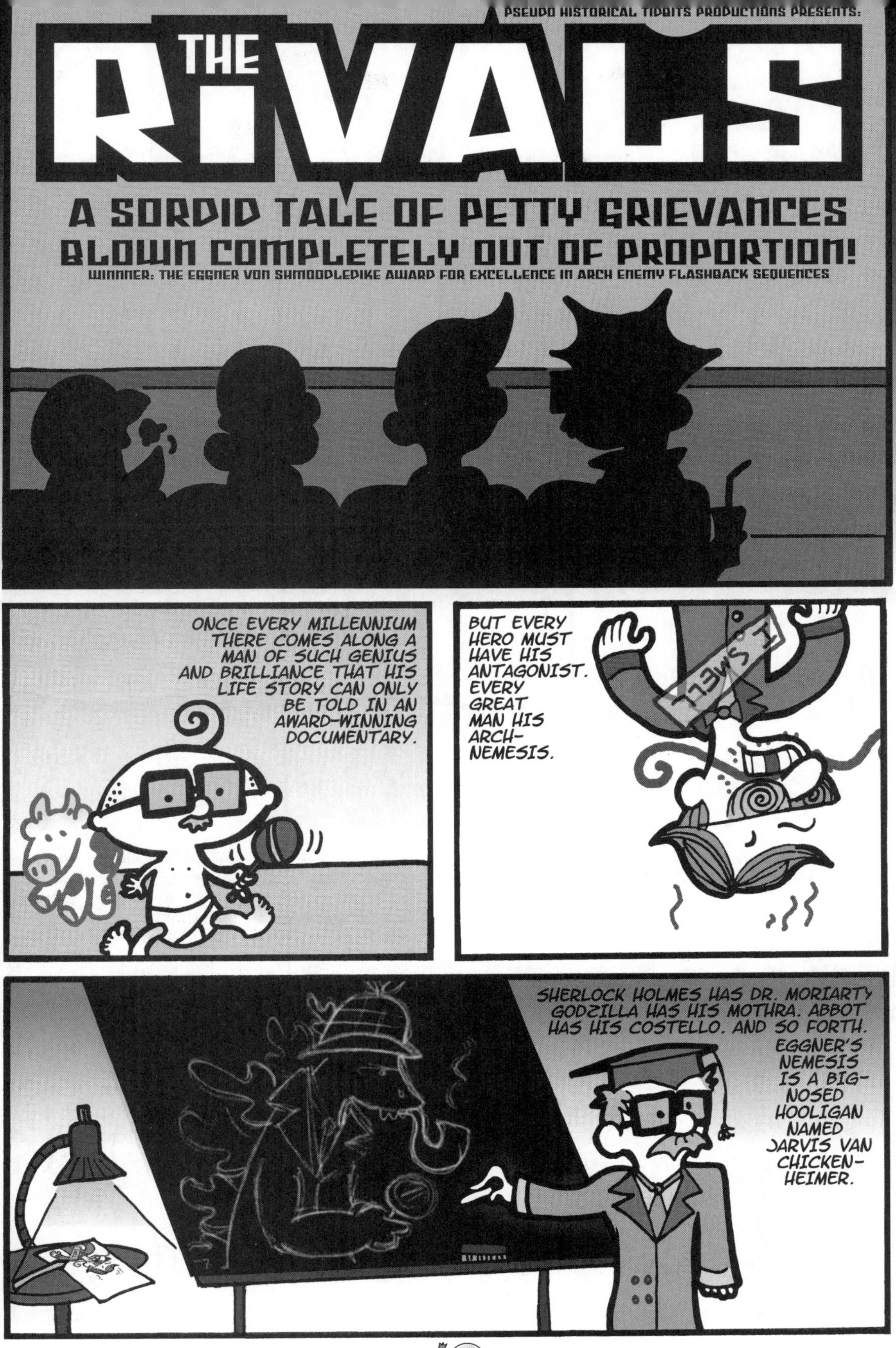
PSEUDO HISTORICAL TIDBITS PRODUCTIONS PRESENTS:
THE RIVALS
A SORDID TALE OF PETTY GRIEVANCES BLOWN COMPLETELY OUT OF PROPORTION!
WINNNER: THE EGGNER VON SHMOODLEDIKE AWARD FOR EXCELLENCE IN ARCH ENEMY FLASHBACK SEQUENCES
ONCE EVERY MILLENNIUM THERE COMES ALONG A MAN OF SUCH GENIUS AND BRILLIANCE THAT HIS LIFE STORY CAN ONLY BE TOLD IN AN AWARD-WINNING DOCUMENTARY.
BUT EVERY HERO MUST HAVE HIS ANTAGONIST. EVERY GREAT MAN HIS ARCH-NEMESIS.
I SMELL
SHERLOCK HOLMES HAS DR. MORIARTY GODZILLA HAS HIS MOTHRA. ABBOT HAS HIS COSTELLO. AND SO FORTH.
EGGNER'S NEMESIS IS A BIG-NOSED HOOLIGAN NAMED JARVIS VAN CHICKEN-HEIMER.

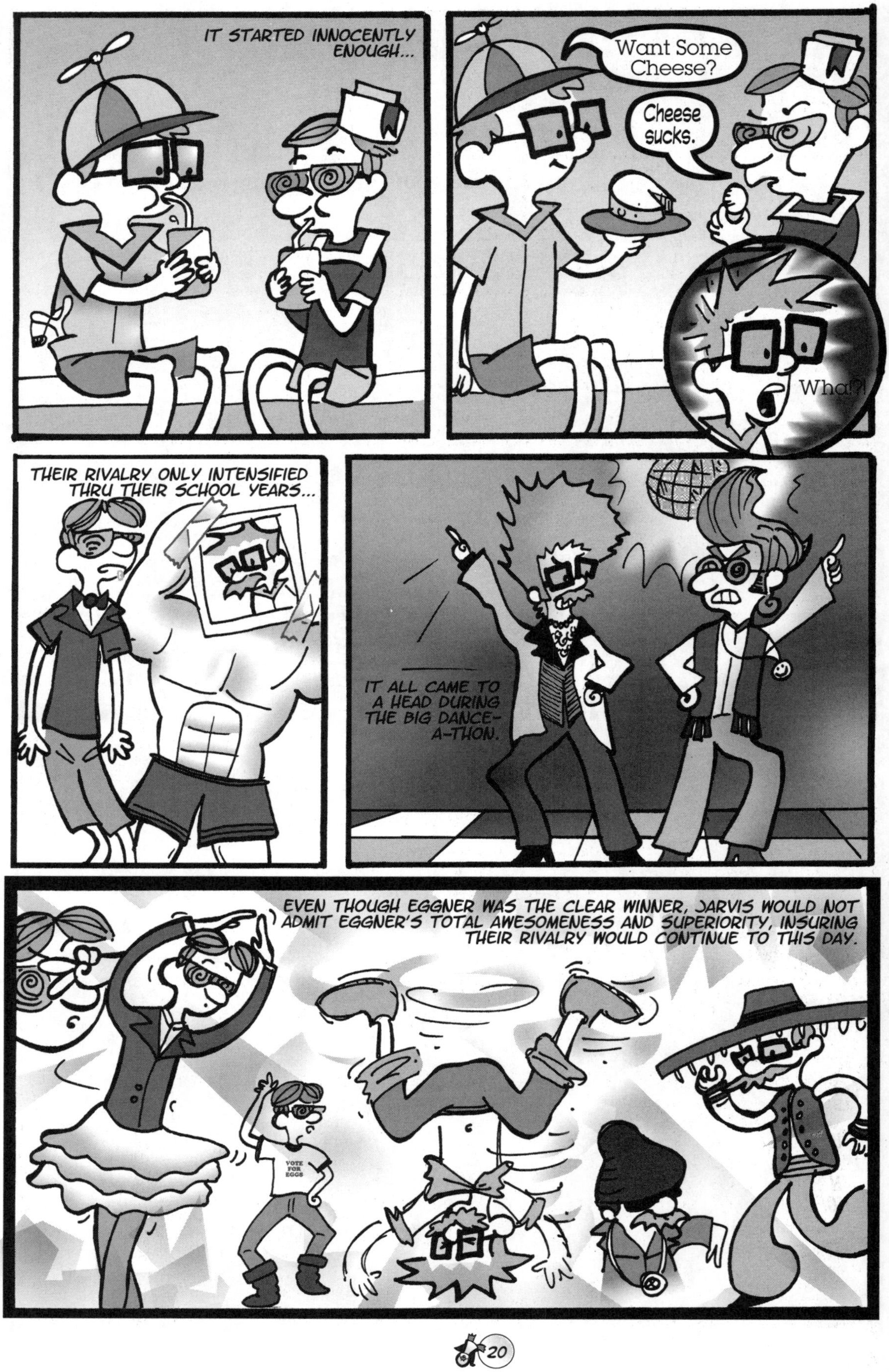
IT STARTED INNOCENTLY ENOUGH...
Want Some Cheese?
Cheese sucks.
Wha!?!
THEIR RIVALRY ONLY INTENSIFIED THRU THEIR SCHOOL YEARS...
IT ALL CAME TO A HEAD DURING THE BIG DANCE-A-THON.
EVEN THOUGH EGGNER WAS THE CLEAR WINNER, JARVIS WOULD NOT ADMIT EGGNER'S TOTAL AWESOMENESS AND SUPERIORITY, INSURING THEIR RIVALRY WOULD CONTINUE TO THIS DAY.
VOTE FOR EGGS

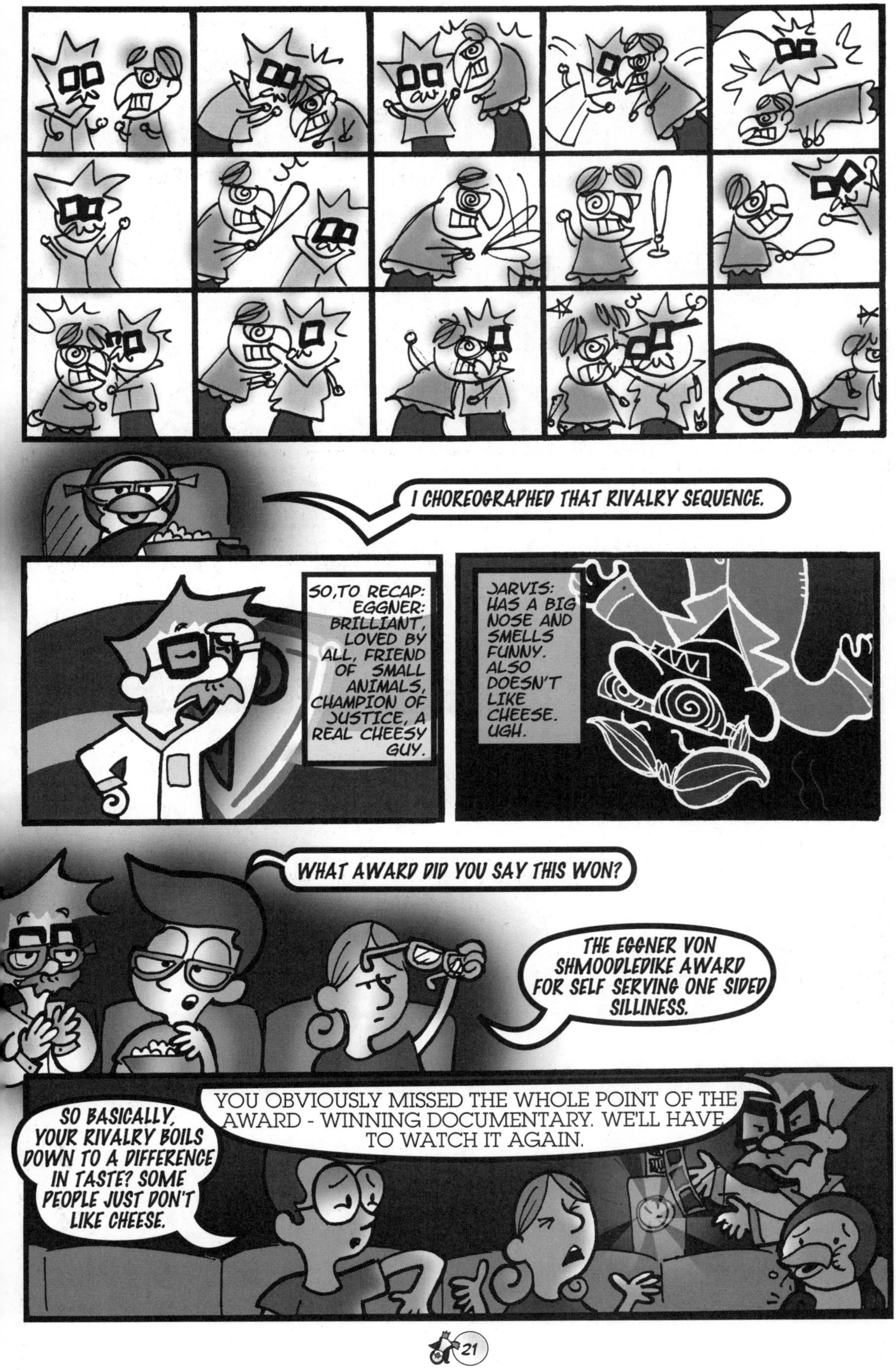
I CHOREOGRAPHED THAT RIVALRY SEQUENCE.
SO,TO RECAP: EGGNER: BRILLIANT, LOVED BY ALL, FRIEND OF SMALL ANIMALS, CHAMPION OF JUSTICE, A REAL CHEESY GUY.
JARVIS: HAS A BIG NOSE AND SMELLS FUNNY. ALSO DOESN'T LIKE CHEESE. UGH.
WHAT AWARD DID YOU SAY THIS WON?
THE EGGNER VON SHMOODLEDIKE AWARD FOR SELF SERVING ONE SIDED SILLINESS.
SO BASICALLY, YOUR RIVALRY BOILS DOWN TO A DIFFERENCE IN TASTE? SOME PEOPLE JUST DON'T LIKE CHEESE.
YOU OBVIOUSLY MISSED THE WHOLE POINT OF THE AWARD - WINNING DOCUMENTARY. WE'LL HAVE TO WATCH IT AGAIN.

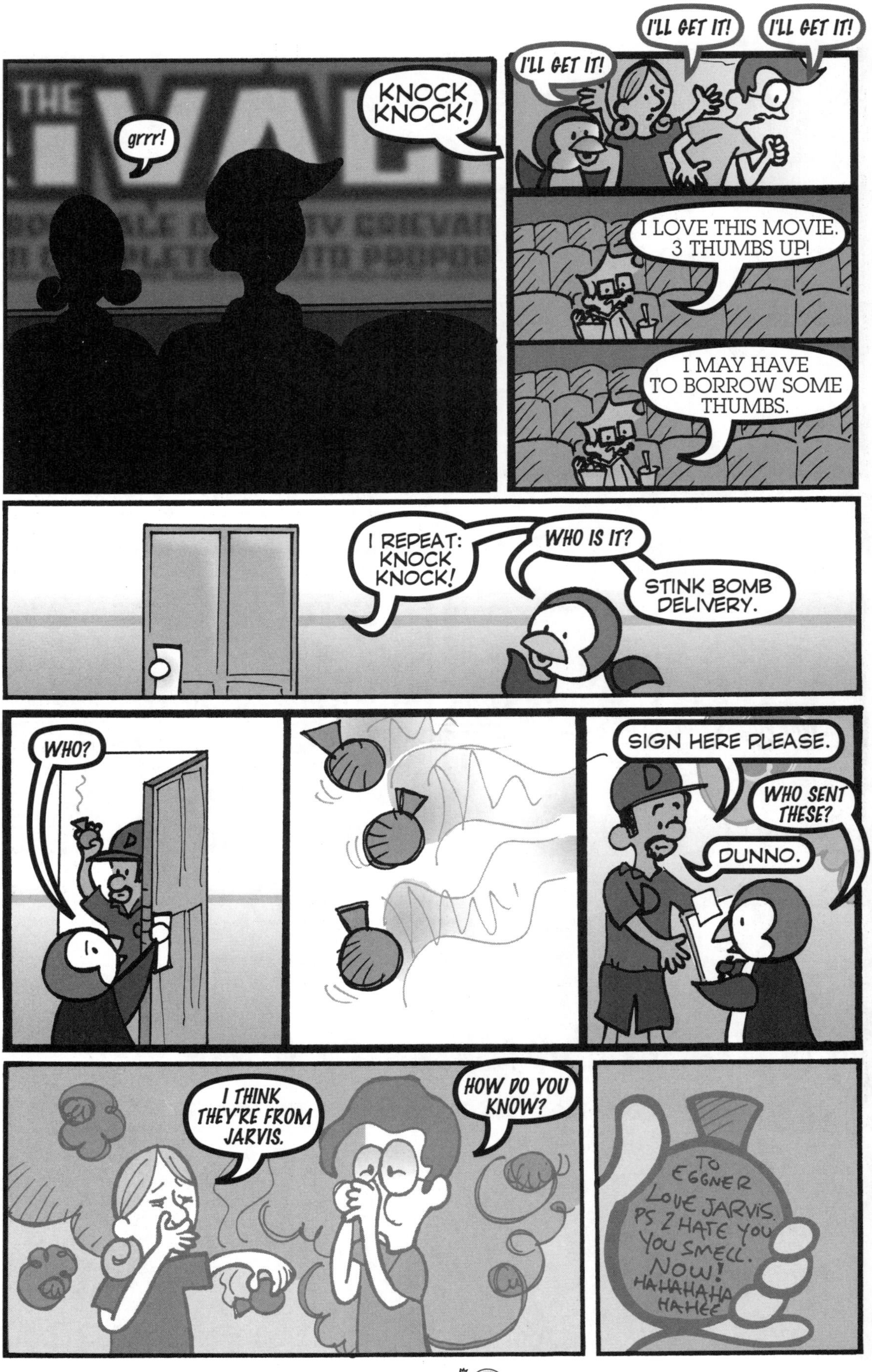
grrr!
KNOCK KNOCK!
I'LL GET IT!
I'LL GET IT!
I'LL GET IT!
I LOVE THIS MOVIE. 3 THUMBS UP!
I MAY HAVE TO BORROW SOME THUMBS.
I REPEAT: KNOCK KNOCK!
WHO IS IT?
STINK BOMB DELIVERY.
WHO?
SIGN HERE PLEASE.
WHO SENT THESE?
DUNNO.
I THINK THEY'RE FROM JARVIS.
HOW DO YOU KNOW?
TO EGGNER
LOVE JARVIS.
PS I HATE YOU
YOU SMELL.
NOW!
HAHAHAHA
HAHEE

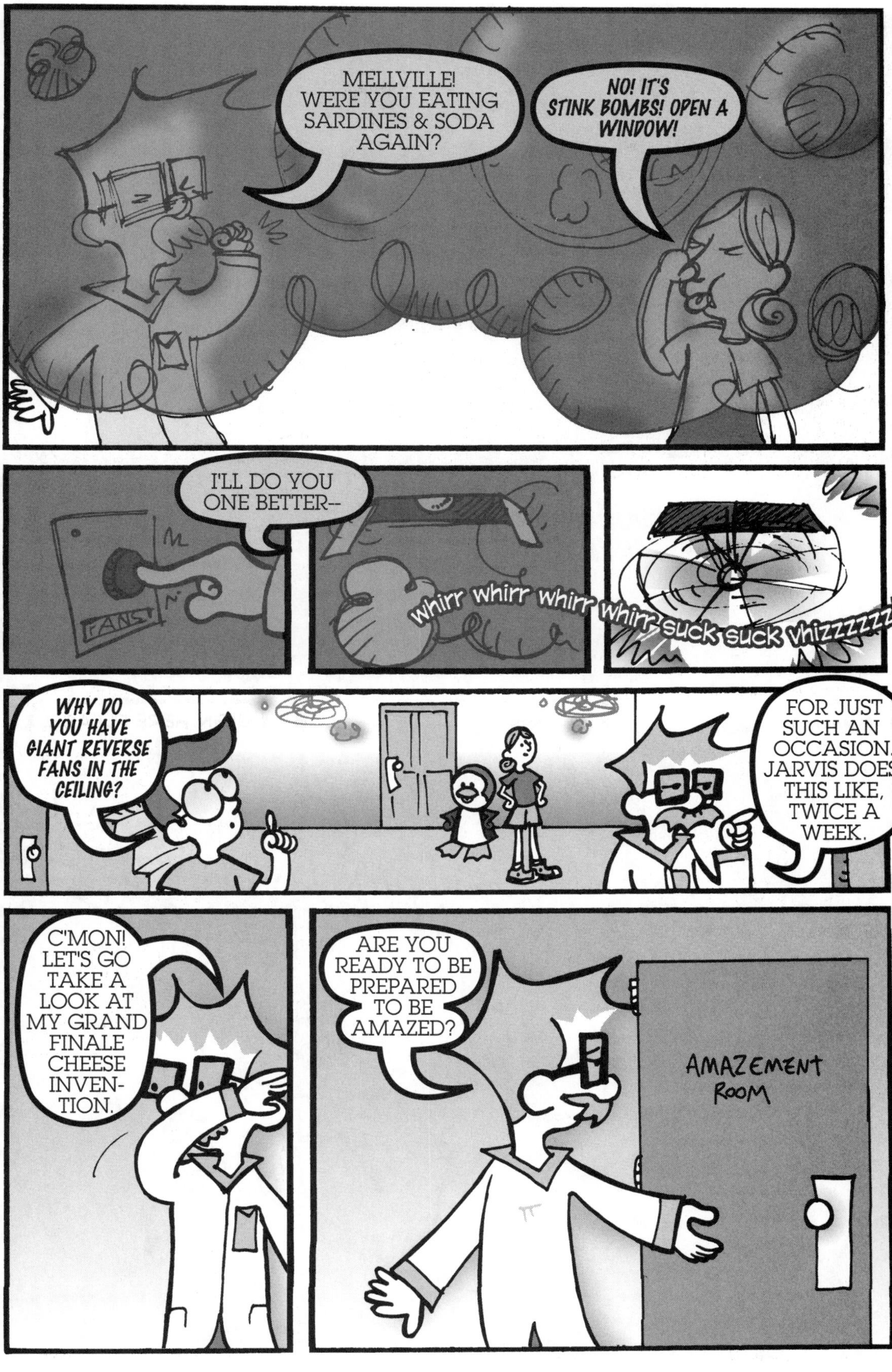
MELLVILLE! WERE YOU EATING SARDINES & SODA AGAIN?
NO! IT'S STINK BOMBS! OPEN A WINDOW!
I'LL DO YOU ONE BETTER--
FANS
whirr whirr whirr whirr suck suck vhizzzzzz!!!
WHY DO YOU HAVE GIANT REVERSE FANS IN THE CEILING?
FOR JUST SUCH AN OCCASION. JARVIS DOES THIS LIKE, TWICE A WEEK.
C'MON! LET'S GO TAKE A LOOK AT MY GRAND FINALE CHEESE INVENTION.
ARE YOU READY TO BE PREPARED TO BE AMAZED?
AMAZEMENT ROOM

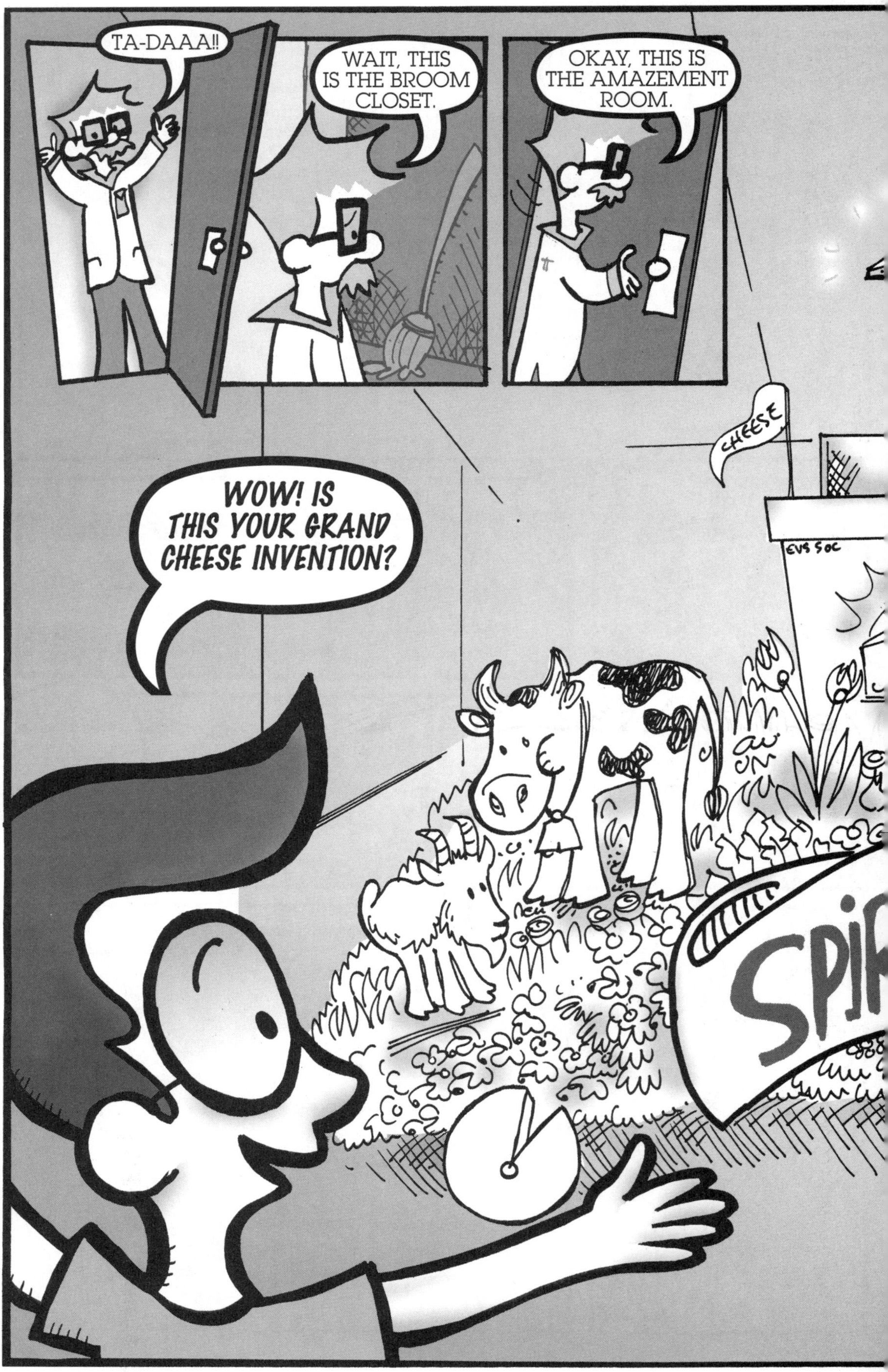
TA-DAAA!!
WAIT, THIS IS THE BROOM CLOSET.
OKAY, THIS IS THE AMAZEMENT ROOM.
CHEESE
EVS SOC
WOW! IS THIS YOUR GRAND CHEESE INVENTION?
SPIR

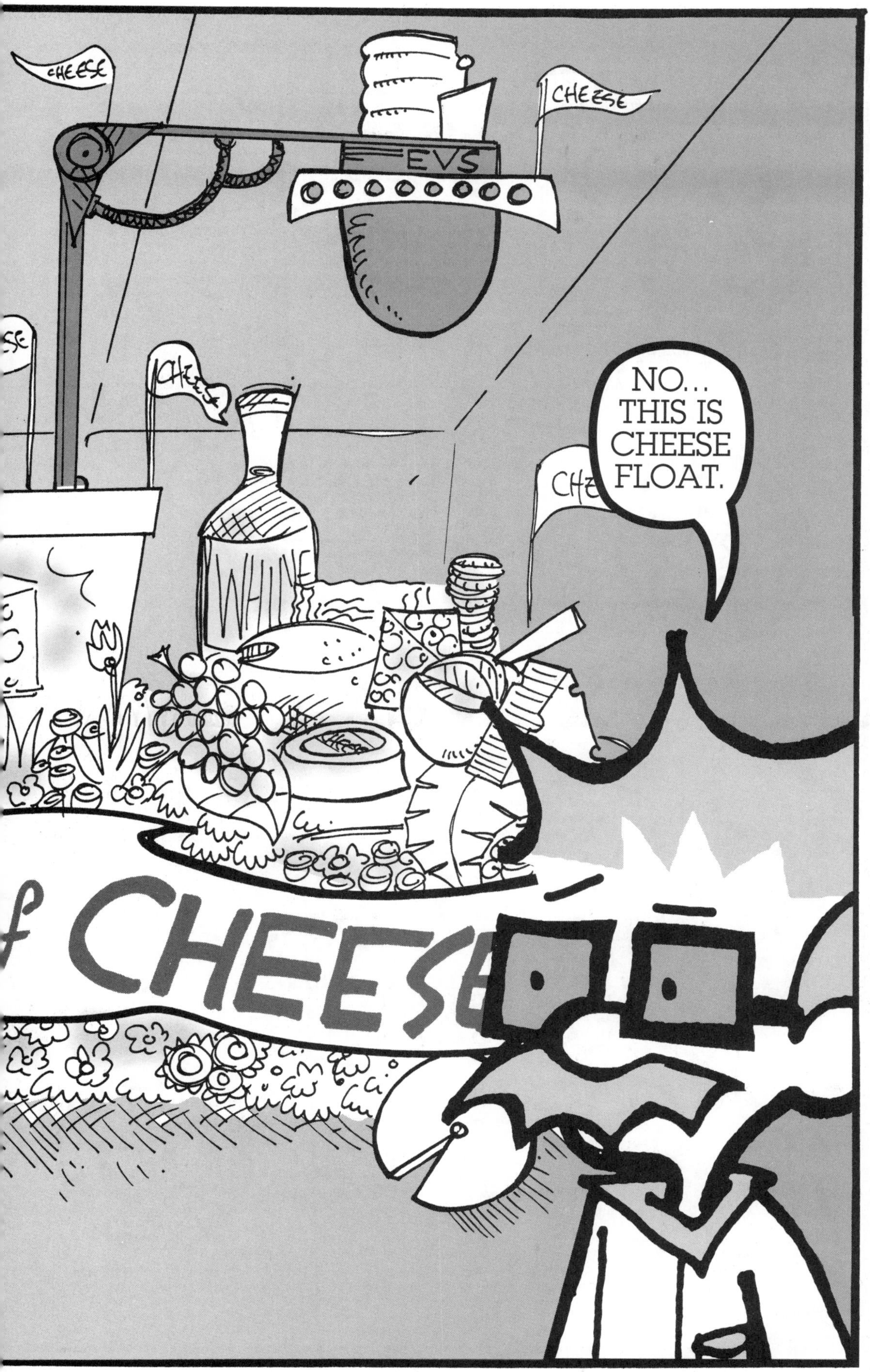
CHEESE
CHEESE
EVS
WHINE
NO... THIS IS CHEESE FLOAT.
CHEESE

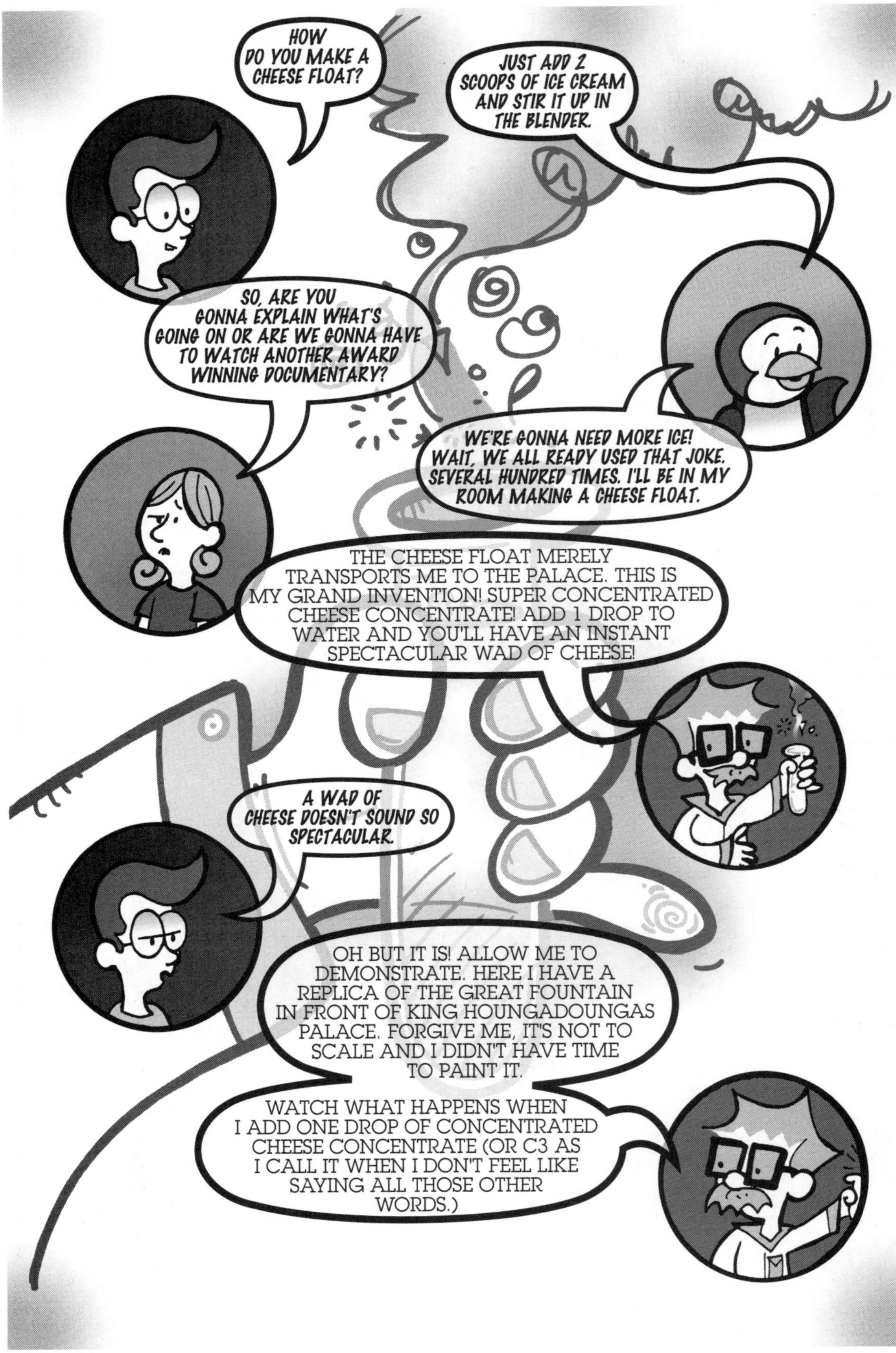
HOW DO YOU MAKE A CHEESE FLOAT?
JUST ADD 2 SCOOPS OF ICE CREAM AND STIR IT UP IN THE BLENDER.
SO, ARE YOU GONNA EXPLAIN WHAT'S GOING ON OR ARE WE GONNA HAVE TO WATCH ANOTHER AWARD WINNING DOCUMENTARY?
WE'RE GONNA NEED MORE ICE! WAIT, WE ALL READY USED THAT JOKE. SEVERAL HUNDRED TIMES. I'LL BE IN MY ROOM MAKING A CHEESE FLOAT.
THE CHEESE FLOAT MERELY TRANSPORTS ME TO THE PALACE. THIS IS MY GRAND INVENTION! SUPER CONCENTRATED CHEESE CONCENTRATE! ADD 1 DROP TO WATER AND YOU'LL HAVE AN INSTANT SPECTACULAR WAD OF CHEESE!
A WAD OF CHEESE DOESN'T SOUND SO SPECTACULAR.
OH BUT IT IS! ALLOW ME TO DEMONSTRATE. HERE I HAVE A REPLICA OF THE GREAT FOUNTAIN IN FRONT OF KING HOUNGADOUNGAS PALACE. FORGIVE ME, IT'S NOT TO SCALE AND I DIDN'T HAVE TIME TO PAINT IT.
WATCH WHAT HAPPENS WHEN I ADD ONE DROP OF CONCENTRATED CHEESE CONCENTRATE (OR C3 AS I CALL IT WHEN I DON'T FEEL LIKE SAYING ALL THOSE OTHER WORDS.)

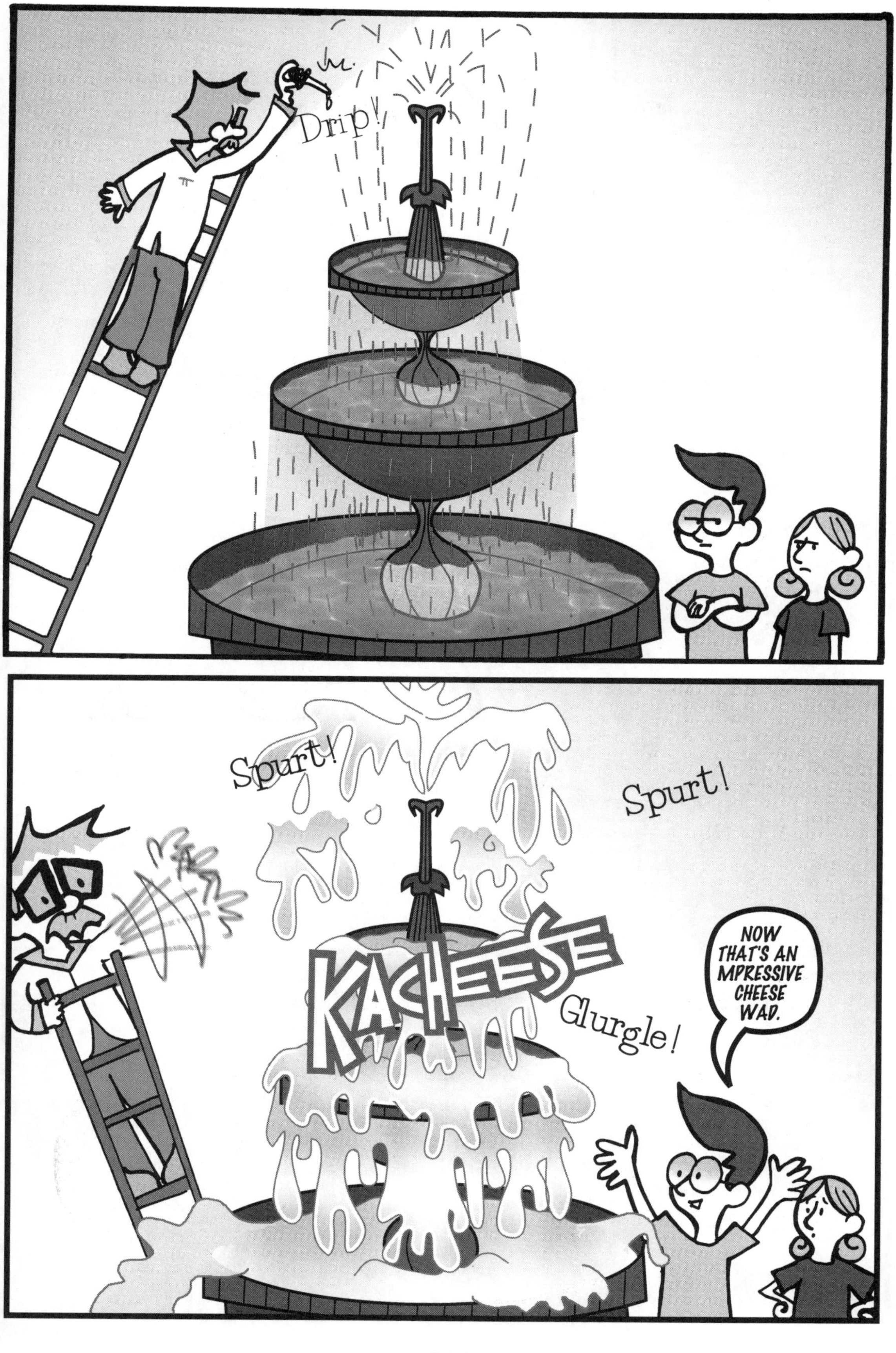
Drip!
Spurt!
Spurt!
KACHEESE
Glurgle!
NOW THAT'S AN MPRESSIVE CHEESE WAD.

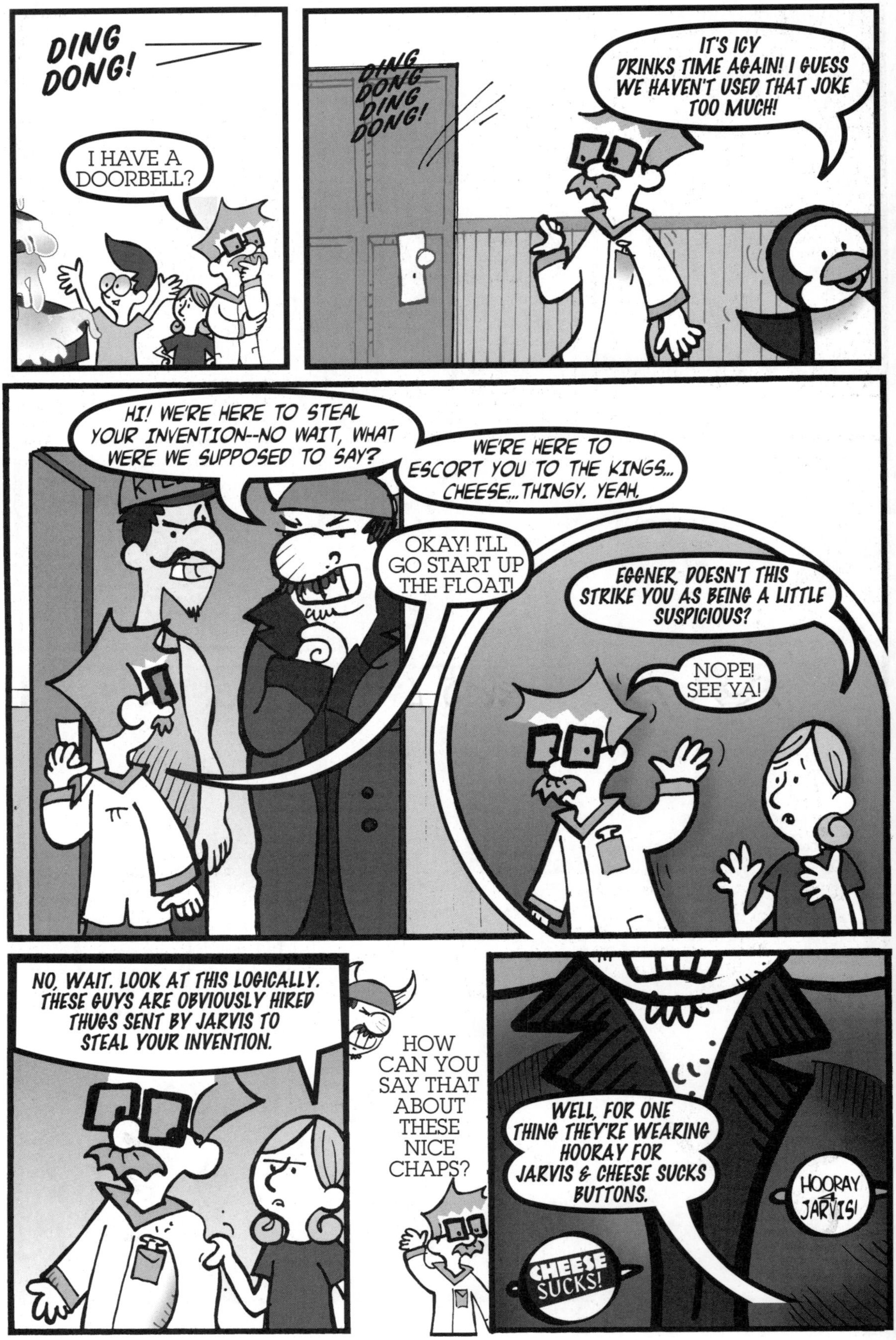
DING DONG!
I HAVE A DOORBELL?
DING DONG DING DONG!
IT'S ICY DRINKS TIME AGAIN! I GUESS WE HAVEN'T USED THAT JOKE TOO MUCH!
HI! WE'RE HERE TO STEAL YOUR INVENTION--NO WAIT, WHAT WERE WE SUPPOSED TO SAY?
WE'RE HERE TO ESCORT YOU TO THE KINGS... CHEESE... THINGY. YEAH.
OKAY! I'LL GO START UP THE FLOAT!
EGGNER, DOESN'T THIS STRIKE YOU AS BEING A LITTLE SUSPICIOUS?
NOPE! SEE YA!
NO, WAIT. LOOK AT THIS LOGICALLY. THESE GUYS ARE OBVIOUSLY HIRED THUGS SENT BY JARVIS TO STEAL YOUR INVENTION.
HOW CAN YOU SAY THAT ABOUT THESE NICE CHAPS?
WELL, FOR ONE THING THEY'RE WEARING HOORAY FOR JARVIS & CHEESE SUCKS BUTTONS.
HOORAY 4 JARVIS!
CHEESE SUCKS!

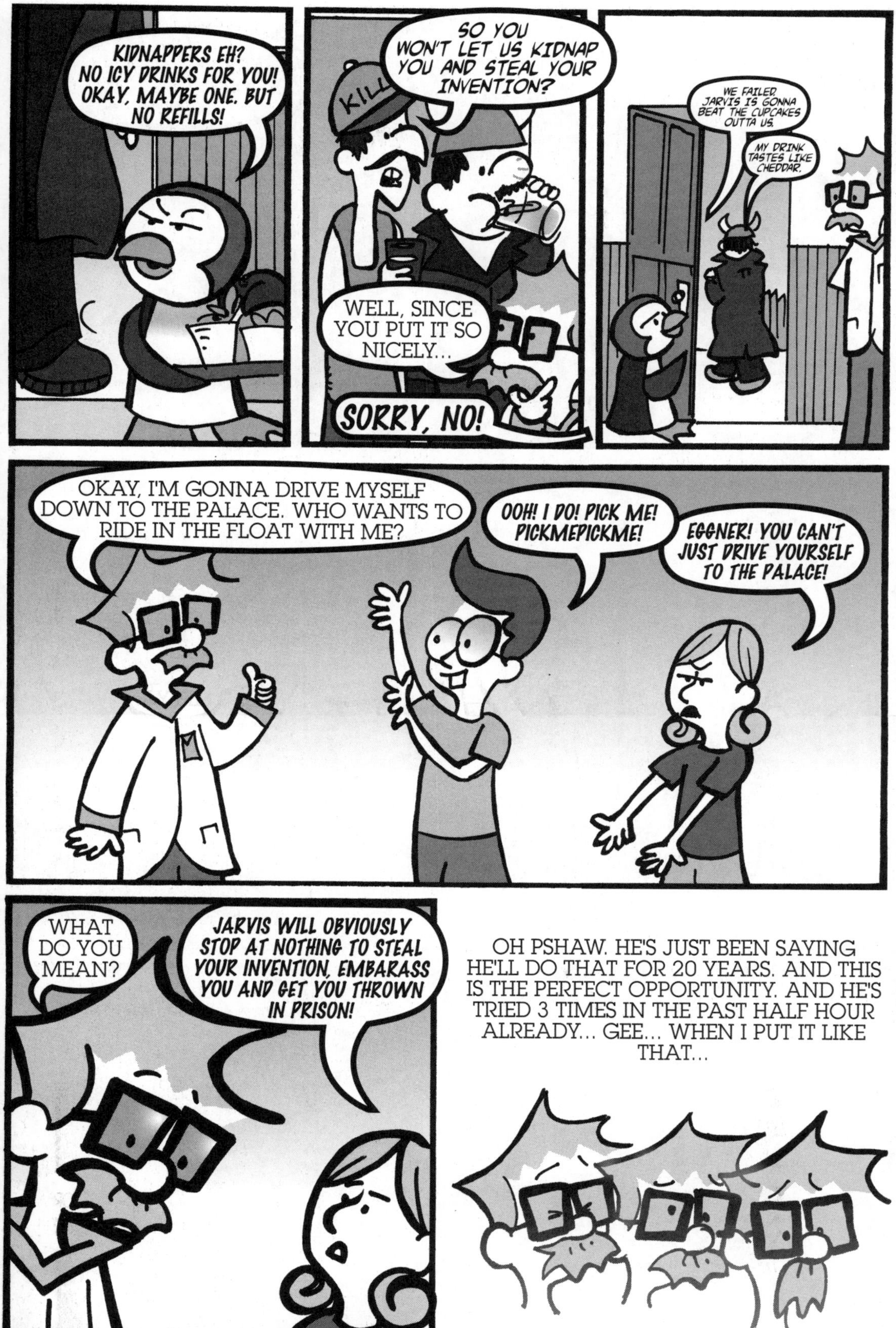
KIDNAPPERS EH? NO ICY DRINKS FOR YOU! OKAY, MAYBE ONE. BUT NO REFILLS!
SO YOU WON'T LET US KIDNAP YOU AND STEAL YOUR INVENTION?
KILL
WELL, SINCE YOU PUT IT SO NICELY...
SORRY, NO!
WE FAILED. JARVIS IS GONNA BEAT THE CUPCAKES OUTTA US.
MY DRINK TASTES LIKE CHEDDAR.
OKAY, I'M GONNA DRIVE MYSELF DOWN TO THE PALACE. WHO WANTS TO RIDE IN THE FLOAT WITH ME?
OOH! I DO! PICK ME! PICKMEPICKME!
EGGNER! YOU CAN'T JUST DRIVE YOURSELF TO THE PALACE!
WHAT DO YOU MEAN?
JARVIS WILL OBVIOUSLY STOP AT NOTHING TO STEAL YOUR INVENTION, EMBARASS YOU AND GET YOU THROWN IN PRISON!
OH PSHAW. HE'S JUST BEEN SAYING HE'LL DO THAT FOR 20 YEARS. AND THIS IS THE PERFECT OPPORTUNITY. AND HE'S TRIED 3 TIMES IN THE PAST HALF HOUR ALREADY... GEE... WHEN I PUT IT LIKE THAT...

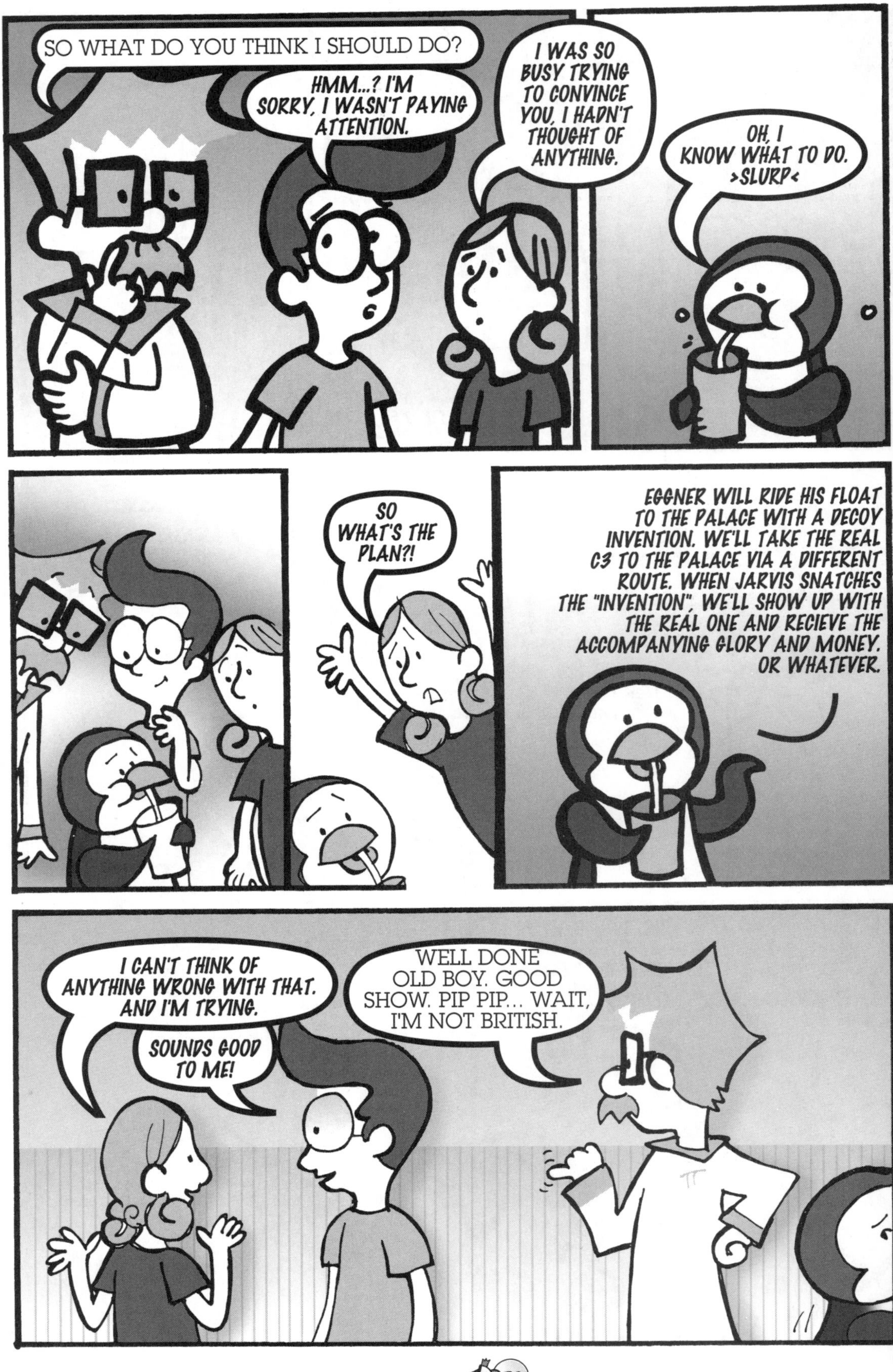
SO WHAT DO YOU THINK I SHOULD DO?
HMM...? I'M SORRY, I WASN'T PAYING ATTENTION.
I WAS SO BUSY TRYING TO CONVINCE YOU, I HADN'T THOUGHT OF ANYTHING.
OH, I KNOW WHAT TO DO. >SLURP<
SO WHAT'S THE PLAN?!
EGGNER WILL RIDE HIS FLOAT TO THE PALACE WITH A DECOY INVENTION. WE'LL TAKE THE REAL C3 TO THE PALACE VIA A DIFFERENT ROUTE. WHEN JARVIS SNATCHES THE "INVENTION", WE'LL SHOW UP WITH THE REAL ONE AND RECIEVE THE ACCOMPANYING GLORY AND MONEY. OR WHATEVER.
I CAN'T THINK OF ANYTHING WRONG WITH THAT. AND I'M TRYING.
SOUNDS GOOD TO ME!
WELL DONE OLD BOY. GOOD SHOW. PIP PIP... WAIT, I'M NOT BRITISH.

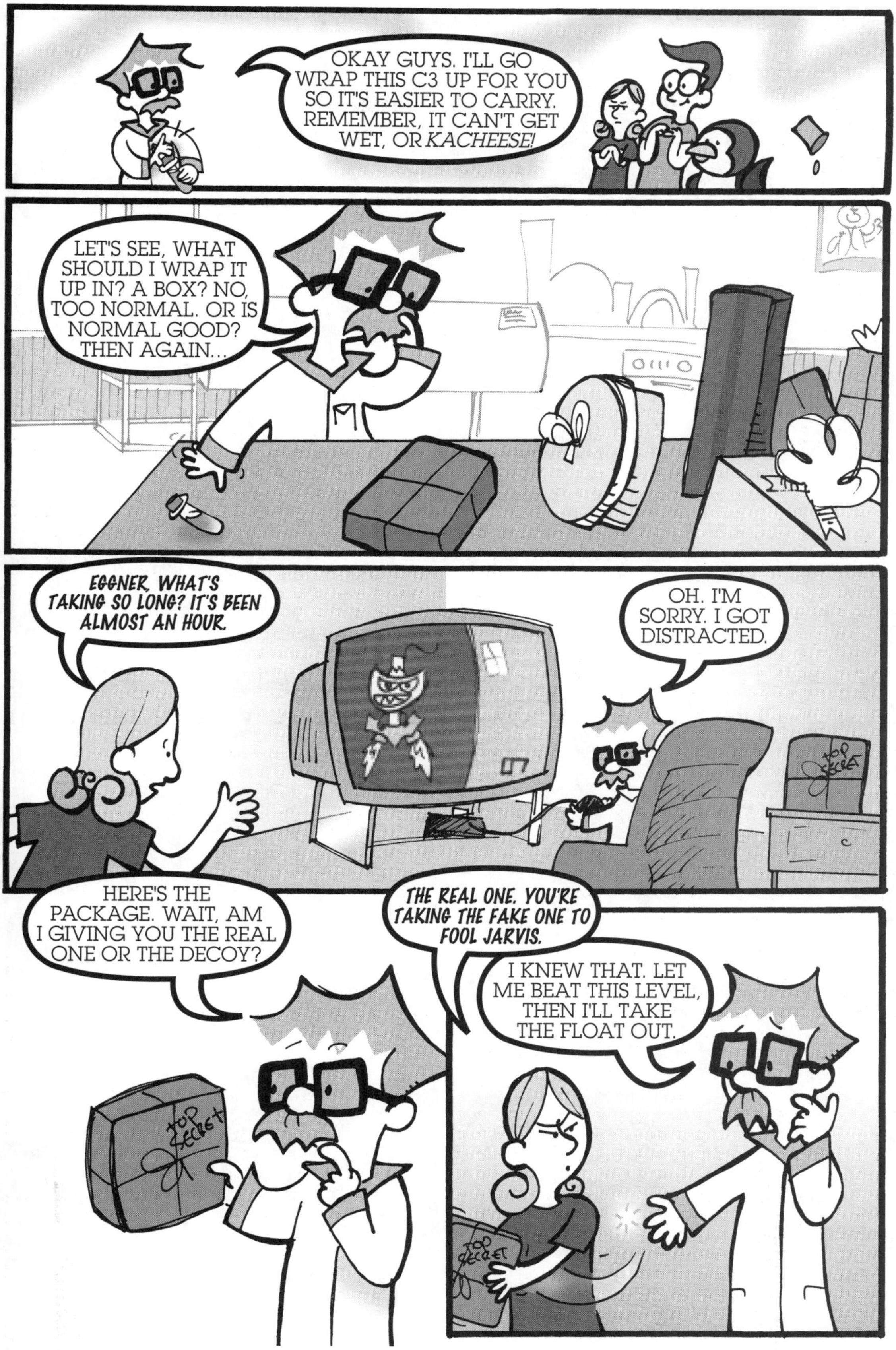

OKAY GUYS. I'LL GO WRAP THIS C3 UP FOR YOU SO IT'S EASIER TO CARRY. REMEMBER, IT CAN'T GET WET, OR *KACHEESE!*
LET'S SEE, WHAT SHOULD I WRAP IT UP IN? A BOX? NO, TOO NORMAL. OR IS NORMAL GOOD? THEN AGAIN...
EGGNER, WHAT'S TAKING SO LONG? IT'S BEEN ALMOST AN HOUR.
OH. I'M SORRY. I GOT DISTRACTED.
TOP SECRET
HERE'S THE PACKAGE. WAIT, AM I GIVING YOU THE REAL ONE OR THE DECOY?
THE REAL ONE. YOU'RE TAKING THE FAKE ONE TO FOOL JARVIS.
I KNEW THAT. LET ME BEAT THIS LEVEL, THEN I'LL TAKE THE FLOAT OUT.
TOP SECRET
TOP SECRET

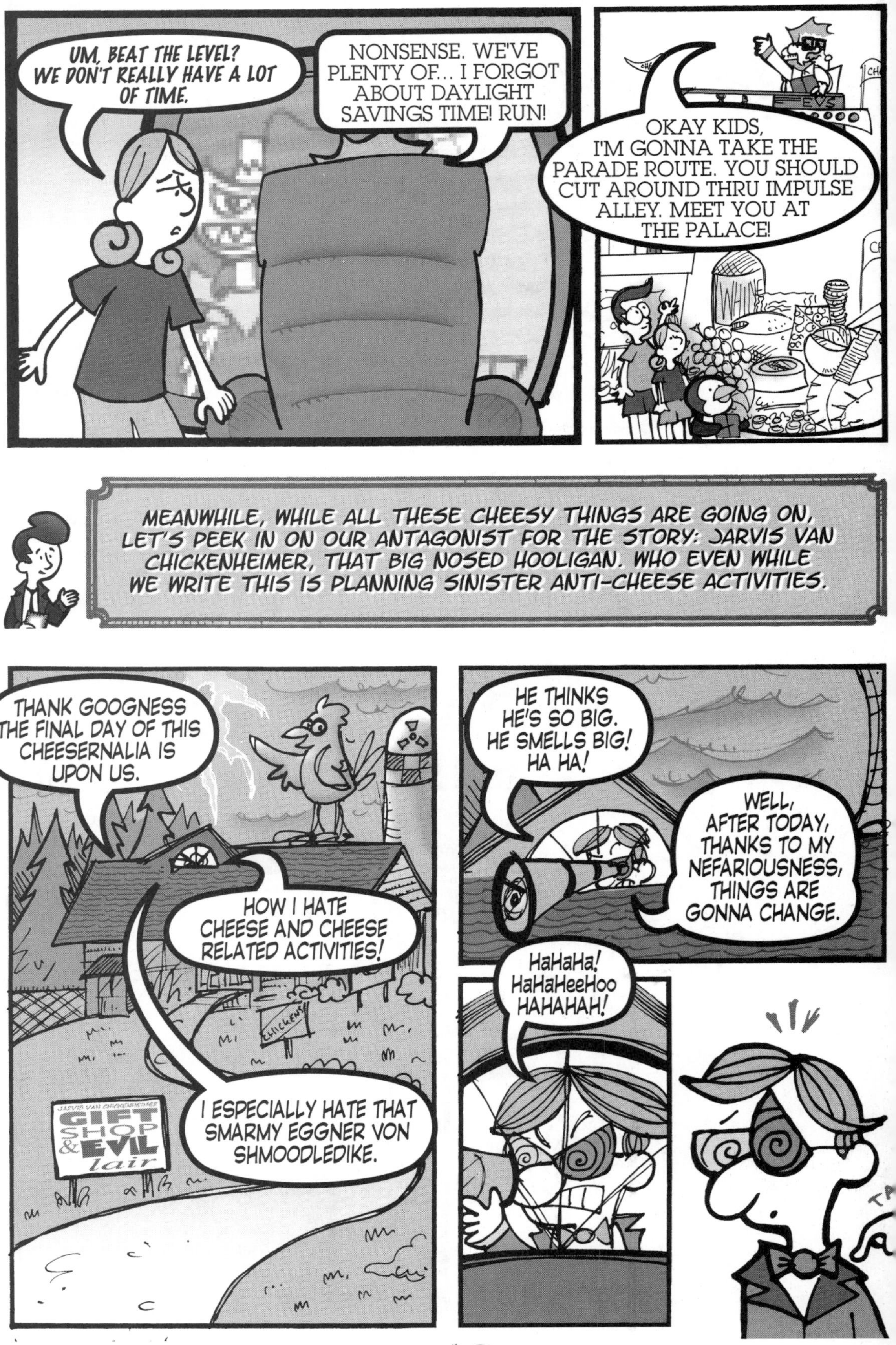
UM, BEAT THE LEVEL? WE DON'T REALLY HAVE A LOT OF TIME.
NONSENSE. WE'VE PLENTY OF... I FORGOT ABOUT DAYLIGHT SAVINGS TIME! RUN!
OKAY KIDS, I'M GONNA TAKE THE PARADE ROUTE. YOU SHOULD CUT AROUND THRU IMPULSE ALLEY. MEET YOU AT THE PALACE!
MEANWHILE, WHILE ALL THESE CHEESY THINGS ARE GOING ON, LET'S PEEK IN ON OUR ANTAGONIST FOR THE STORY: JARVIS VAN CHICKENHEIMER, THAT BIG NOSED HOOLIGAN. WHO EVEN WHILE WE WRITE THIS IS PLANNING SINISTER ANTI-CHEESE ACTIVITIES.
THANK GOOGNESS THE FINAL DAY OF THIS CHEESERNALIA IS UPON US.
HOW I HATE CHEESE AND CHEESE RELATED ACTIVITIES!
CHICKENS
GIFT SHOP & EVIL lair
I ESPECIALLY HATE THAT SMARMY EGGNER VON SHMOODLEDIKE.
HE THINKS HE'S SO BIG. HE SMELLS BIG! HA HA!
WELL, AFTER TODAY, THANKS TO MY NEFARIOUSNESS, THINGS ARE GONNA CHANGE.
HaHaHa! HaHaHeeHoo HAHAHAH!

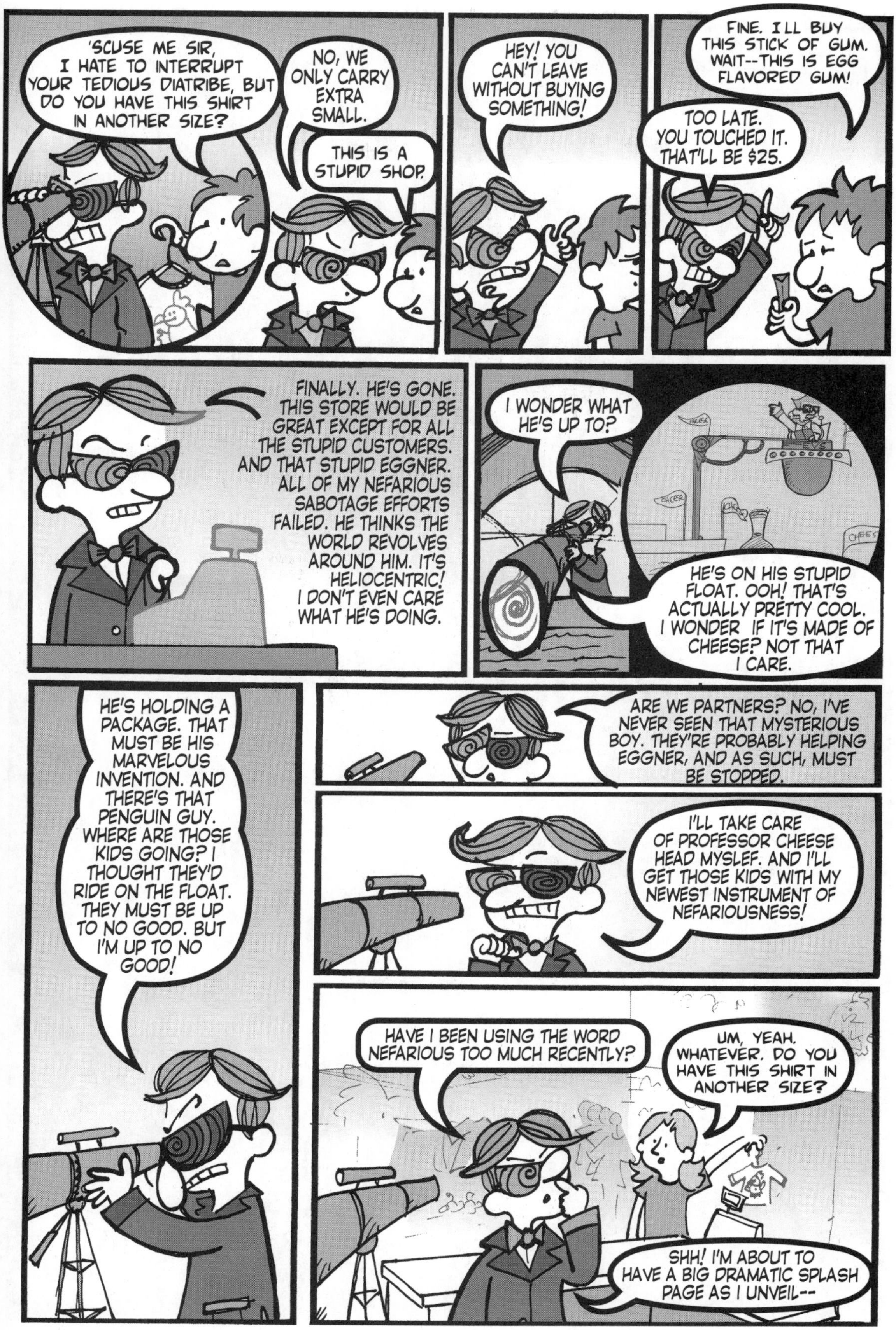
'SCUSE ME SIR, I HATE TO INTERRUPT YOUR TEDIOUS DIATRIBE, BUT DO YOU HAVE THIS SHIRT IN ANOTHER SIZE?
NO, WE ONLY CARRY EXTRA SMALL.
THIS IS A STUPID SHOP.
HEY! YOU CAN'T LEAVE WITHOUT BUYING SOMETHING!
FINE. I'LL BUY THIS STICK OF GUM. WAIT--THIS IS EGG FLAVORED GUM!
TOO LATE. YOU TOUCHED IT. THAT'LL BE $25.
FINALLY. HE'S GONE. THIS STORE WOULD BE GREAT EXCEPT FOR ALL THE STUPID CUSTOMERS. AND THAT STUPID EGGNER. ALL OF MY NEFARIOUS SABOTAGE EFFORTS FAILED. HE THINKS THE WORLD REVOLVES AROUND HIM. IT'S HELIOCENTRIC! I DON'T EVEN CARE WHAT HE'S DOING.
I WONDER WHAT HE'S UP TO?
HE'S ON HIS STUPID FLOAT. OOH! THAT'S ACTUALLY PRETTY COOL. I WONDER IF IT'S MADE OF CHEESE? NOT THAT I CARE.
HE'S HOLDING A PACKAGE. THAT MUST BE HIS MARVELOUS INVENTION. AND THERE'S THAT PENGUIN GUY. WHERE ARE THOSE KIDS GOING? I THOUGHT THEY'D RIDE ON THE FLOAT. THEY MUST BE UP TO NO GOOD. BUT I'M UP TO NO GOOD!
ARE WE PARTNERS? NO, I'VE NEVER SEEN THAT MYSTERIOUS BOY. THEY'RE PROBABLY HELPING EGGNER, AND AS SUCH, MUST BE STOPPED.
I'LL TAKE CARE OF PROFESSOR CHEESE HEAD MYSLEF. AND I'LL GET THOSE KIDS WITH MY NEWEST INSTRUMENT OF NEFARIOUSNESS!
HAVE I BEEN USING THE WORD NEFARIOUS TOO MUCH RECENTLY?
UM, YEAH. WHATEVER. DO YOU HAVE THIS SHIRT IN ANOTHER SIZE?
SHH! I'M ABOUT TO HAVE A BIG DRAMATIC SPLASH PAGE AS I UNVEIL--

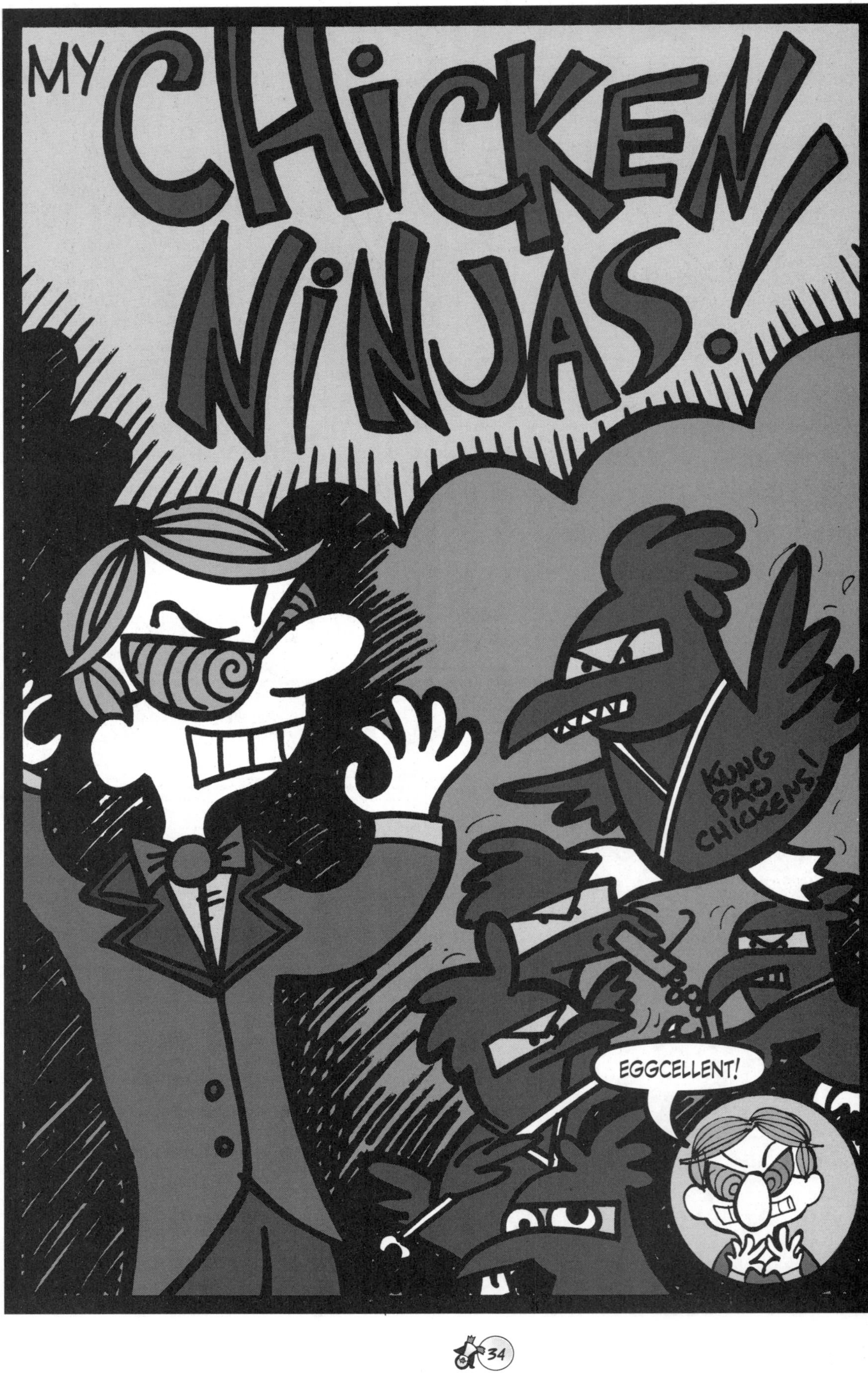
MY CHICKEN NINJAS!
KUNG PAO CHICKENS!
EGGCELLENT!

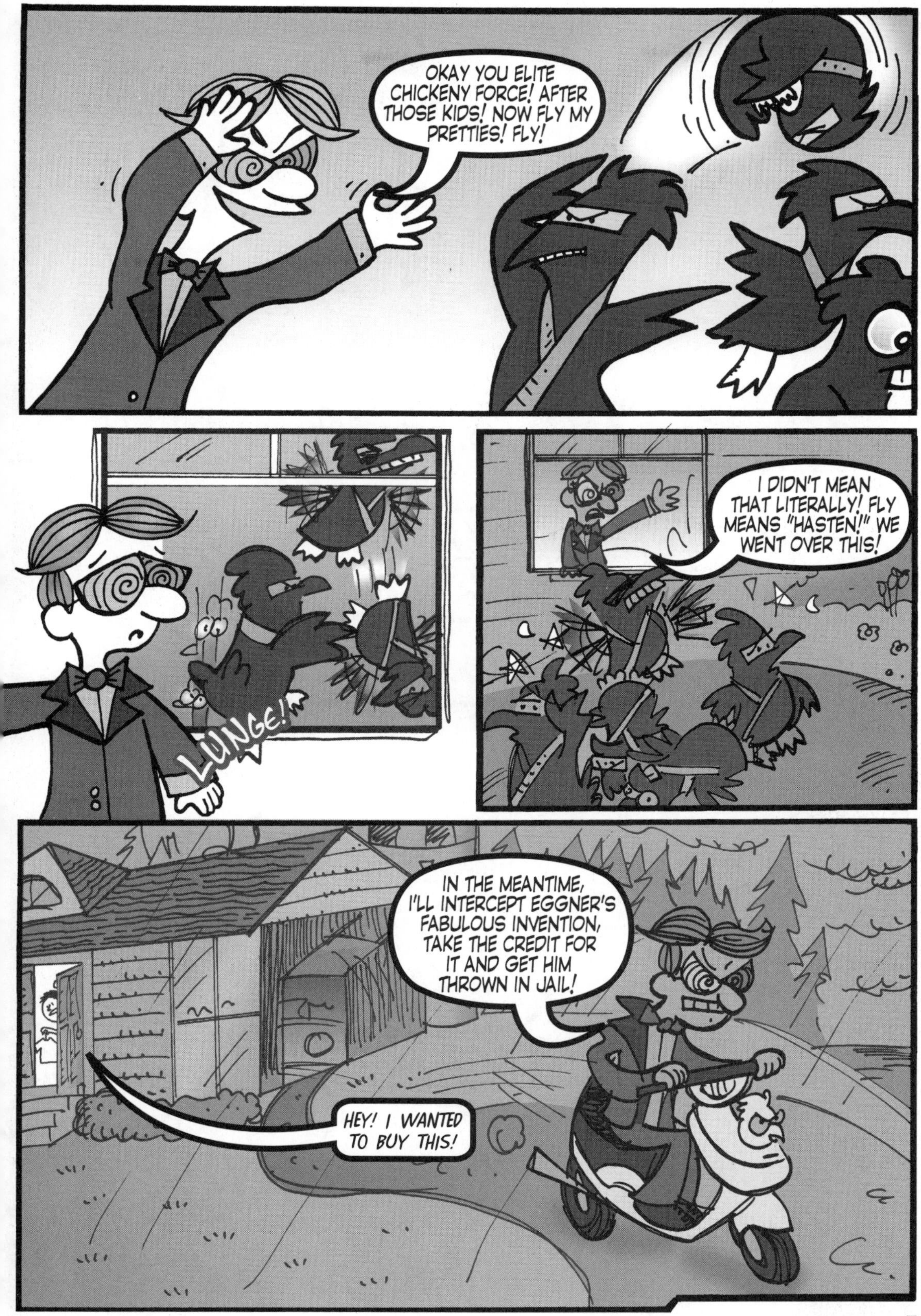
OKAY YOU ELITE CHICKENY FORCE! AFTER THOSE KIDS! NOW FLY MY PRETTIES! FLY!
LUNGE!
I DIDN'T MEAN THAT LITERALLY! FLY MEANS "HASTEN!" WE WENT OVER THIS!
IN THE MEANTIME, I'LL INTERCEPT EGGNER'S FABULOUS INVENTION, TAKE THE CREDIT FOR IT AND GET HIM THROWN IN JAIL!
HEY! I WANTED TO BUY THIS!

END OF CHAPTER 1

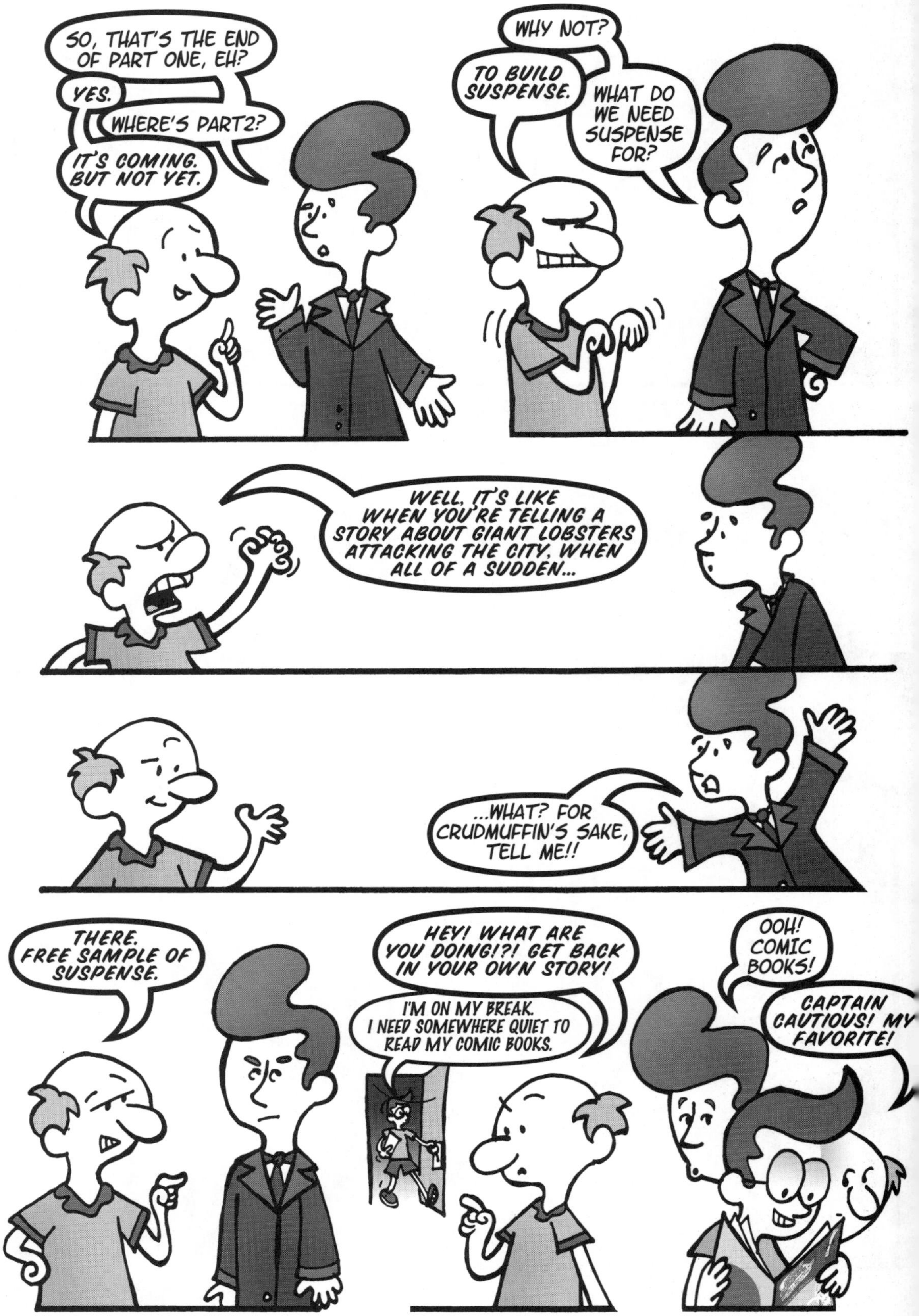
SO, THAT'S THE END OF PART ONE, EH?
YES.
WHERE'S PART2?
IT'S COMING. BUT NOT YET.
WHY NOT?
TO BUILD SUSPENSE.
WHAT DO WE NEED SUSPENSE FOR?
WELL, IT'S LIKE WHEN YOU'RE TELLING A STORY ABOUT GIANT LOBSTERS ATTACKING THE CITY, WHEN ALL OF A SUDDEN...
...WHAT? FOR CRUDMUFFIN'S SAKE, TELL ME!!
THERE. FREE SAMPLE OF SUSPENSE.
HEY! WHAT ARE YOU DOING!?! GET BACK IN YOUR OWN STORY!
I'M ON MY BREAK. I NEED SOMEWHERE QUIET TO READ MY COMIC BOOKS.
OOH! COMIC BOOKS!
CAPTAIN CAUTIOUS! MY FAVORITE!

CAPTAIN CAUTIOUS &
WILLIAM J. WOOLINGTON III
THE SIX MILLION DOLLAR LAMB

in:"BACON & SPANDEX"
and:"SHOVING GLOVES"
also:"HECK ON WHEELS"

What do you get for the person who has everything? *A* super hero, of course! When William J. Woolington III (the world's richest sheep) hires Captain Cautious (a wimpy neat-freak superhero) as his sidekick, oh the hilarity that ensues! All they need is some pint-sized flying comic-relief. *E*nter batguin, his auxillary. *W*ith this combination of wealthy brashness, timid super-strength and random goofy-ness, every adventure is 100% guaranteed.

You heard me.

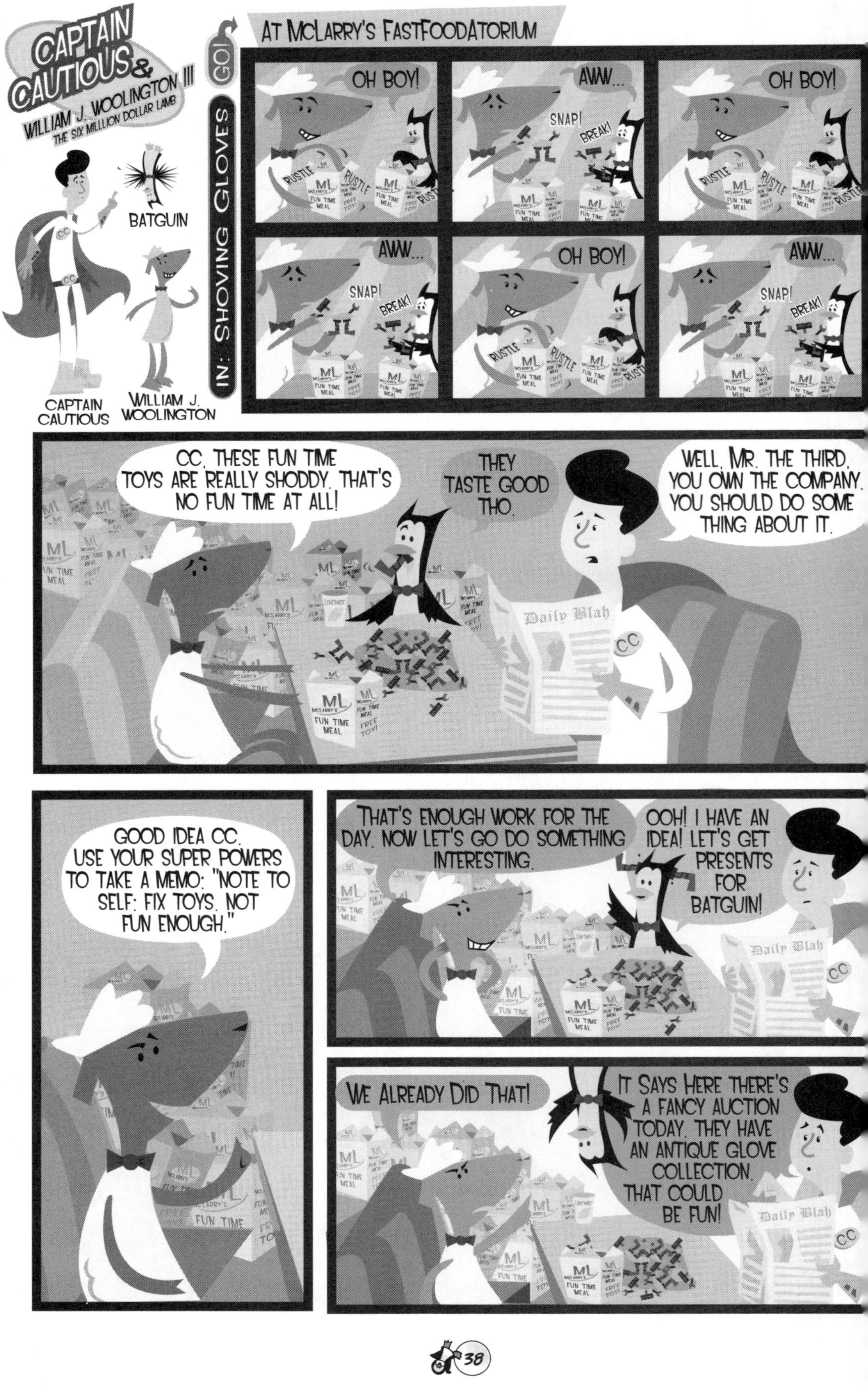
CAPTAIN CAUTIOUS &
WILLIAM J. WOOLINGTON III
THE SIX MILLION DOLLAR LAMB
BATGUIN
CAPTAIN CAUTIOUS
WILLIAM J. WOOLINGTON
GO!
IN: SHOVING GLOVES
AT McLARRY'S FASTFOODATORIUM
OH BOY!
RUSTLE
RUSTLE
AWW...
SNAP!
BREAK!
OH BOY!
AWW...
SNAP!
BREAK!
OH BOY!
AWW...
SNAP!
BREAK!
CC, THESE FUN TIME TOYS ARE REALLY SHODDY. THAT'S NO FUN TIME AT ALL!
THEY TASTE GOOD THO.
WELL, MR. THE THIRD, YOU OWN THE COMPANY. YOU SHOULD DO SOME THING ABOUT IT.
Daily Blah
GOOD IDEA CC. USE YOUR SUPER POWERS TO TAKE A MEMO: "NOTE TO SELF: FIX TOYS. NOT FUN ENOUGH."
THAT'S ENOUGH WORK FOR THE DAY. NOW LET'S GO DO SOMETHING INTERESTING.
OOH! I HAVE AN IDEA! LET'S GET PRESENTS FOR BATGUIN!
WE ALREADY DID THAT!
IT SAYS HERE THERE'S A FANCY AUCTION TODAY. THEY HAVE AN ANTIQUE GLOVE COLLECTION. THAT COULD BE FUN!

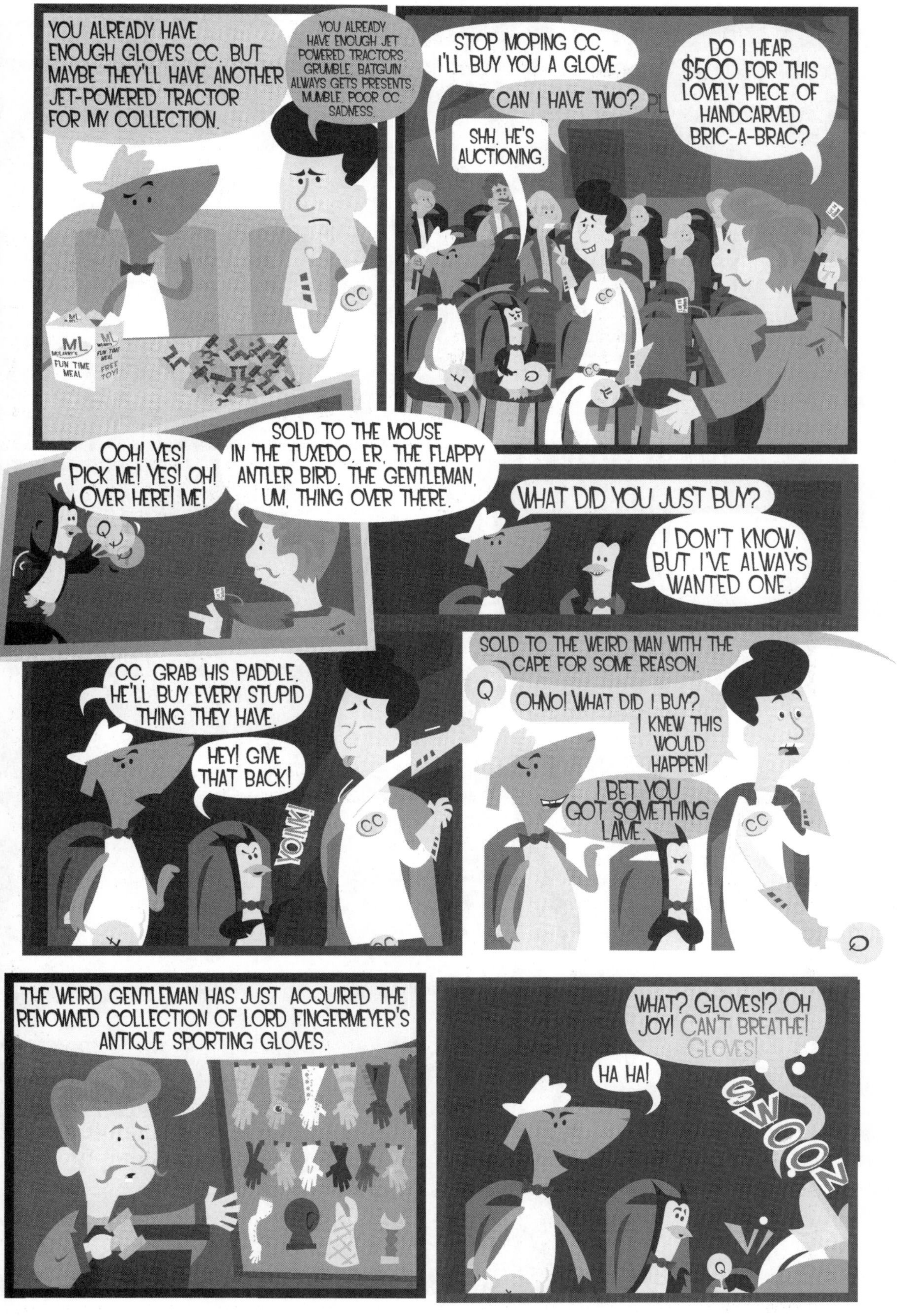

YOU ALREADY HAVE ENOUGH GLOVES CC. BUT MAYBE THEY'LL HAVE ANOTHER JET-POWERED TRACTOR FOR MY COLLECTION.
YOU ALREADY HAVE ENOUGH JET POWERED TRACTORS. GRUMBLE. BATGUIN ALWAYS GETS PRESENTS. MUMBLE. POOR CC. SADNESS.
ML McLARRY'S FUN TIME MEAL
FREE TOY!
STOP MOPING CC. I'LL BUY YOU A GLOVE.
CAN I HAVE TWO?
SHH. HE'S AUCTIONING.
DO I HEAR $500 FOR THIS LOVELY PIECE OF HANDCARVED BRIC-A-BRAC?
OOH! YES! PICK ME! YES! OH! OVER HERE! ME!
SOLD TO THE MOUSE IN THE TUXEDO. ER, THE FLAPPY ANTLER BIRD. THE GENTLEMAN, UM, THING OVER THERE.
WHAT DID YOU JUST BUY?
I DON'T KNOW. BUT I'VE ALWAYS WANTED ONE.
CC, GRAB HIS PADDLE. HE'LL BUY EVERY STUPID THING THEY HAVE.
HEY! GIVE THAT BACK!
YOINK!
SOLD TO THE WEIRD MAN WITH THE CAPE FOR SOME REASON.
OHNO! WHAT DID I BUY? I KNEW THIS WOULD HAPPEN!
I BET YOU GOT SOMETHING LAME.
THE WEIRD GENTLEMAN HAS JUST ACQUIRED THE RENOWNED COLLECTION OF LORD FINGERMEYER'S ANTIQUE SPORTING GLOVES.
WHAT? GLOVES!? OH JOY! CAN'T BREATHE! GLOVES!
HA HA!
SWOON

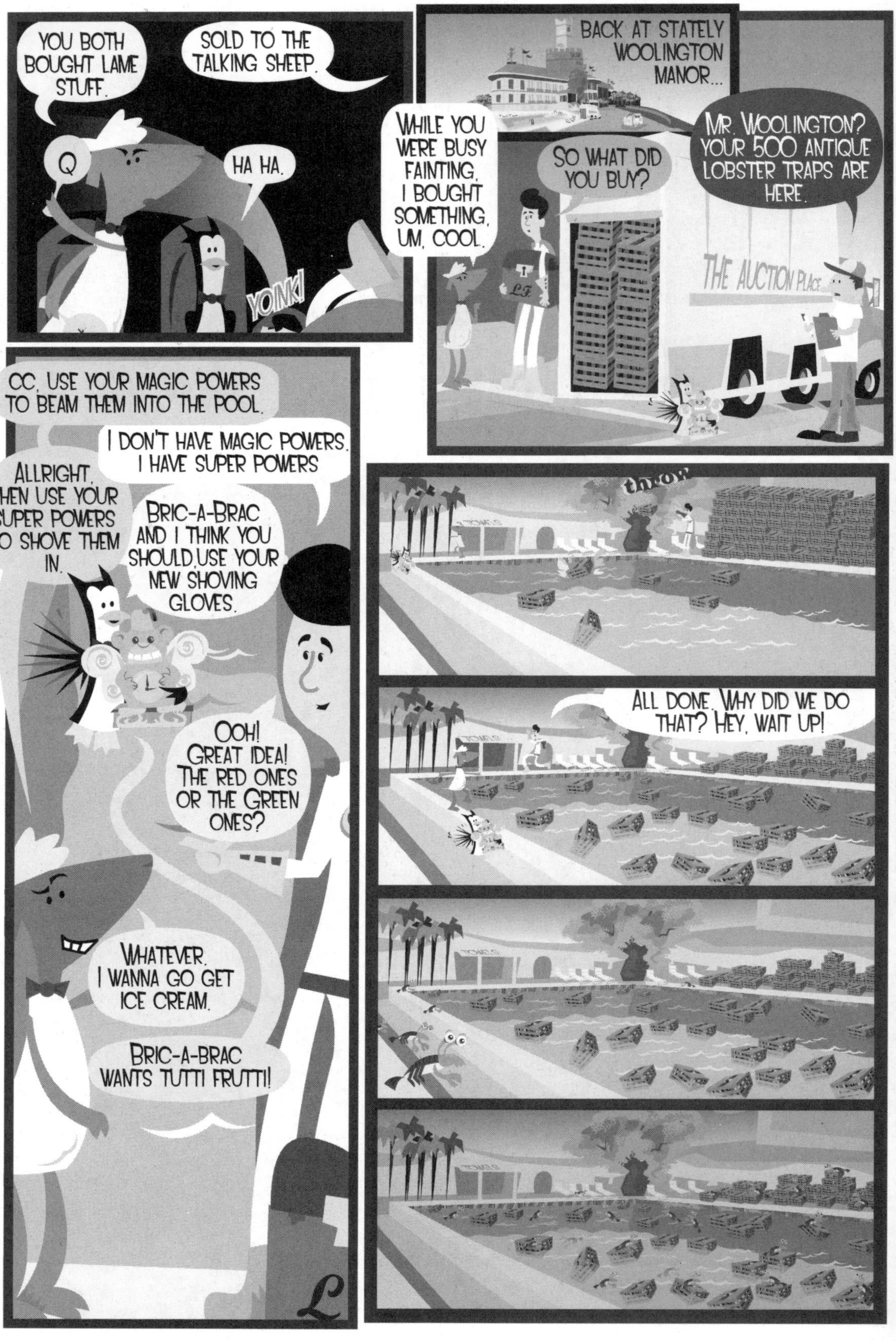
YOU BOTH BOUGHT LAME STUFF.
SOLD TO THE TALKING SHEEP.
Q
HA HA.
YOINK!
BACK AT STATELY WOOLINGTON MANOR...
WHILE YOU WERE BUSY FAINTING, I BOUGHT SOMETHING, UM, COOL.
SO WHAT DID YOU BUY?
MR. WOOLINGTON? YOUR 500 ANTIQUE LOBSTER TRAPS ARE HERE.
THE AUCTION PLACE
CC, USE YOUR MAGIC POWERS TO BEAM THEM INTO THE POOL.
I DON'T HAVE MAGIC POWERS. I HAVE SUPER POWERS
ALLRIGHT, THEN USE YOUR SUPER POWERS TO SHOVE THEM IN.
BRIC-A-BRAC AND I THINK YOU SHOULD,USE YOUR NEW SHOVING GLOVES.
OOH! GREAT IDEA! THE RED ONES OR THE GREEN ONES?
WHATEVER. I WANNA GO GET ICE CREAM.
BRIC-A-BRAC WANTS TUTTI FRUTTI!
throw
ALL DONE. WHY DID WE DO THAT? HEY, WAIT UP!

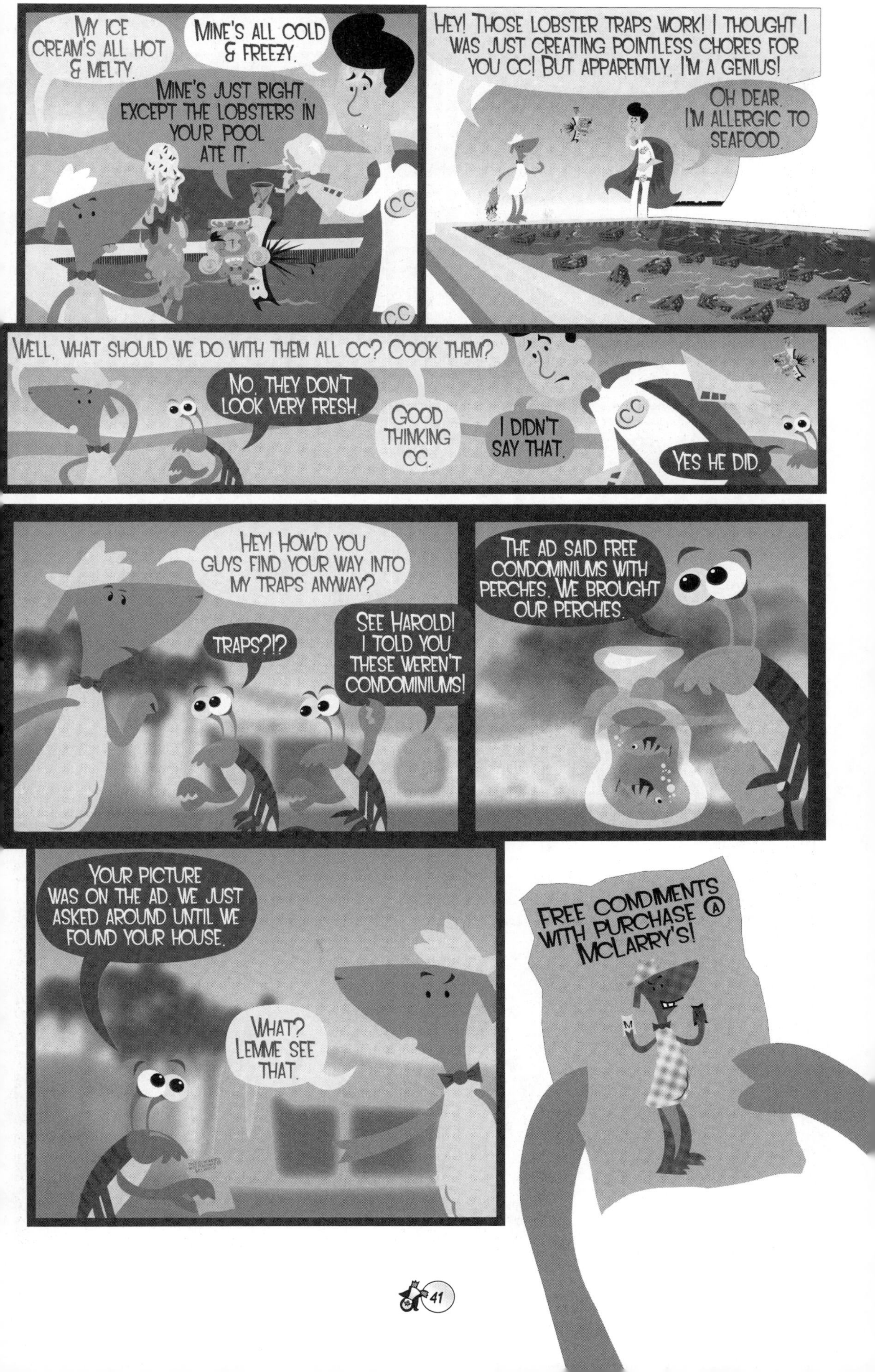
MY ICE CREAM'S ALL HOT & MELTY.
MINE'S ALL COLD & FREEZY.
MINE'S JUST RIGHT, EXCEPT THE LOBSTERS IN YOUR POOL ATE IT.
HEY! THOSE LOBSTER TRAPS WORK! I THOUGHT I WAS JUST CREATING POINTLESS CHORES FOR YOU CC! BUT APPARENTLY, I'M A GENIUS!
OH DEAR. I'M ALLERGIC TO SEAFOOD.
WELL, WHAT SHOULD WE DO WITH THEM ALL CC? COOK THEM?
NO, THEY DON'T LOOK VERY FRESH.
GOOD THINKING CC.
I DIDN'T SAY THAT.
YES HE DID.
HEY! HOW'D YOU GUYS FIND YOUR WAY INTO MY TRAPS ANYWAY?
TRAPS?!?
SEE HAROLD! I TOLD YOU THESE WEREN'T CONDOMINIUMS!
THE AD SAID FREE CONDOMINIUMS WITH PERCHES. WE BROUGHT OUR PERCHES.
YOUR PICTURE WAS ON THE AD. WE JUST ASKED AROUND UNTIL WE FOUND YOUR HOUSE.
WHAT? LEMME SEE THAT.
FREE CONDIMENTS WITH PURCHASE @ MCLARRY'S!

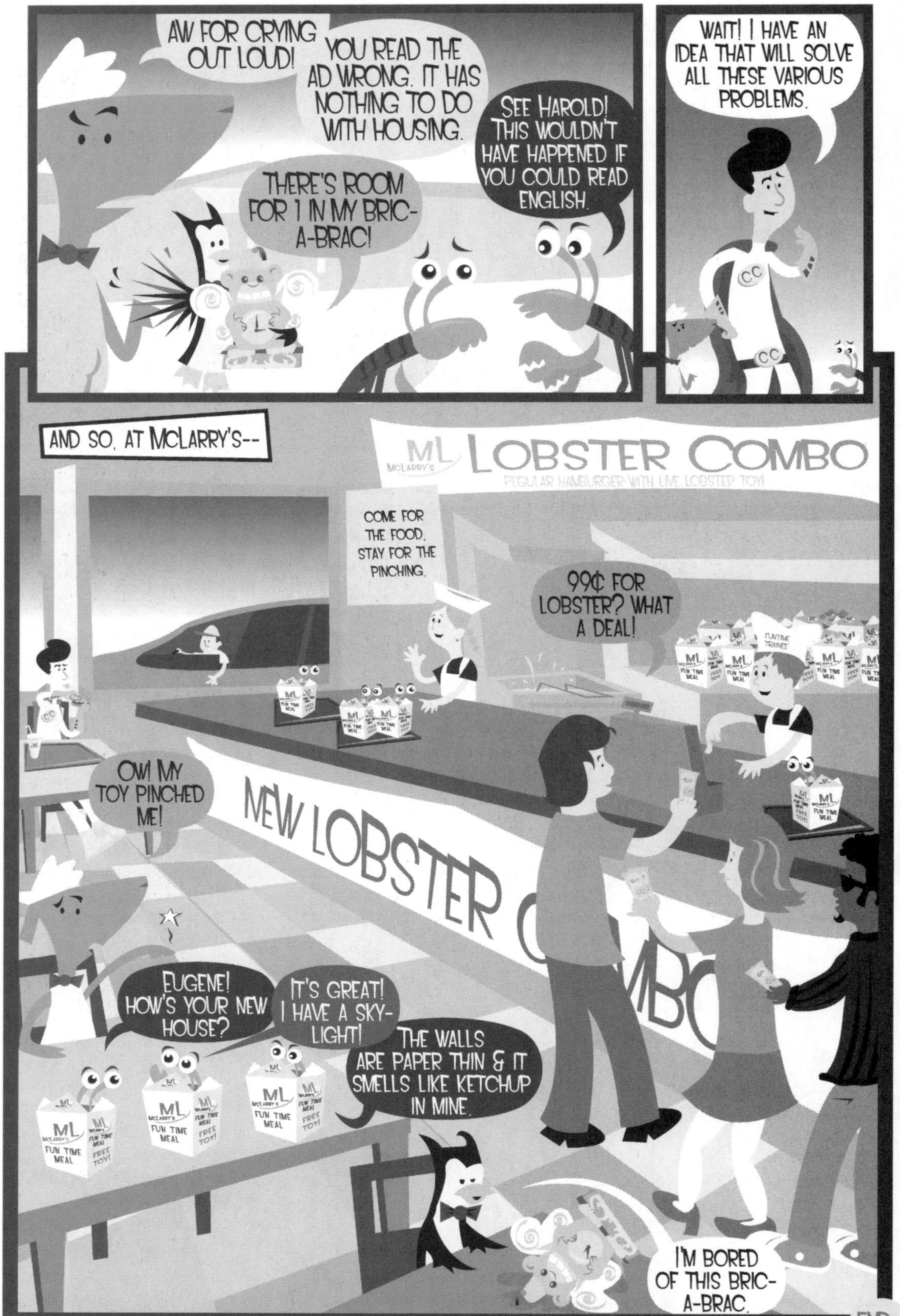

AW FOR CRYING OUT LOUD!
YOU READ THE AD WRONG. IT HAS NOTHING TO DO WITH HOUSING.
SEE HAROLD! THIS WOULDN'T HAVE HAPPENED IF YOU COULD READ ENGLISH.
THERE'S ROOM FOR 1 IN MY BRIC-A-BRAC!
WAIT! I HAVE AN IDEA THAT WILL SOLVE ALL THESE VARIOUS PROBLEMS.
AND SO, AT McLARRY'S--
ML McLARRY'S LOBSTER COMBO
REGULAR HAMBURGER WITH LIVE LOBSTER TOY!
COME FOR THE FOOD, STAY FOR THE PINCHING.
99¢ FOR LOBSTER? WHAT A DEAL!
FUNTIME TRAINEE
ML McLARRY'S FUN TIME MEAL FREE TOY!
OW! MY TOY PINCHED ME!
NEW LOBSTER COMBO
EUGENE! HOW'S YOUR NEW HOUSE?
IT'S GREAT! I HAVE A SKY-LIGHT!
THE WALLS ARE PAPER THIN & IT SMELLS LIKE KETCHUP IN MINE.
I'M BORED OF THIS BRIC-A-BRAC.
END.

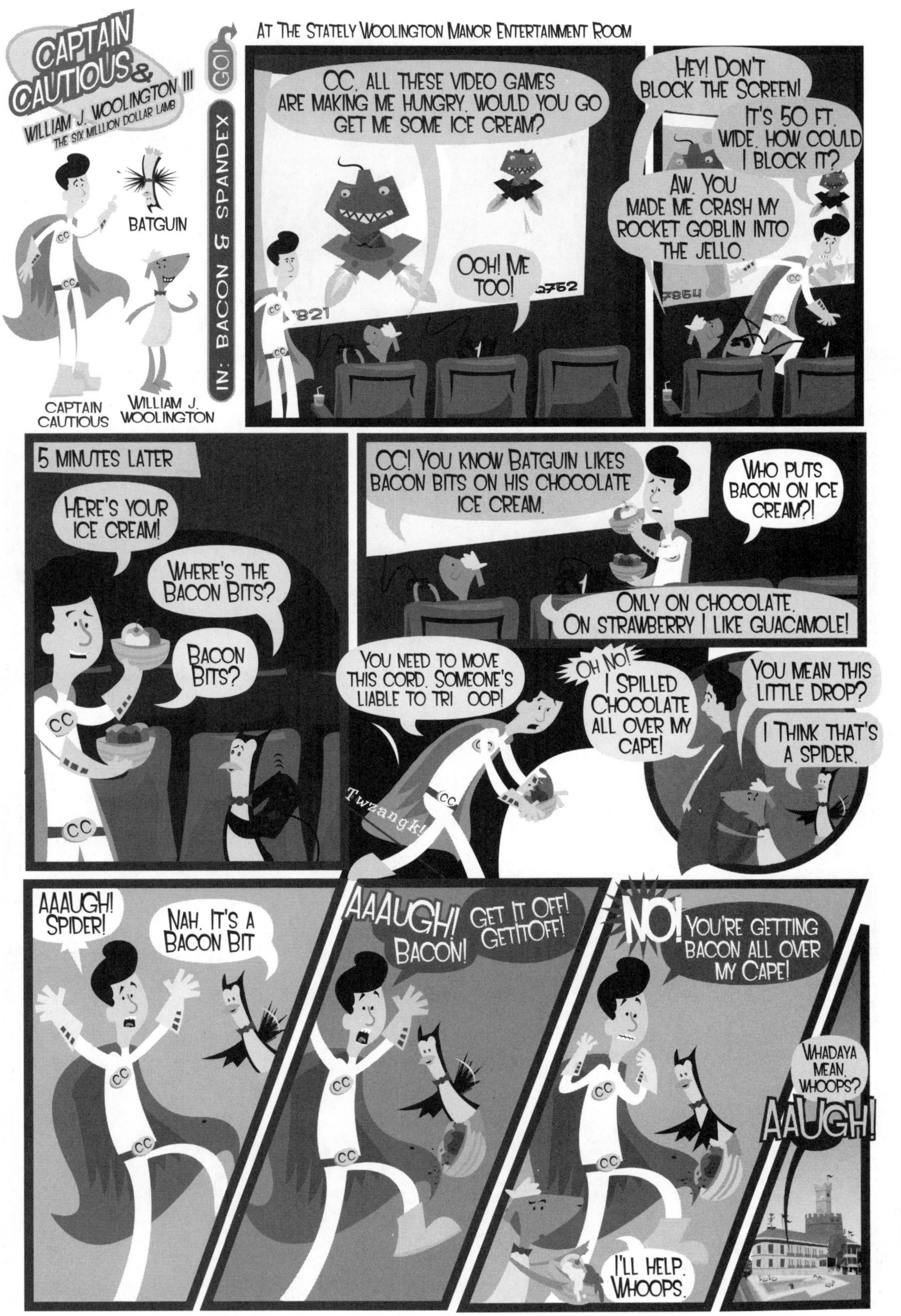
CAPTAIN CAUTIOUS & WILLIAM J. WOOLINGTON III
THE SIX MILLION DOLLAR LAMB
BATGUIN
CAPTAIN CAUTIOUS
WILLIAM J. WOOLINGTON
GO!
IN: BACON & SPANDEX
AT THE STATELY WOOLINGTON MANOR ENTERTAINMENT ROOM
CC, ALL THESE VIDEO GAMES ARE MAKING ME HUNGRY. WOULD YOU GO GET ME SOME ICE CREAM?
OOH! ME TOO!
HEY! DON'T BLOCK THE SCREEN!
IT'S 50 FT. WIDE. HOW COULD I BLOCK IT?
AW. YOU MADE ME CRASH MY ROCKET GOBLIN INTO THE JELLO.
5 MINUTES LATER
HERE'S YOUR ICE CREAM!
WHERE'S THE BACON BITS?
BACON BITS?
CC! YOU KNOW BATGUIN LIKES BACON BITS ON HIS CHOCOLATE ICE CREAM.
WHO PUTS BACON ON ICE CREAM?!
ONLY ON CHOCOLATE. ON STRAWBERRY I LIKE GUACAMOLE!
YOU NEED TO MOVE THIS CORD. SOMEONE'S LIABLE TO TRI OOP!
Twzangk!
OH NO! I SPILLED CHOCOLATE ALL OVER MY CAPE!
YOU MEAN THIS LITTLE DROP?
I THINK THAT'S A SPIDER.
AAAUGH! SPIDER!
NAH. IT'S A BACON BIT
AAAUGH! BACON!
GET IT OFF! GETITOFF!
NO! YOU'RE GETTING BACON ALL OVER MY CAPE!
I'LL HELP. WHOOPS.
WHADAYA MEAN, WHOOPS?
AAUGH!

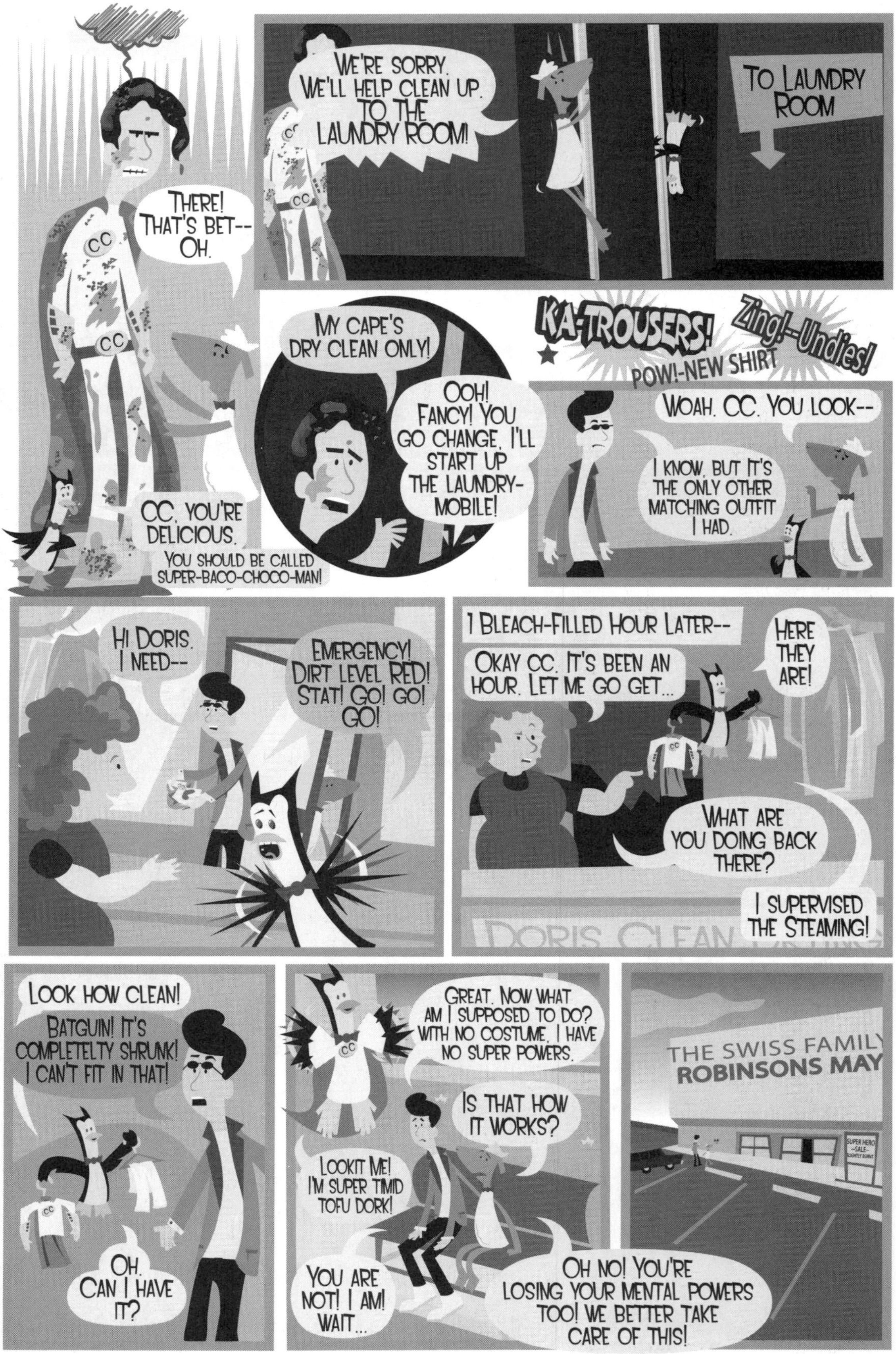
THERE! THAT'S BET-- OH.
CC, YOU'RE DELICIOUS.
YOU SHOULD BE CALLED SUPER-BACO-CHOCO-MAN!
WE'RE SORRY. WE'LL HELP CLEAN UP. TO THE LAUNDRY ROOM!
TO LAUNDRY ROOM
MY CAPE'S DRY CLEAN ONLY!
OOH! FANCY! YOU GO CHANGE, I'LL START UP THE LAUNDRY-MOBILE!
KA-TROUSERS!
Zing!-Undies!
POW!-NEW SHIRT
WOAH. CC. YOU LOOK--
I KNOW, BUT IT'S THE ONLY OTHER MATCHING OUTFIT I HAD.
HI DORIS. I NEED--
EMERGENCY! DIRT LEVEL RED! STAT! GO! GO! GO!
1 BLEACH-FILLED HOUR LATER--
OKAY CC. IT'S BEEN AN HOUR. LET ME GO GET...
HERE THEY ARE!
WHAT ARE YOU DOING BACK THERE?
I SUPERVISED THE STEAMING!
LOOK HOW CLEAN!
BATGUIN! IT'S COMPLETELTY SHRUNK! I CAN'T FIT IN THAT!
OH. CAN I HAVE IT?
GREAT. NOW WHAT AM I SUPPOSED TO DO? WITH NO COSTUME, I HAVE NO SUPER POWERS.
IS THAT HOW IT WORKS?
LOOKIT ME! I'M SUPER TIMID TOFU DORK!
YOU ARE NOT! I AM! WAIT...
OH NO! YOU'RE LOSING YOUR MENTAL POWERS TOO! WE BETTER TAKE CARE OF THIS!
THE SWISS FAMILY ROBINSONS MAY
SUPER HERO -SALE-

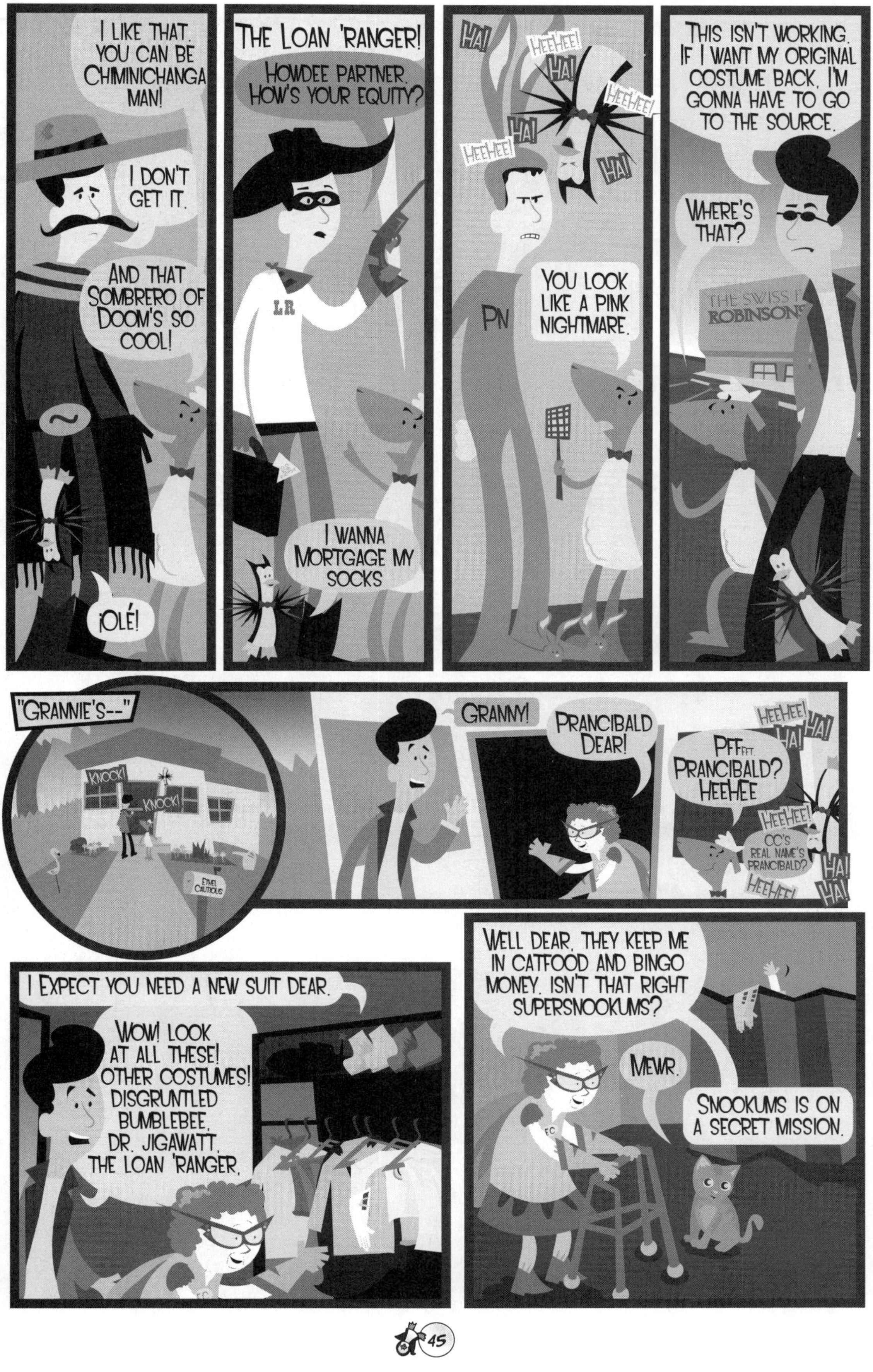
I LIKE THAT. YOU CAN BE CHIMINICHANGA MAN!
I DON'T GET IT.
AND THAT SOMBRERO OF DOOM'S SO COOL!
¡OLÉ!
THE LOAN 'RANGER!
HOWDEE PARTNER. HOW'S YOUR EQUITY?
LR
I WANNA MORTGAGE MY SOCKS
HA!
HEEHEE!
HA!
HEEHEE!
HA!
HEEHEE!
HA!
PN
YOU LOOK LIKE A PINK NIGHTMARE.
THIS ISN'T WORKING. IF I WANT MY ORIGINAL COSTUME BACK, I'M GONNA HAVE TO GO TO THE SOURCE.
WHERE'S THAT?
THE SWISS F ROBINSONS
"GRANNIE'S--"
KNOCK!
KNOCK!
ETHEL CAUTIOUS
GRANNY!
PRANCIBALD DEAR!
HEEHEE!
HA!
HA!
PFFFFT. PRANCIBALD? HEEHEE
HEEHEE!
CC'S REAL NAME'S PRANCIBALD?
HA!
HA!
HEEHEE!
I EXPECT YOU NEED A NEW SUIT DEAR.
WOW! LOOK AT ALL THESE! OTHER COSTUMES! DISGRUNTLED BUMBLEBEE, DR. JIGAWATT, THE LOAN 'RANGER,
WELL DEAR, THEY KEEP ME IN CATFOOD AND BINGO MONEY. ISN'T THAT RIGHT SUPERSNOOKUMS?
MEWR.
SNOOKUMS IS ON A SECRET MISSION.

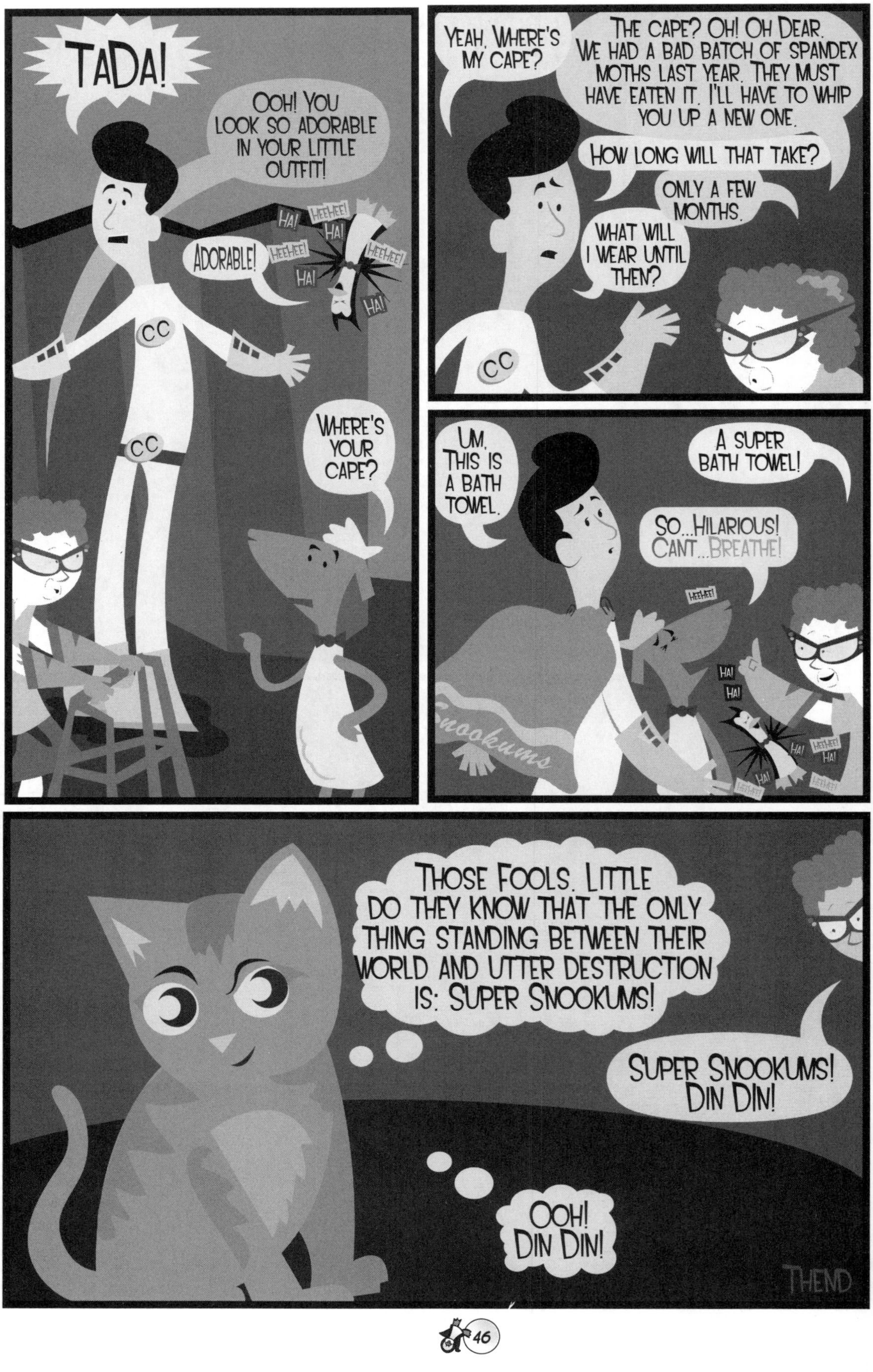
TADA!
OOH! YOU LOOK SO ADORABLE IN YOUR LITTLE OUTFIT!
HA! HEEHEE! HA!
ADORABLE! HEEHEE! HEEHEE!
HA! HA!
WHERE'S YOUR CAPE?
YEAH, WHERE'S MY CAPE?
THE CAPE? OH! OH DEAR. WE HAD A BAD BATCH OF SPANDEX MOTHS LAST YEAR. THEY MUST HAVE EATEN IT. I'LL HAVE TO WHIP YOU UP A NEW ONE.
HOW LONG WILL THAT TAKE?
ONLY A FEW MONTHS.
WHAT WILL I WEAR UNTIL THEN?
UM, THIS IS A BATH TOWEL.
A SUPER BATH TOWEL!
SO...HILARIOUS! CANT...BREATHE!
Snookums
HEEHEE!
HA! HA!
HA! HEEHEE! HA!
THOSE FOOLS. LITTLE DO THEY KNOW THAT THE ONLY THING STANDING BETWEEN THEIR WORLD AND UTTER DESTRUCTION IS: SUPER SNOOKUMS!
SUPER SNOOKUMS! DIN DIN!
OOH! DIN DIN!
THEND

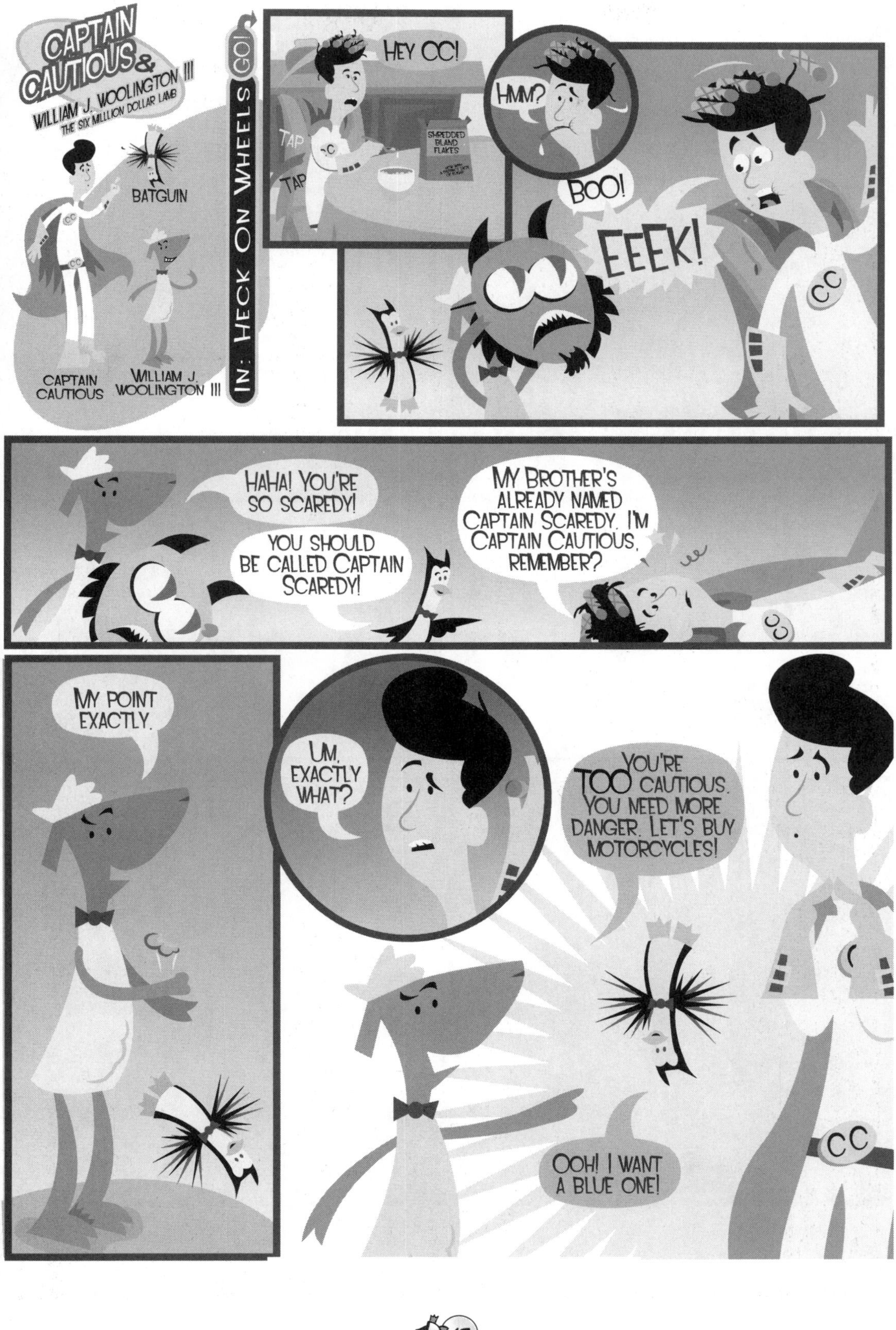
CAPTAIN CAUTIOUS & WILLIAM J. WOOLINGTON III
THE SIX MILLION DOLLAR LAMB
BATGUIN
CAPTAIN CAUTIOUS
WILLIAM J. WOOLINGTON III
IN: HECK ON WHEELS GO!
HEY CC!
TAP
TAP
SHREDDED BLAND FLAKES
HMM?
BOO!
EEEK!
HAHA! YOU'RE SO SCAREDY!
YOU SHOULD BE CALLED CAPTAIN SCAREDY!
MY BROTHER'S ALREADY NAMED CAPTAIN SCAREDY. I'M CAPTAIN CAUTIOUS, REMEMBER?
MY POINT EXACTLY.
UM, EXACTLY WHAT?
YOU'RE TOO CAUTIOUS. YOU NEED MORE DANGER. LET'S BUY MOTORCYCLES!
OOH! I WANT A BLUE ONE!

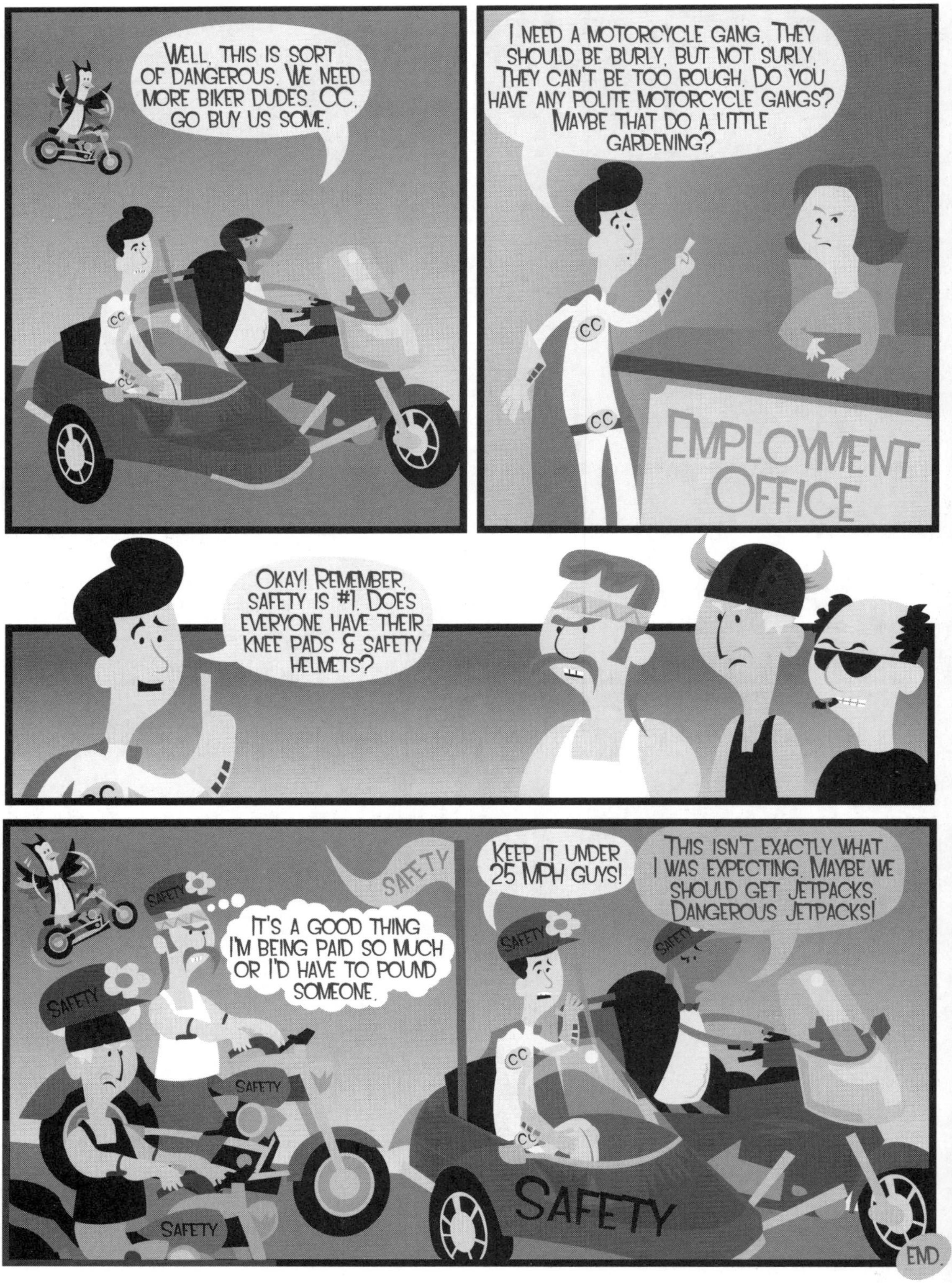
WELL, THIS IS SORT OF DANGEROUS. WE NEED MORE BIKER DUDES. CC, GO BUY US SOME.
I NEED A MOTORCYCLE GANG. THEY SHOULD BE BURLY, BUT NOT SURLY. THEY CAN'T BE TOO ROUGH. DO YOU HAVE ANY POLITE MOTORCYCLE GANGS? MAYBE THAT DO A LITTLE GARDENING?
EMPLOYMENT OFFICE
OKAY! REMEMBER, SAFETY IS #1. DOES EVERYONE HAVE THEIR KNEE PADS & SAFETY HELMETS?
SAFETY
IT'S A GOOD THING I'M BEING PAID SO MUCH OR I'D HAVE TO POUND SOMEONE.
KEEP IT UNDER 25 MPH GUYS!
THIS ISN'T EXACTLY WHAT I WAS EXPECTING. MAYBE WE SHOULD GET JETPACKS. DANGEROUS JETPACKS!
SAFETY
END.

t BYRD fearlessness

in: "The Saga of
Scruffy & Mcbeens"

BACK IN THE OLD
WEST, WHEN BIRDS
WERE BIRDS AND FROGS
WEREN'T, AND A MAN'S
BEST FRIEND WAS HIS
SPOON, THERE STOOD
A FIGURE. A TALL FIGURE.
A TALL GANGLY FIGURE IN
DESPERATE NEED OF A
BATH: TBYRD FEARLESSNESS.
ALONG WITH HIS SIDEKICK,
HOPALONG CASSOWARY, THE
OBTUSE OUTLAWS ARE IN
SEARCH OF FAME, FORTUNE
OR LUNCH.

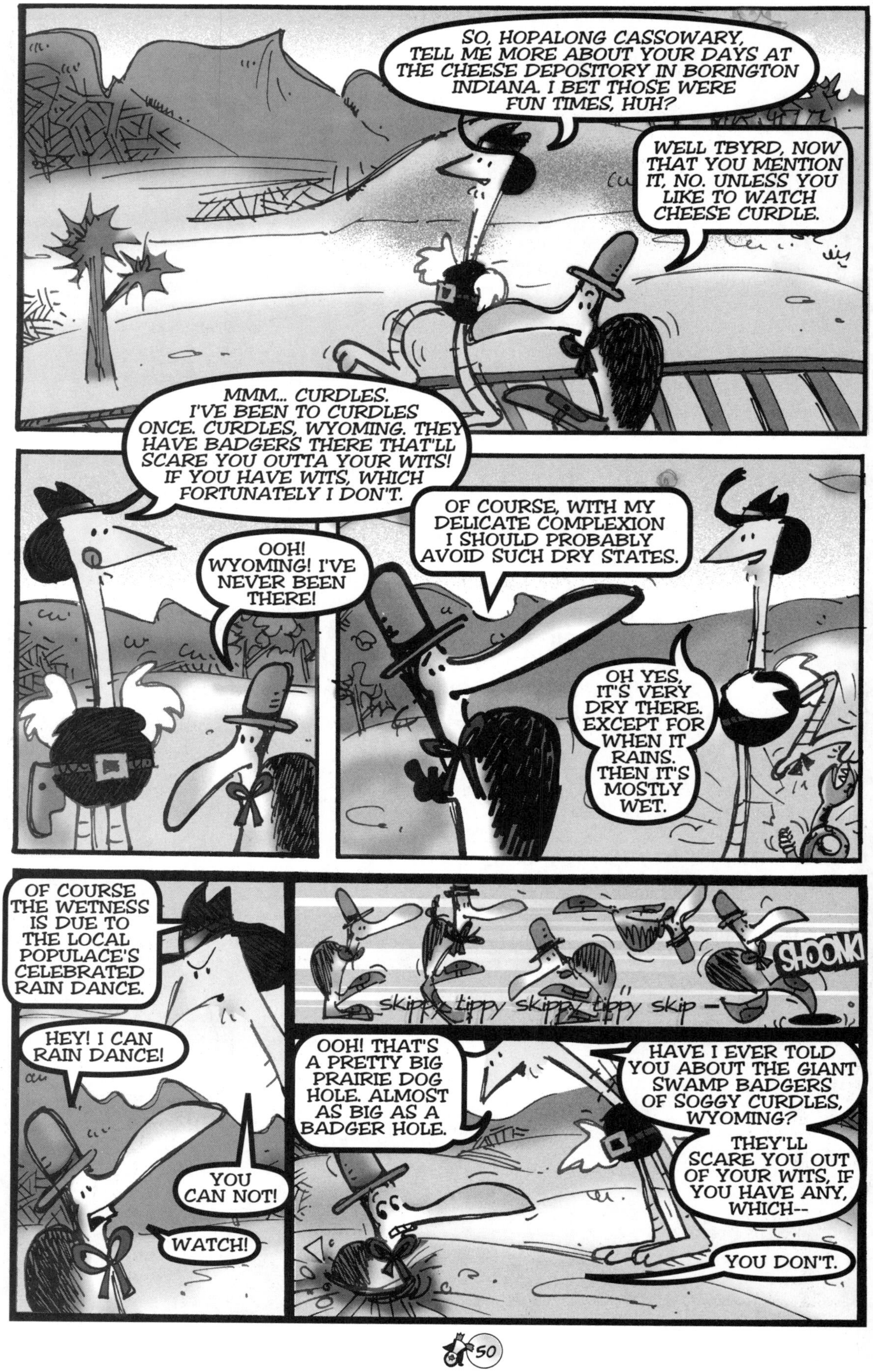
SO, HOPALONG CASSOWARY, TELL ME MORE ABOUT YOUR DAYS AT THE CHEESE DEPOSITORY IN BORINGTON INDIANA. I BET THOSE WERE FUN TIMES, HUH?
WELL TBYRD, NOW THAT YOU MENTION IT, NO. UNLESS YOU LIKE TO WATCH CHEESE CURDLE.
MMM... CURDLES. I'VE BEEN TO CURDLES ONCE. CURDLES, WYOMING. THEY HAVE BADGERS THERE THAT'LL SCARE YOU OUTTA YOUR WITS! IF YOU HAVE WITS, WHICH FORTUNATELY I DON'T.
OOH! WYOMING! I'VE NEVER BEEN THERE!
OF COURSE, WITH MY DELICATE COMPLEXION I SHOULD PROBABLY AVOID SUCH DRY STATES.
OH YES, IT'S VERY DRY THERE. EXCEPT FOR WHEN IT RAINS. THEN IT'S MOSTLY WET.
OF COURSE THE WETNESS IS DUE TO THE LOCAL POPULACE'S CELEBRATED RAIN DANCE.
HEY! I CAN RAIN DANCE!
YOU CAN NOT!
WATCH!
skippy tippy skippy tippy skip
SHOONK!
OOH! THAT'S A PRETTY BIG PRAIRIE DOG HOLE. ALMOST AS BIG AS A BADGER HOLE.
HAVE I EVER TOLD YOU ABOUT THE GIANT SWAMP BADGERS OF SOGGY CURDLES, WYOMING?
THEY'LL SCARE YOU OUT OF YOUR WITS, IF YOU HAVE ANY, WHICH--
YOU DON'T.

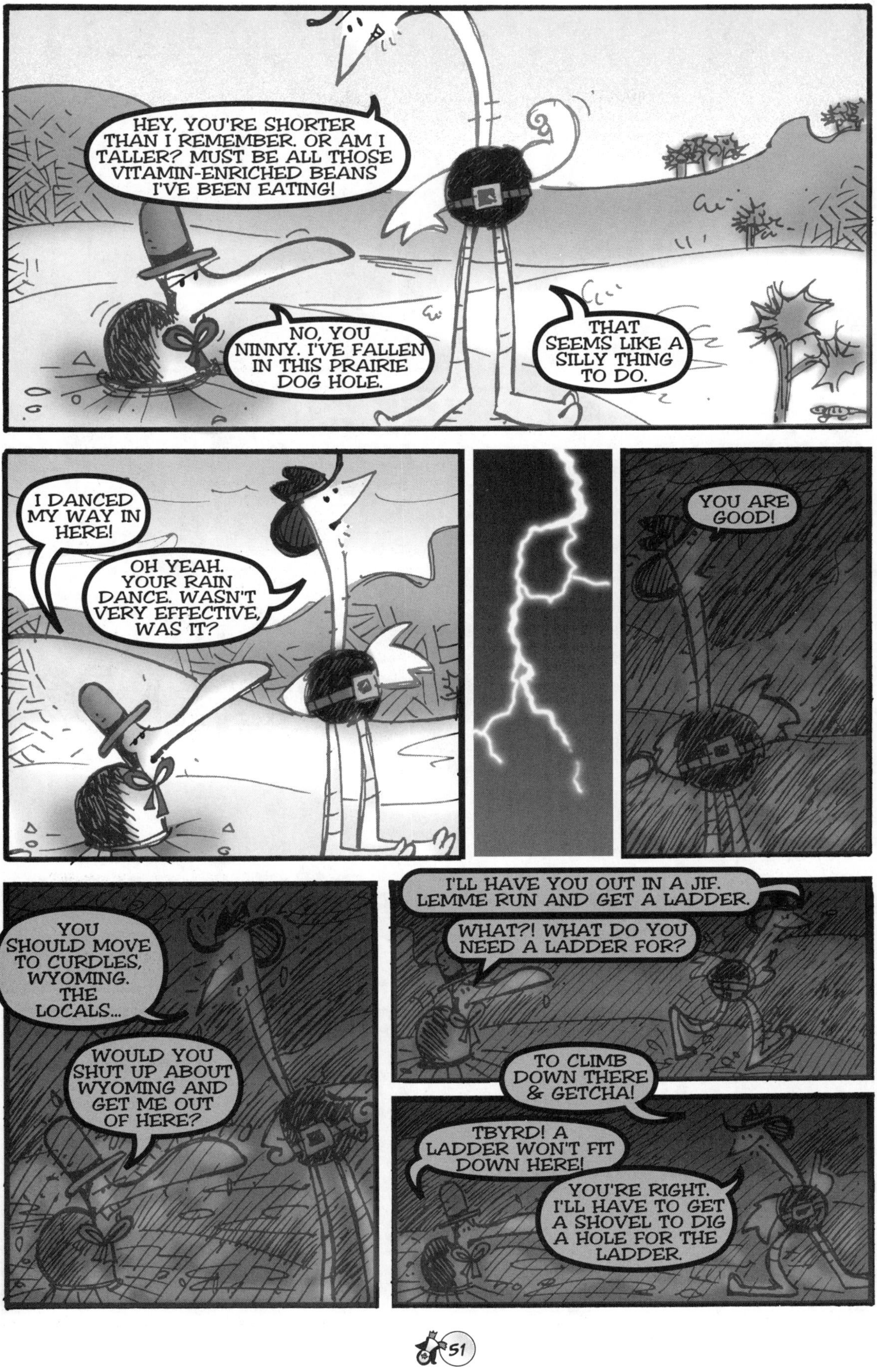
HEY, YOU'RE SHORTER THAN I REMEMBER. OR AM I TALLER? MUST BE ALL THOSE VITAMIN-ENRICHED BEANS I'VE BEEN EATING!
NO, YOU NINNY. I'VE FALLEN IN THIS PRAIRIE DOG HOLE.
THAT SEEMS LIKE A SILLY THING TO DO.
I DANCED MY WAY IN HERE!
OH YEAH. YOUR RAIN DANCE. WASN'T VERY EFFECTIVE, WAS IT?
YOU ARE GOOD!
YOU SHOULD MOVE TO CURDLES, WYOMING. THE LOCALS...
WOULD YOU SHUT UP ABOUT WYOMING AND GET ME OUT OF HERE?
I'LL HAVE YOU OUT IN A JIF. LEMME RUN AND GET A LADDER.
WHAT?! WHAT DO YOU NEED A LADDER FOR?
TO CLIMB DOWN THERE & GETCHA!
TBYRD! A LADDER WON'T FIT DOWN HERE!
YOU'RE RIGHT. I'LL HAVE TO GET A SHOVEL TO DIG A HOLE FOR THE LADDER.

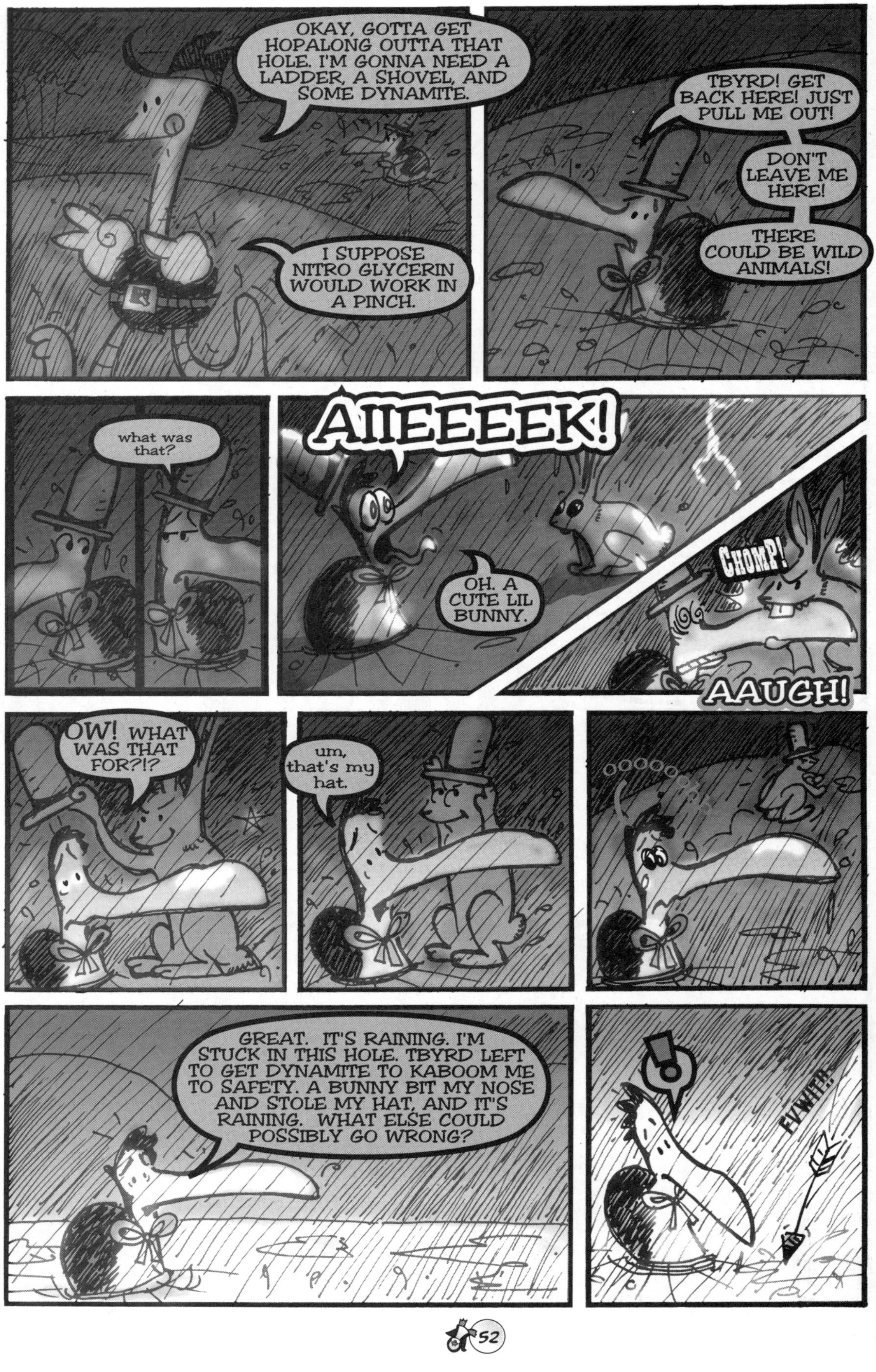
OKAY, GOTTA GET HOPALONG OUTTA THAT HOLE. I'M GONNA NEED A LADDER, A SHOVEL, AND SOME DYNAMITE.
I SUPPOSE NITRO GLYCERIN WOULD WORK IN A PINCH.
TBYRD! GET BACK HERE! JUST PULL ME OUT!
DON'T LEAVE ME HERE!
THERE COULD BE WILD ANIMALS!
what was that?
AIIEEEEK!
OH. A CUTE LIL BUNNY.
CHOMP!
AAUGH!
OW! WHAT WAS THAT FOR?!?
um, that's my hat.
GREAT. IT'S RAINING. I'M STUCK IN THIS HOLE. TBYRD LEFT TO GET DYNAMITE TO KABOOM ME TO SAFETY. A BUNNY BIT MY NOSE AND STOLE MY HAT, AND IT'S RAINING. WHAT ELSE COULD POSSIBLY GO WRONG?
!
FVWIT!!

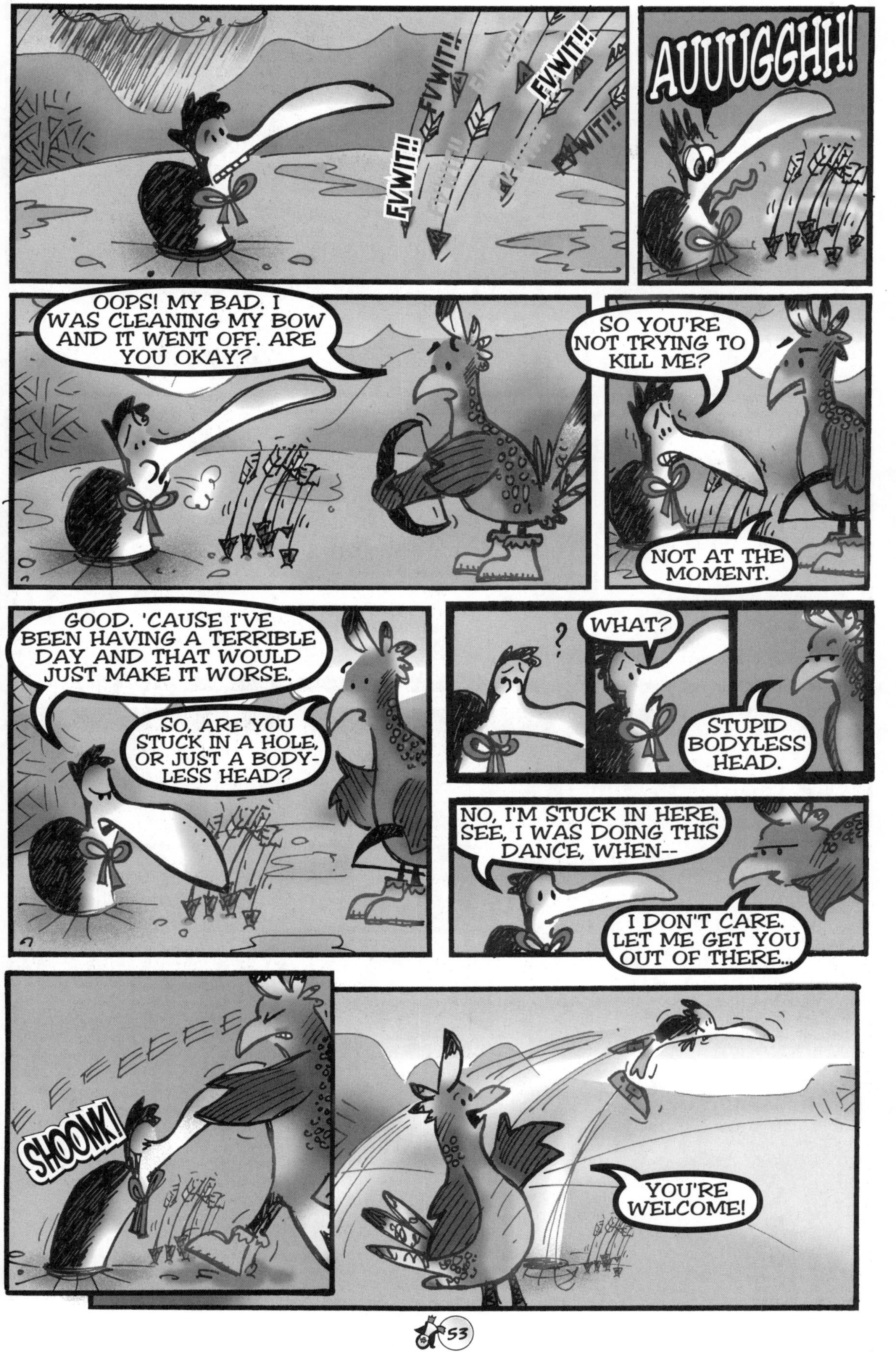
FVWIT!!
FVWIT!!
FVWIT!!
FVWIT!!
AUUUGGHH!
OOPS! MY BAD. I WAS CLEANING MY BOW AND IT WENT OFF. ARE YOU OKAY?
SO YOU'RE NOT TRYING TO KILL ME?
NOT AT THE MOMENT.
GOOD. 'CAUSE I'VE BEEN HAVING A TERRIBLE DAY AND THAT WOULD JUST MAKE IT WORSE.
SO, ARE YOU STUCK IN A HOLE, OR JUST A BODY-LESS HEAD?
?
WHAT?
STUPID BODYLESS HEAD.
NO, I'M STUCK IN HERE. SEE, I WAS DOING THIS DANCE, WHEN--
I DON'T CARE. LET ME GET YOU OUT OF THERE...
EEEEEEEE
SHOONK!
YOU'RE WELCOME!

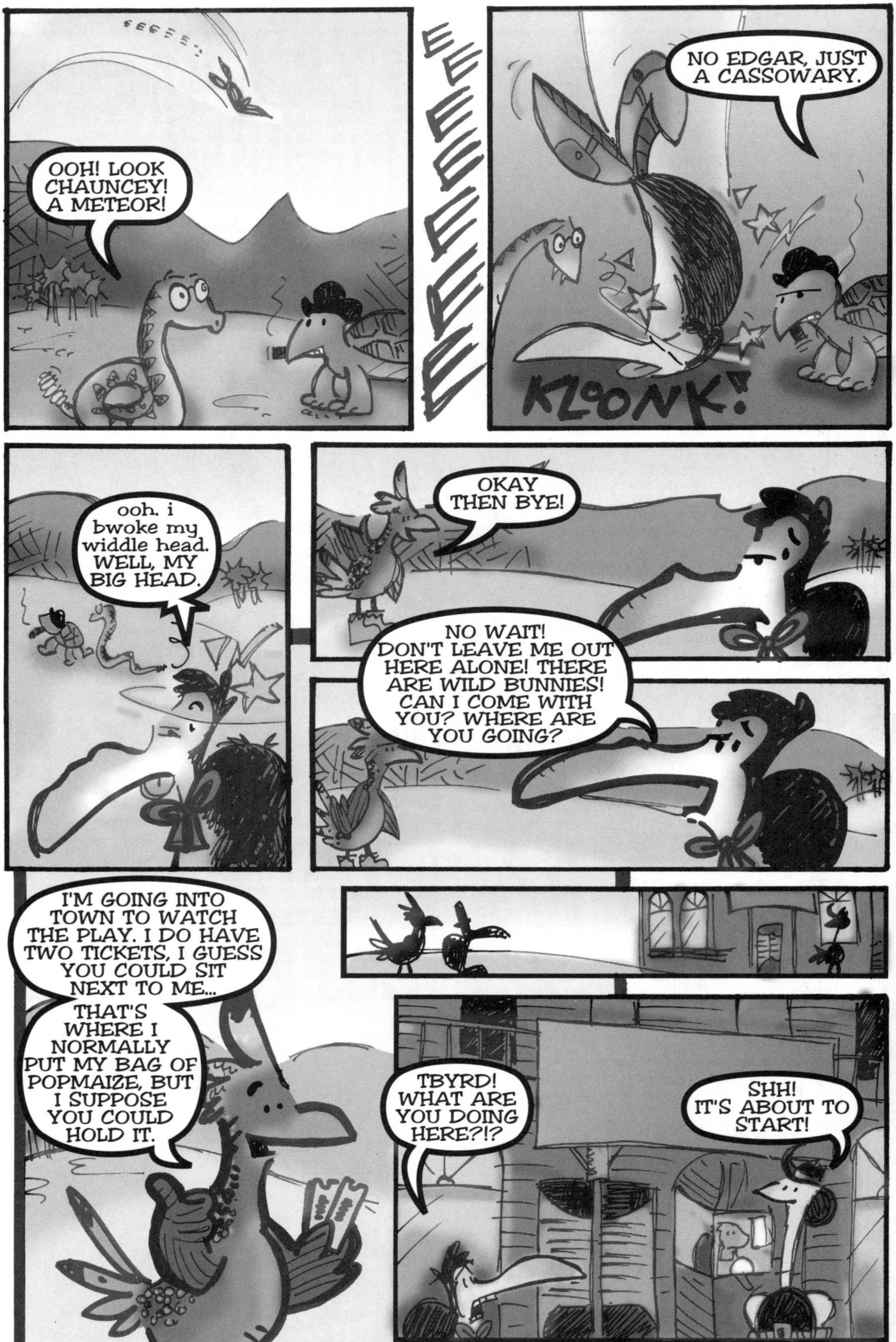

EEEEE
OOH! LOOK CHAUNCEY! A METEOR!
EEEEEEEEEE
NO EDGAR, JUST A CASSOWARY.
KLOONK!
ooh. i bwoke my widdle head. WELL, MY BIG HEAD.
OKAY THEN BYE!
NO WAIT! DON'T LEAVE ME OUT HERE ALONE! THERE ARE WILD BUNNIES! CAN I COME WITH YOU? WHERE ARE YOU GOING?
I'M GOING INTO TOWN TO WATCH THE PLAY. I DO HAVE TWO TICKETS, I GUESS YOU COULD SIT NEXT TO ME...
THAT'S WHERE I NORMALLY PUT MY BAG OF POPMAIZE, BUT I SUPPOSE YOU COULD HOLD IT.
TBYRD! WHAT ARE YOU DOING HERE?!?
SHH! IT'S ABOUT TO START!

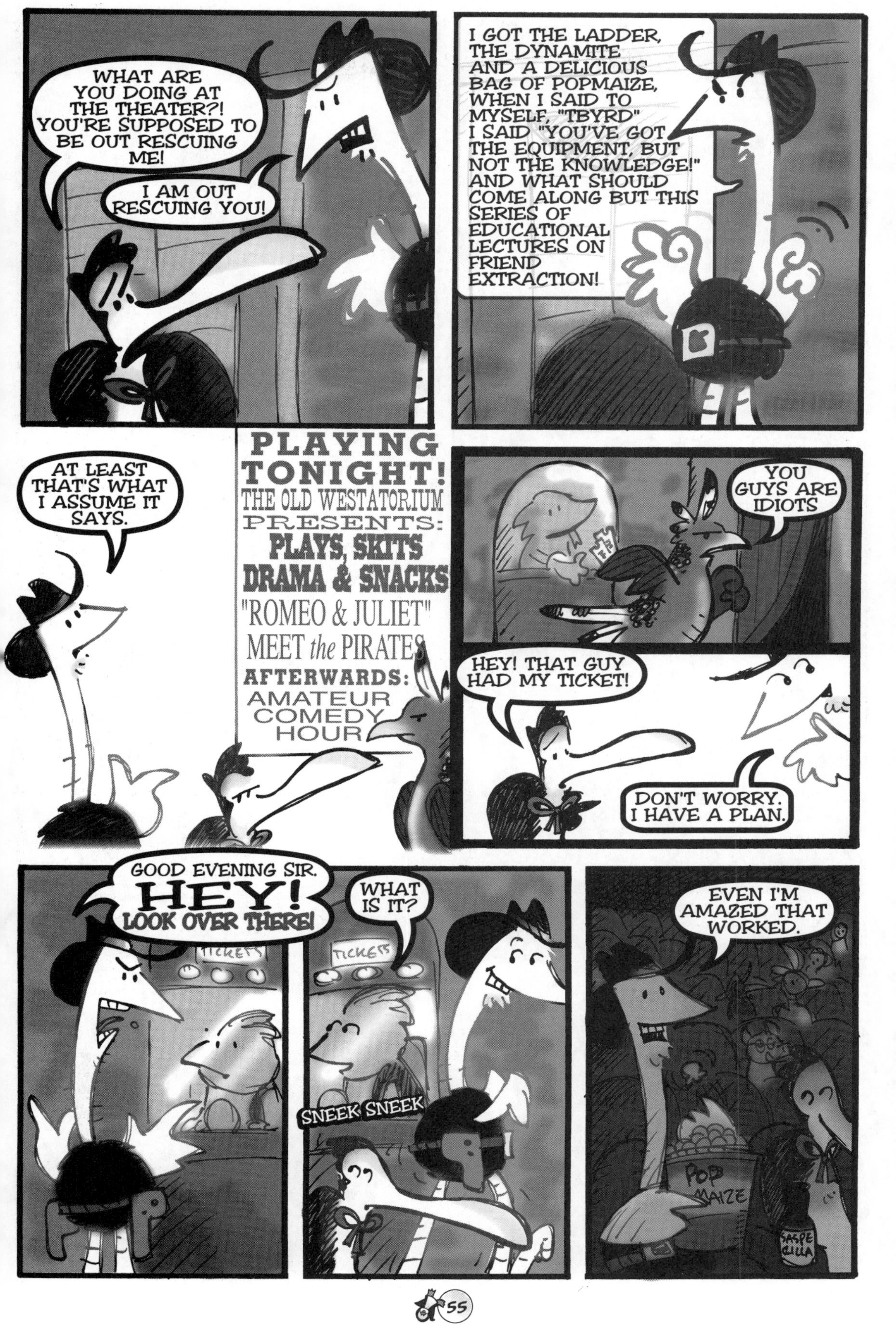
WHAT ARE YOU DOING AT THE THEATER?! YOU'RE SUPPOSED TO BE OUT RESCUING ME!
I AM OUT RESCUING YOU!
I GOT THE LADDER, THE DYNAMITE AND A DELICIOUS BAG OF POPMAIZE, WHEN I SAID TO MYSELF, "TBYRD" I SAID "YOU'VE GOT THE EQUIPMENT, BUT NOT THE KNOWLEDGE!" AND WHAT SHOULD COME ALONG BUT THIS SERIES OF EDUCATIONAL LECTURES ON FRIEND EXTRACTION!
AT LEAST THAT'S WHAT I ASSUME IT SAYS.
PLAYING TONIGHT!
THE OLD WESTATORIUM
PRESENTS:
PLAYS, SKITS DRAMA & SNACKS
"ROMEO & JULIET" MEET the PIRATES
AFTERWARDS: AMATEUR COMEDY HOUR
YOU GUYS ARE IDIOTS
HEY! THAT GUY HAD MY TICKET!
DON'T WORRY. I HAVE A PLAN.
GOOD EVENING SIR. HEY! LOOK OVER THERE!
TICKETS
WHAT IS IT?
TICKETS
SNEEK SNEEK
EVEN I'M AMAZED THAT WORKED.
POP MAIZE
SASPE CILLA

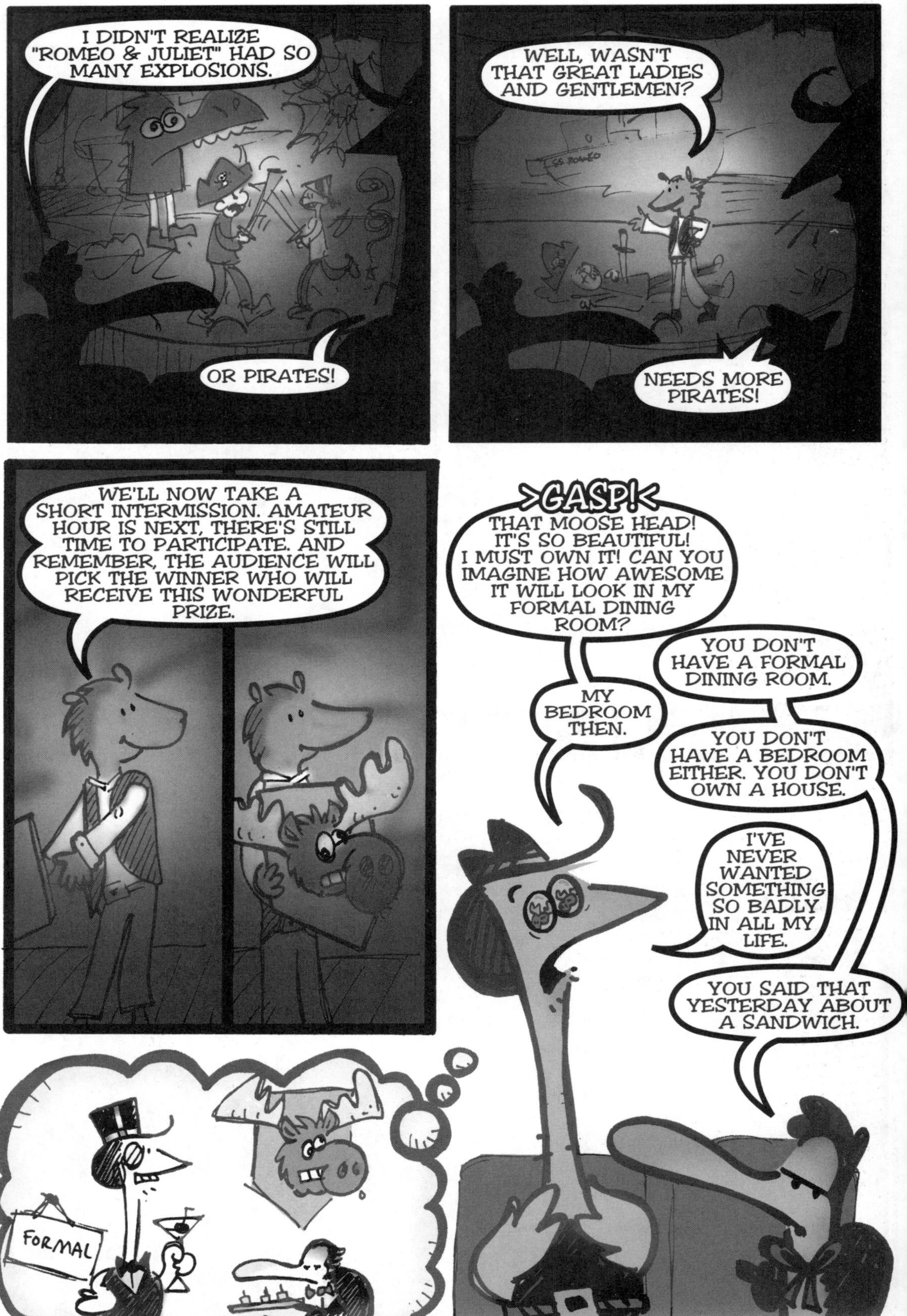
I DIDN'T REALIZE "ROMEO & JULIET" HAD SO MANY EXPLOSIONS.
OR PIRATES!
WELL, WASN'T THAT GREAT LADIES AND GENTLEMEN?
NEEDS MORE PIRATES!
WE'LL NOW TAKE A SHORT INTERMISSION. AMATEUR HOUR IS NEXT, THERE'S STILL TIME TO PARTICIPATE. AND REMEMBER, THE AUDIENCE WILL PICK THE WINNER WHO WILL RECEIVE THIS WONDERFUL PRIZE.
>GASP!<
THAT MOOSE HEAD! IT'S SO BEAUTIFUL! I MUST OWN IT! CAN YOU IMAGINE HOW AWESOME IT WILL LOOK IN MY FORMAL DINING ROOM?
YOU DON'T HAVE A FORMAL DINING ROOM.
MY BEDROOM THEN.
YOU DON'T HAVE A BEDROOM EITHER. YOU DON'T OWN A HOUSE.
I'VE NEVER WANTED SOMETHING SO BADLY IN ALL MY LIFE.
YOU SAID THAT YESTERDAY ABOUT A SANDWICH.
FORMAL

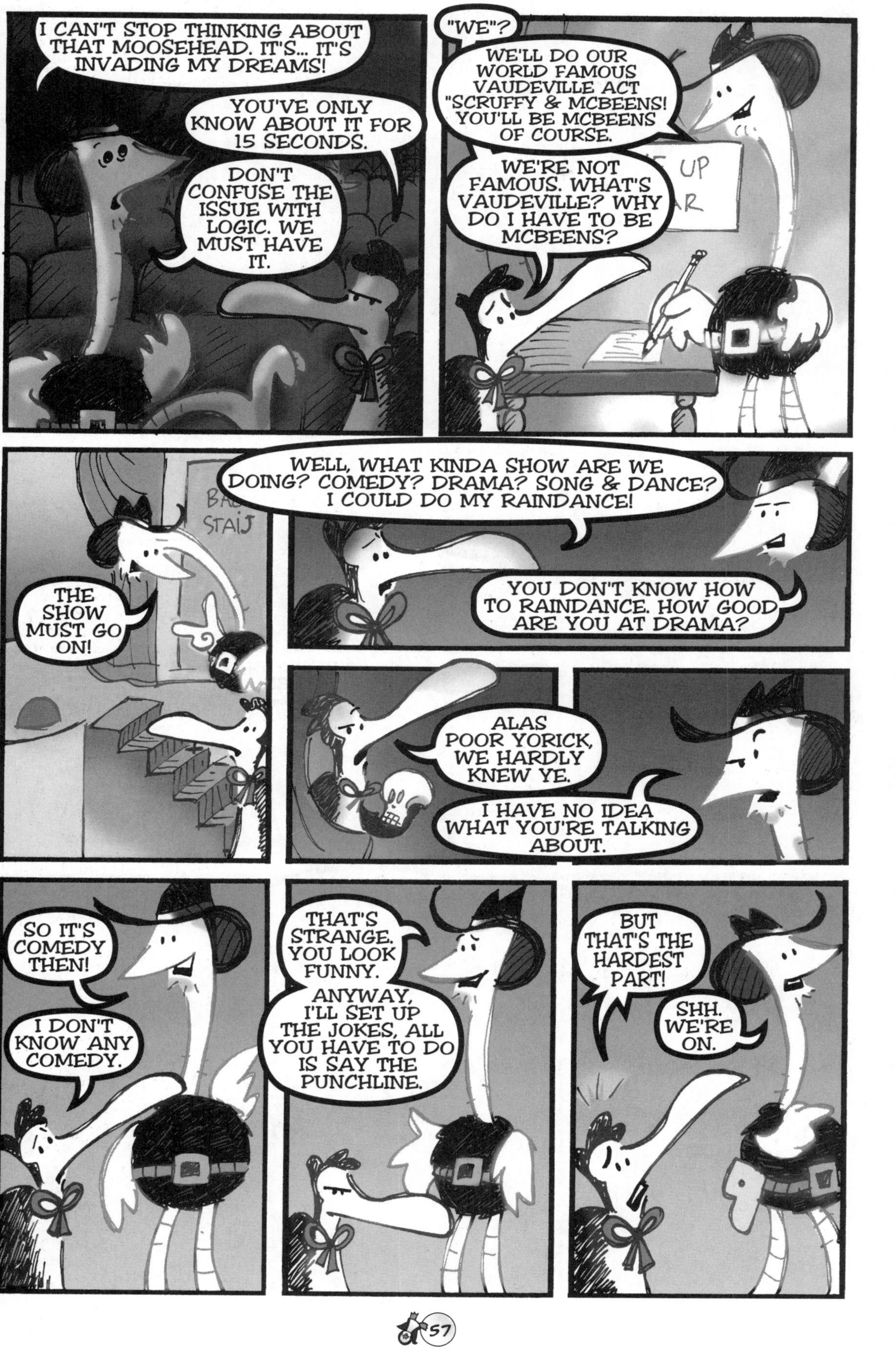
I CAN'T STOP THINKING ABOUT THAT MOOSEHEAD. IT'S... IT'S INVADING MY DREAMS!
YOU'VE ONLY KNOW ABOUT IT FOR 15 SECONDS.
DON'T CONFUSE THE ISSUE WITH LOGIC. WE MUST HAVE IT.
"WE"?
WE'LL DO OUR WORLD FAMOUS VAUDEVILLE ACT "SCRUFFY & MCBEENS! YOU'LL BE MCBEENS OF COURSE.
WE'RE NOT FAMOUS. WHAT'S VAUDEVILLE? WHY DO I HAVE TO BE MCBEENS?
THE SHOW MUST GO ON!
WELL, WHAT KINDA SHOW ARE WE DOING? COMEDY? DRAMA? SONG & DANCE? I COULD DO MY RAINDANCE!
YOU DON'T KNOW HOW TO RAINDANCE. HOW GOOD ARE YOU AT DRAMA?
ALAS POOR YORICK, WE HARDLY KNEW YE.
I HAVE NO IDEA WHAT YOU'RE TALKING ABOUT.
SO IT'S COMEDY THEN!
I DON'T KNOW ANY COMEDY.
THAT'S STRANGE. YOU LOOK FUNNY.
ANYWAY, I'LL SET UP THE JOKES, ALL YOU HAVE TO DO IS SAY THE PUNCHLINE.
BUT THAT'S THE HARDEST PART!
SHH. WE'RE ON.

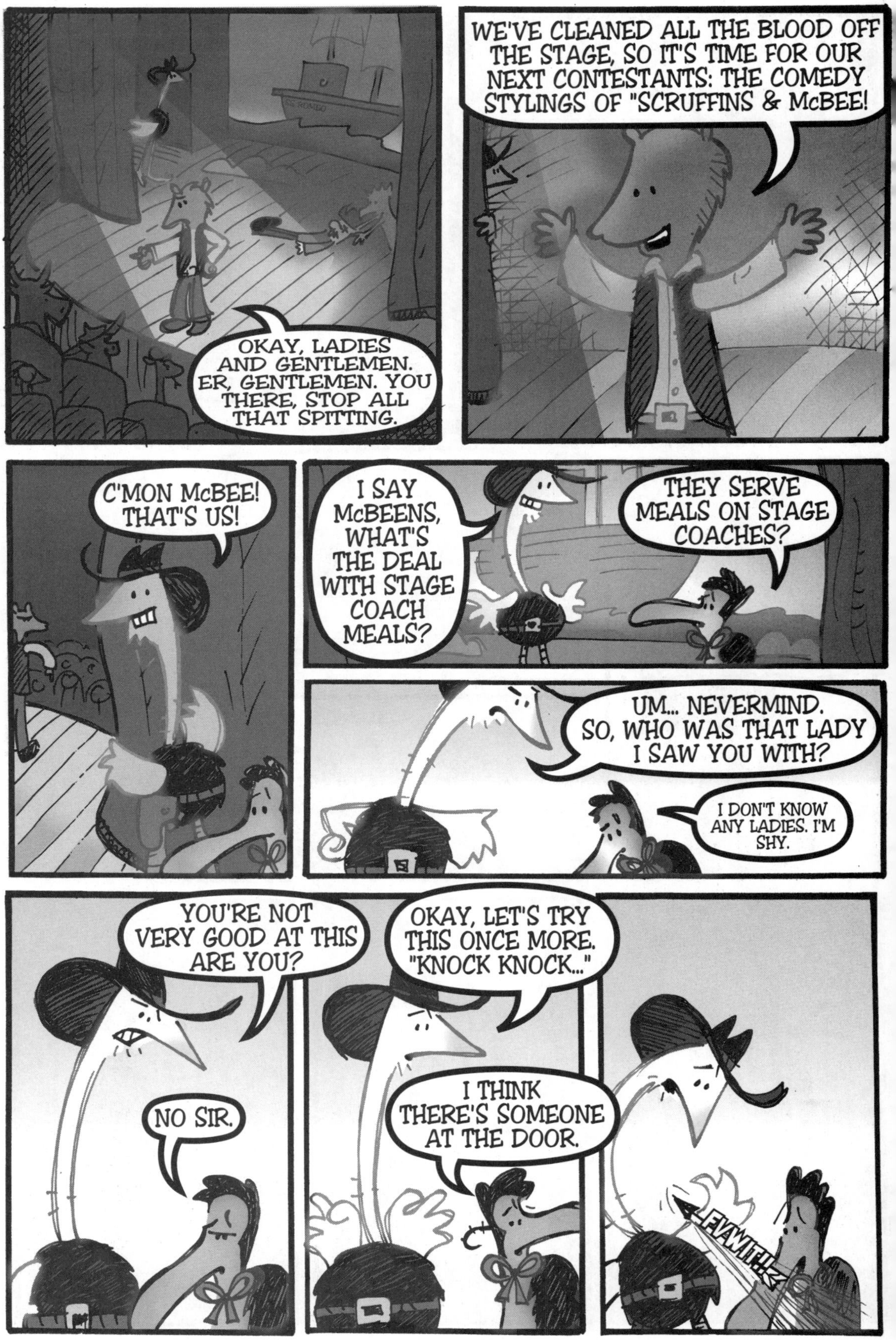
OKAY, LADIES AND GENTLEMEN. ER, GENTLEMEN. YOU THERE, STOP ALL THAT SPITTING.
WE'VE CLEANED ALL THE BLOOD OFF THE STAGE, SO IT'S TIME FOR OUR NEXT CONTESTANTS: THE COMEDY STYLINGS OF "SCRUFFINS & McBEE!
C'MON McBEE! THAT'S US!
I SAY McBEENS, WHAT'S THE DEAL WITH STAGE COACH MEALS?
THEY SERVE MEALS ON STAGE COACHES?
UM... NEVERMIND. SO, WHO WAS THAT LADY I SAW YOU WITH?
I DON'T KNOW ANY LADIES. I'M SHY.
YOU'RE NOT VERY GOOD AT THIS ARE YOU?
NO SIR.
OKAY, LET'S TRY THIS ONCE MORE. "KNOCK KNOCK..."
I THINK THERE'S SOMEONE AT THE DOOR.
FVAWITH!

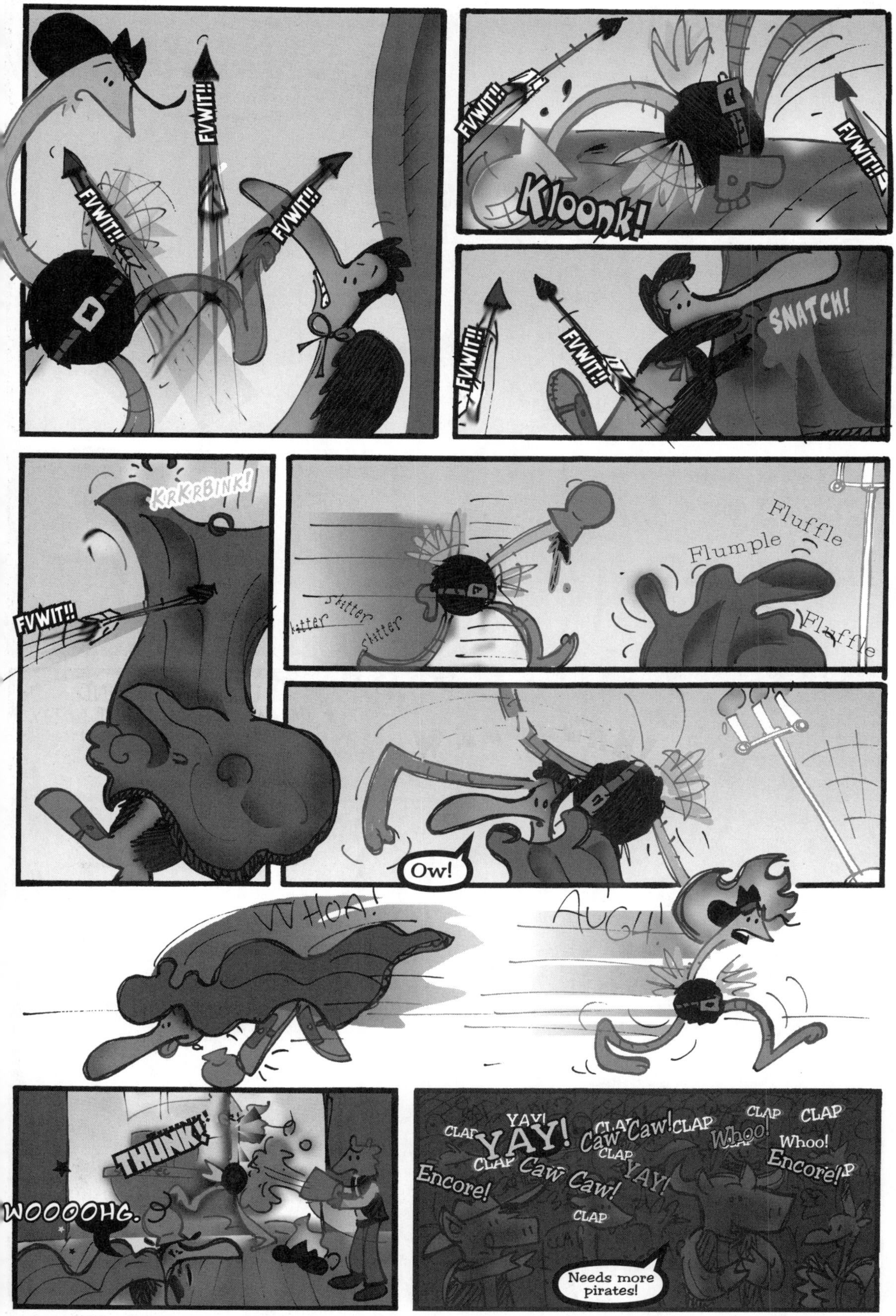
FVWIT!!
FVWIT!!
FVWIT!!
FVWIT!!
Kloonk!
FVWIT!!
FVWIT!!
FVWIT!!
SNATCH!
KRKRBINK!
FVWIT!!
Skitter
Skitter
Skitter
Flumple
Fluffle
Fluffle
Ow!
WHOA!
AUGH!
THUNK!
WOOOOHG.
CLAP
YAY!
YAY!
Caw Caw!
CLAP
CLAP
Whoo!
CLAP
CLAP
Whoo!
CLAP
Caw Caw!
YAY!
Encore!
Encore!
CLAP
Needs more pirates!

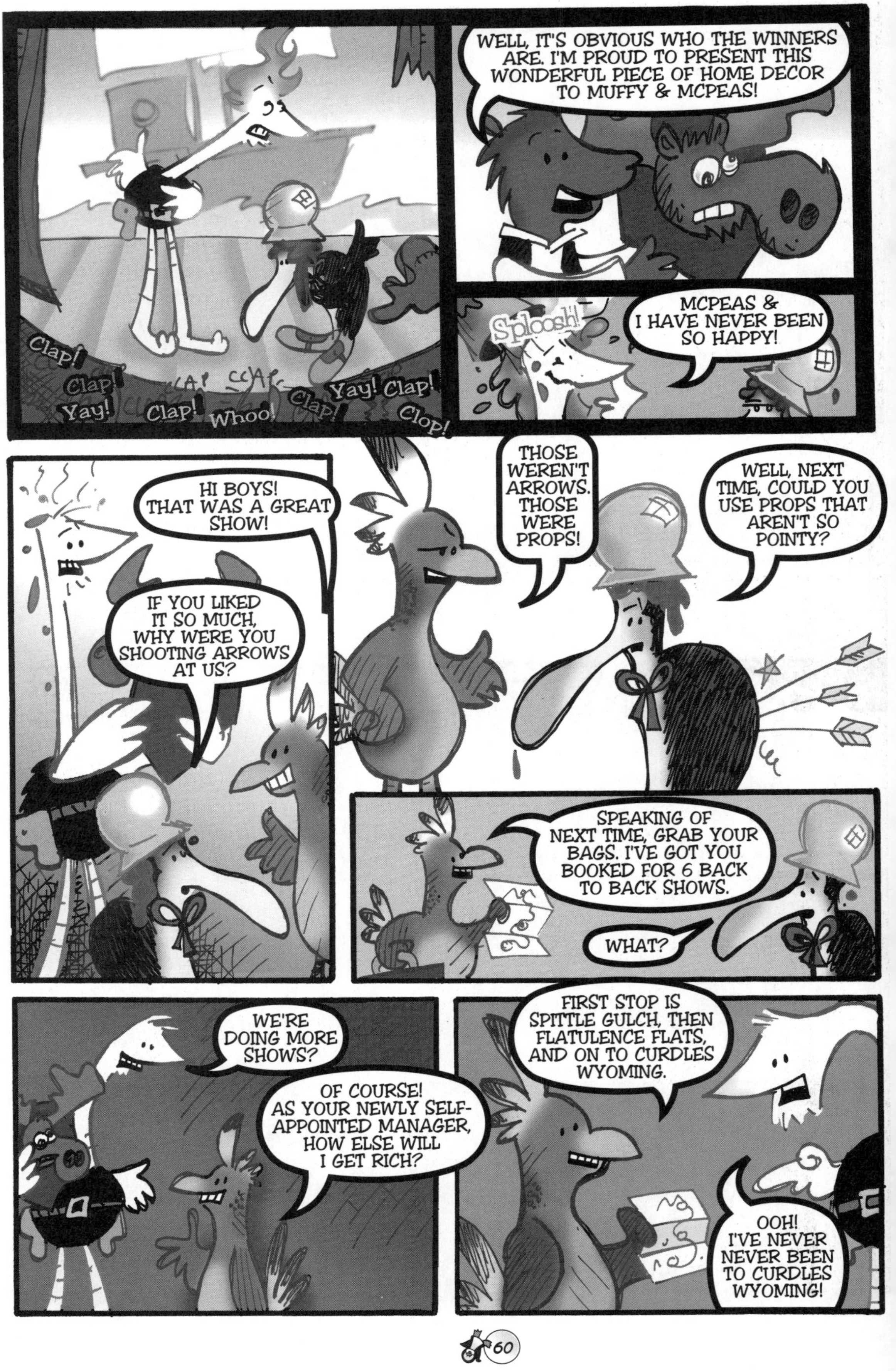

Clap!
Clap!
Yay!
Clap!
Whoo!
Clap!
Yay!
Clap!
Clop!
WELL, IT'S OBVIOUS WHO THE WINNERS ARE. I'M PROUD TO PRESENT THIS WONDERFUL PIECE OF HOME DECOR TO MUFFY & MCPEAS!
Sploosh!
MCPEAS & I HAVE NEVER BEEN SO HAPPY!
HI BOYS! THAT WAS A GREAT SHOW!
IF YOU LIKED IT SO MUCH, WHY WERE YOU SHOOTING ARROWS AT US?
THOSE WEREN'T ARROWS. THOSE WERE PROPS!
WELL, NEXT TIME, COULD YOU USE PROPS THAT AREN'T SO POINTY?
SPEAKING OF NEXT TIME, GRAB YOUR BAGS. I'VE GOT YOU BOOKED FOR 6 BACK TO BACK SHOWS.
WHAT?
WE'RE DOING MORE SHOWS?
OF COURSE! AS YOUR NEWLY SELF-APPOINTED MANAGER, HOW ELSE WILL I GET RICH?
FIRST STOP IS SPITTLE GULCH, THEN FLATULENCE FLATS, AND ON TO CURDLES WYOMING.
OOH! I'VE NEVER NEVER BEEN TO CURDLES WYOMING!

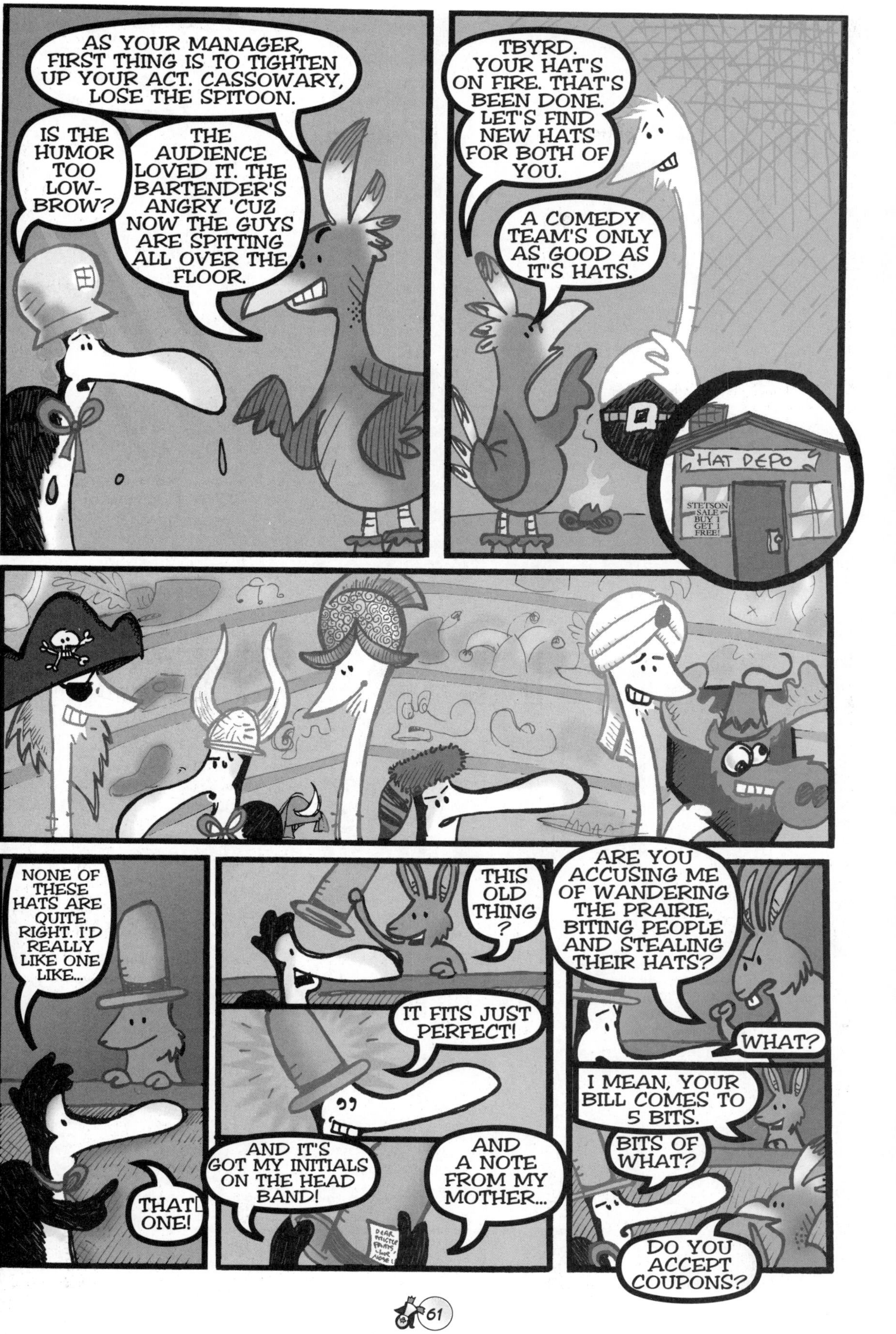
AS YOUR MANAGER, FIRST THING IS TO TIGHTEN UP YOUR ACT. CASSOWARY, LOSE THE SPITOON.
IS THE HUMOR TOO LOW-BROW?
THE AUDIENCE LOVED IT. THE BARTENDER'S ANGRY 'CUZ NOW THE GUYS ARE SPITTING ALL OVER THE FLOOR.
TBYRD. YOUR HAT'S ON FIRE. THAT'S BEEN DONE. LET'S FIND NEW HATS FOR BOTH OF YOU.
A COMEDY TEAM'S ONLY AS GOOD AS IT'S HATS.
HAT DEPO
STETSON SALE BUY 1 GET 1 FREE!
NONE OF THESE HATS ARE QUITE RIGHT. I'D REALLY LIKE ONE LIKE...
THAT ONE!
THIS OLD THING?
ARE YOU ACCUSING ME OF WANDERING THE PRAIRIE, BITING PEOPLE AND STEALING THEIR HATS?
WHAT?
IT FITS JUST PERFECT!
AND IT'S GOT MY INITIALS ON THE HEAD BAND!
AND A NOTE FROM MY MOTHER...
I MEAN, YOUR BILL COMES TO 5 BITS.
BITS OF WHAT?
DO YOU ACCEPT COUPONS?

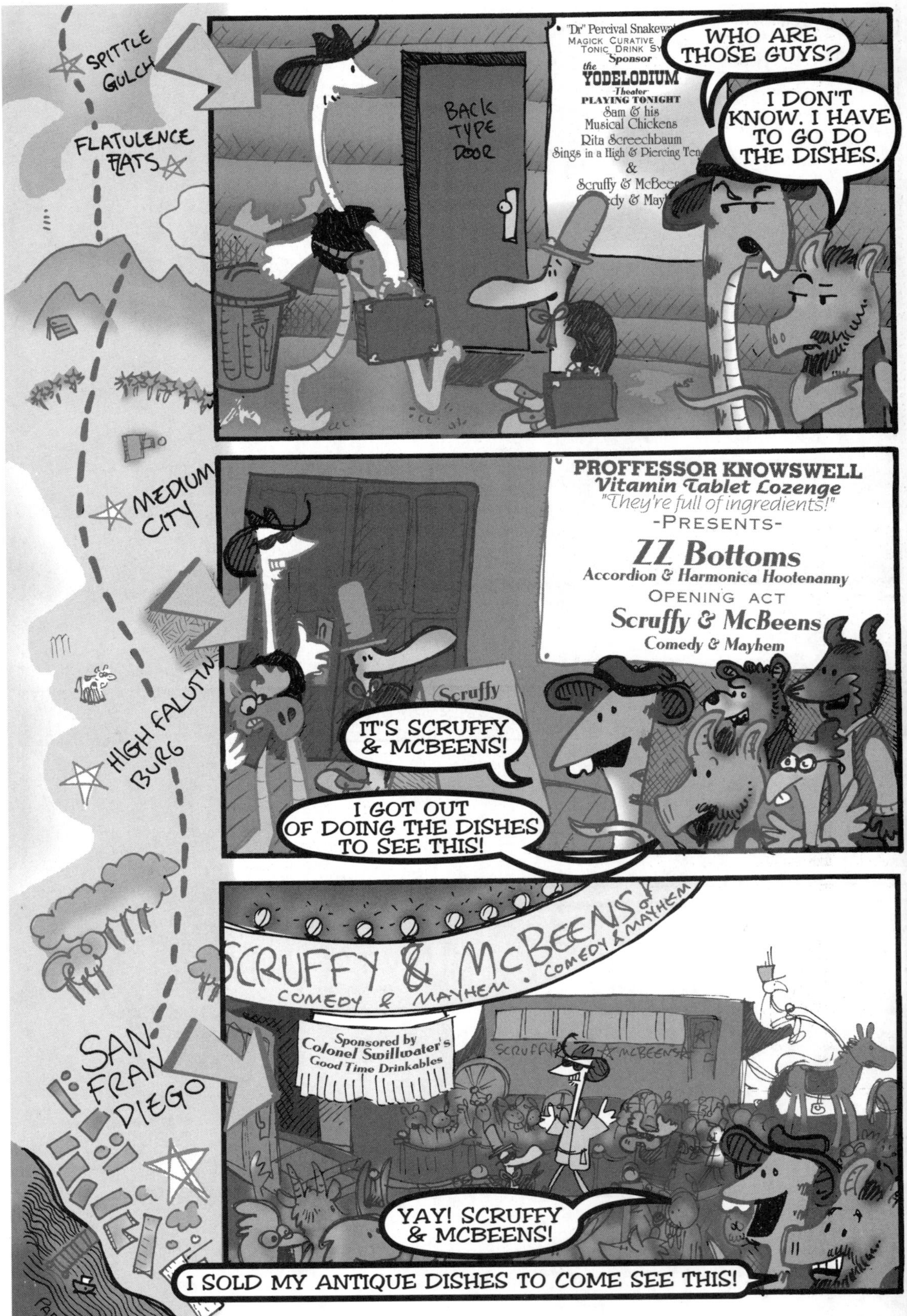
SPITTLE GULCH
FLATULENCE FLATS
BACK TYPE DOOR
the YODELODIUM Theater
PLAYING TONIGHT
Sam & his Musical Chickens
Rita Screechbaum
&
WHO ARE THOSE GUYS?
I DON'T KNOW. I HAVE TO GO DO THE DISHES.
MEDIUM CITY
HIGH FALUTIN BURG
PROFFESSOR KNOWSWELL
Vitamin Tablet Lozenge
"They're full of ingredients!"
-PRESENTS-
ZZ Bottoms
Accordion & Harmonica Hootenanny
OPENING ACT
Scruffy & McBeens
Comedy & Mayhem
Scruffy
IT'S SCRUFFY & MCBEENS!
I GOT OUT OF DOING THE DISHES TO SEE THIS!
SAN FRAN DIEGO
PACIFIC OCEAN
SCRUFFY & McBEENS COMEDY & MAYHEM
COMEDY & MAYHEM
Sponsored by Colonel Swillwater's Good Time Drinkables
SCRUFFY & McBEENS
YAY! SCRUFFY & MCBEENS!
I SOLD MY ANTIQUE DISHES TO COME SEE THIS!

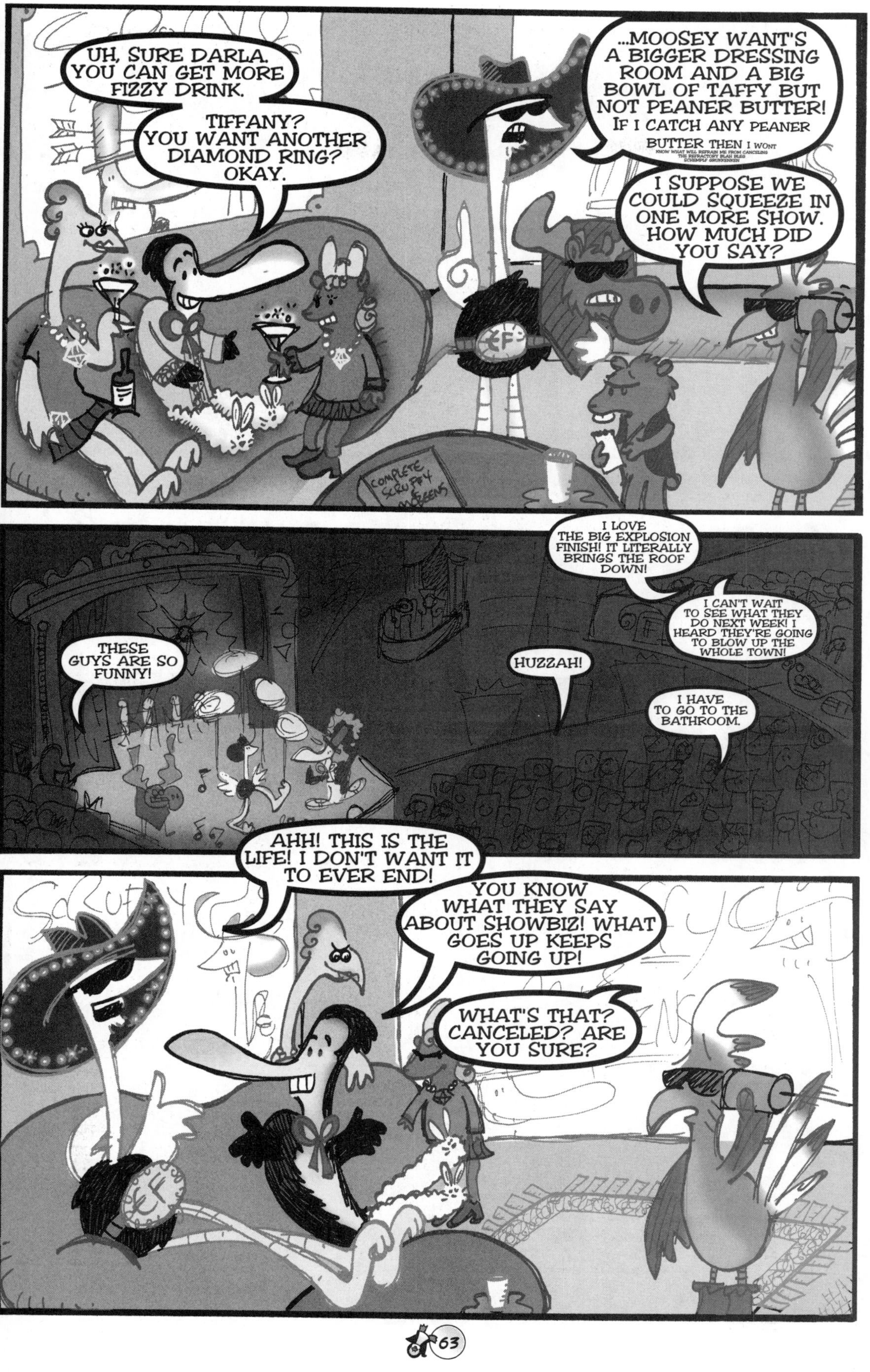
UH, SURE DARLA. YOU CAN GET MORE FIZZY DRINK.
TIFFANY? YOU WANT ANOTHER DIAMOND RING? OKAY.
...MOOSEY WANT'S A BIGGER DRESSING ROOM AND A BIG BOWL OF TAFFY BUT NOT PEANER BUTTER! IF I CATCH ANY PEANER BUTTER THEN I WONT KNOW WHAT WILL REFRAIN ME FROM CANCELING THE REFRACTORY BLAH BLEG SCHEMPLF GRUKKENKEN
I SUPPOSE WE COULD SQUEEZE IN ONE MORE SHOW. HOW MUCH DID YOU SAY?
COMPLETE SCRUFFY & MOSSENS
THESE GUYS ARE SO FUNNY!
HUZZAH!
I LOVE THE BIG EXPLOSION FINISH! IT LITERALLY BRINGS THE ROOF DOWN!
I CAN'T WAIT TO SEE WHAT THEY DO NEXT WEEK! I HEARD THEY'RE GOING TO BLOW UP THE WHOLE TOWN!
I HAVE TO GO TO THE BATHROOM.
AHH! THIS IS THE LIFE! I DON'T WANT IT TO EVER END!
YOU KNOW WHAT THEY SAY ABOUT SHOWBIZ! WHAT GOES UP KEEPS GOING UP!
WHAT'S THAT? CANCELED? ARE YOU SURE?

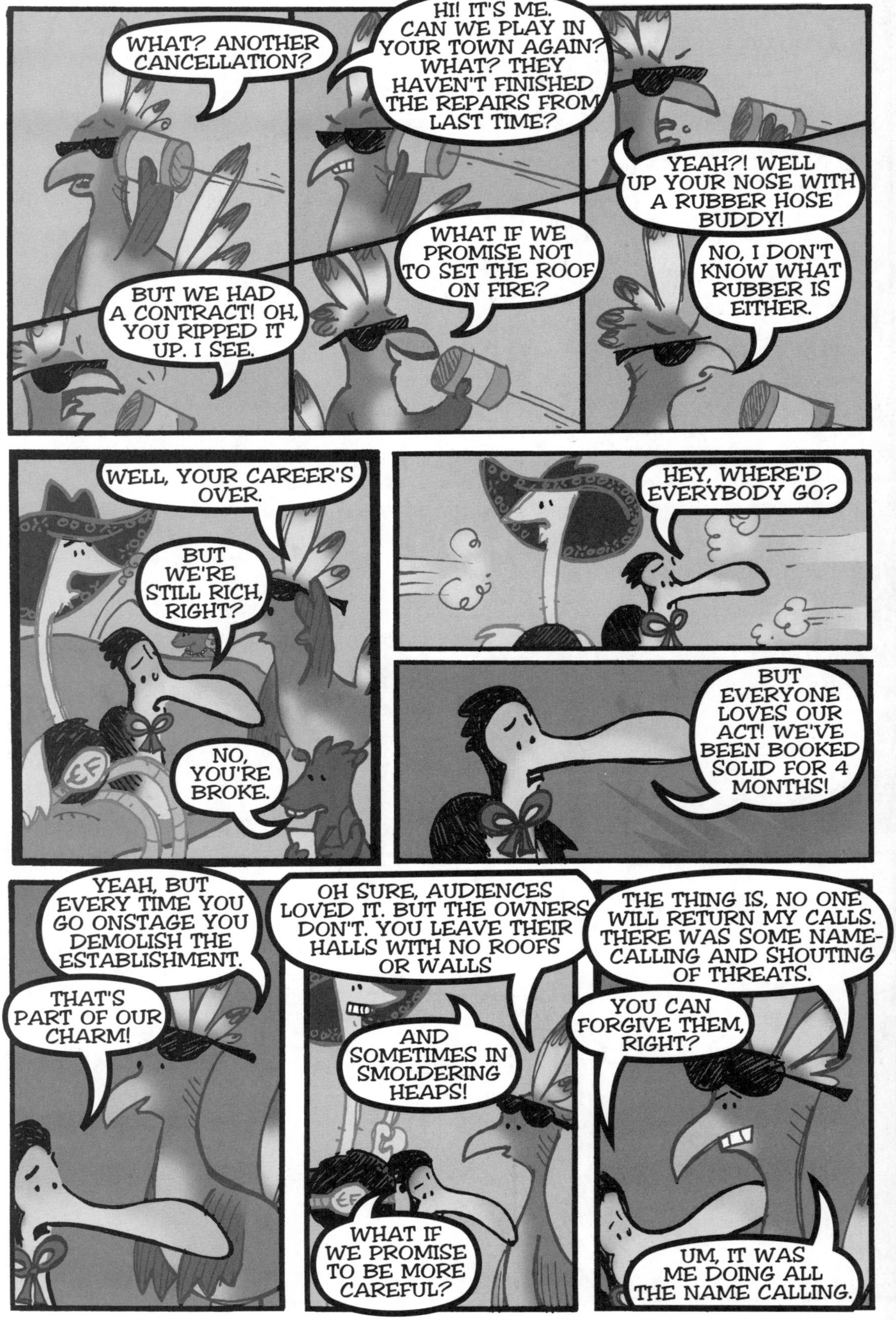
WHAT? ANOTHER CANCELLATION?
BUT WE HAD A CONTRACT! OH, YOU RIPPED IT UP. I SEE.
HI! IT'S ME. CAN WE PLAY IN YOUR TOWN AGAIN? WHAT? THEY HAVEN'T FINISHED THE REPAIRS FROM LAST TIME?
WHAT IF WE PROMISE NOT TO SET THE ROOF ON FIRE?
YEAH?! WELL UP YOUR NOSE WITH A RUBBER HOSE BUDDY!
NO, I DON'T KNOW WHAT RUBBER IS EITHER.
WELL, YOUR CAREER'S OVER.
BUT WE'RE STILL RICH, RIGHT?
NO, YOU'RE BROKE.
HEY, WHERE'D EVERYBODY GO?
BUT EVERYONE LOVES OUR ACT! WE'VE BEEN BOOKED SOLID FOR 4 MONTHS!
YEAH, BUT EVERY TIME YOU GO ONSTAGE YOU DEMOLISH THE ESTABLISHMENT.
THAT'S PART OF OUR CHARM!
OH SURE, AUDIENCES LOVED IT. BUT THE OWNERS DON'T. YOU LEAVE THEIR HALLS WITH NO ROOFS OR WALLS
AND SOMETIMES IN SMOLDERING HEAPS!
WHAT IF WE PROMISE TO BE MORE CAREFUL?
THE THING IS, NO ONE WILL RETURN MY CALLS. THERE WAS SOME NAME-CALLING AND SHOUTING OF THREATS.
YOU CAN FORGIVE THEM, RIGHT?
UM, IT WAS ME DOING ALL THE NAME CALLING.

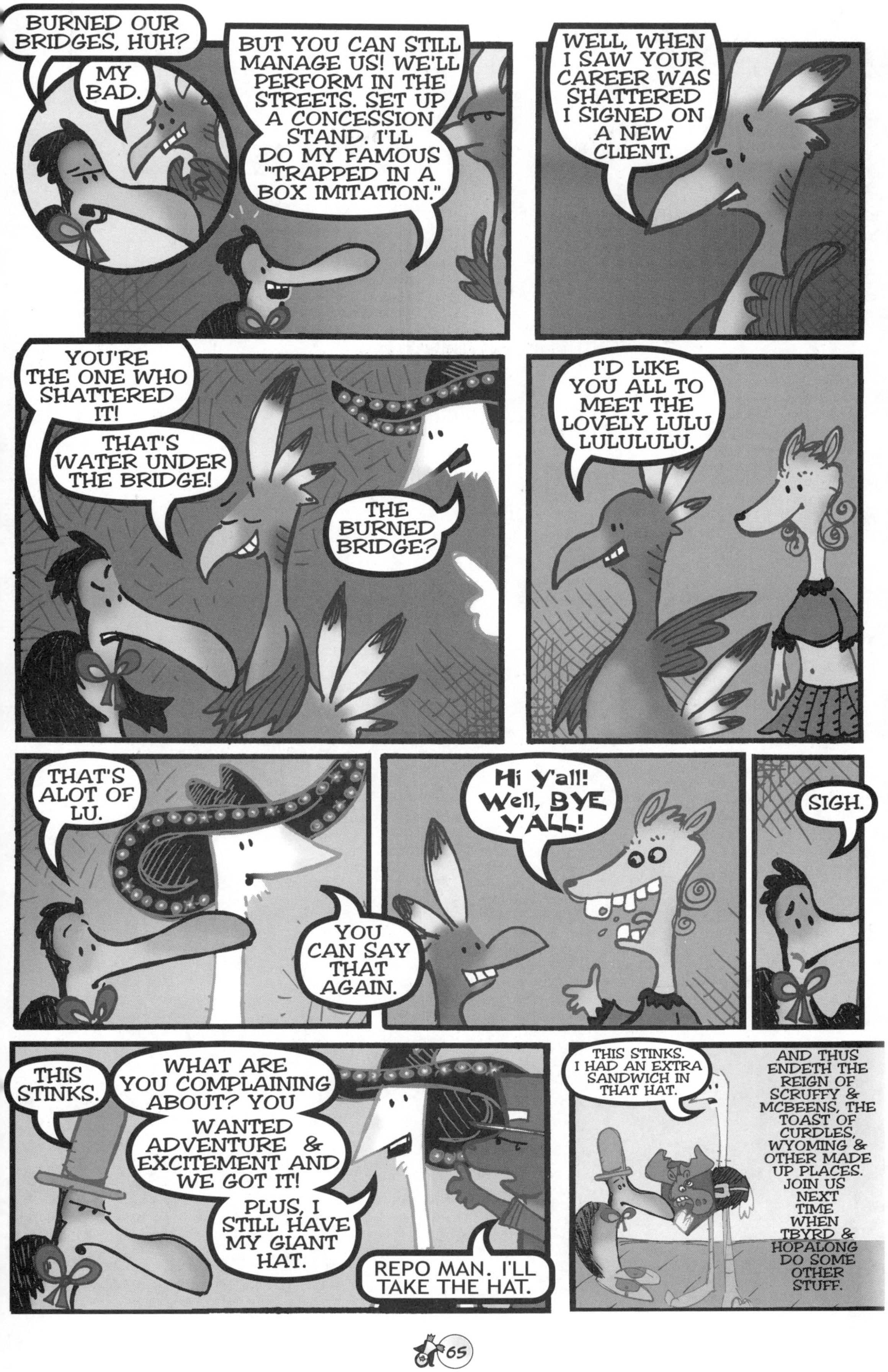
BURNED OUR BRIDGES, HUH?
MY BAD.
BUT YOU CAN STILL MANAGE US! WE'LL PERFORM IN THE STREETS. SET UP A CONCESSION STAND. I'LL DO MY FAMOUS "TRAPPED IN A BOX IMITATION."
WELL, WHEN I SAW YOUR CAREER WAS SHATTERED I SIGNED ON A NEW CLIENT.
YOU'RE THE ONE WHO SHATTERED IT!
THAT'S WATER UNDER THE BRIDGE!
THE BURNED BRIDGE?
I'D LIKE YOU ALL TO MEET THE LOVELY LULU LULULULU.
THAT'S ALOT OF LU.
YOU CAN SAY THAT AGAIN.
Hi Y'all! Well, BYE Y'ALL!
SIGH.
THIS STINKS.
WHAT ARE YOU COMPLAINING ABOUT? YOU WANTED ADVENTURE & EXCITEMENT AND WE GOT IT!
PLUS, I STILL HAVE MY GIANT HAT.
REPO MAN. I'LL TAKE THE HAT.
THIS STINKS. I HAD AN EXTRA SANDWICH IN THAT HAT.
AND THUS ENDETH THE REIGN OF SCRUFFY & MCBEENS, THE TOAST OF CURDLES, WYOMING & OTHER MADE UP PLACES. JOIN US NEXT TIME WHEN TBYRD & HOPALONG DO SOME OTHER STUFF.

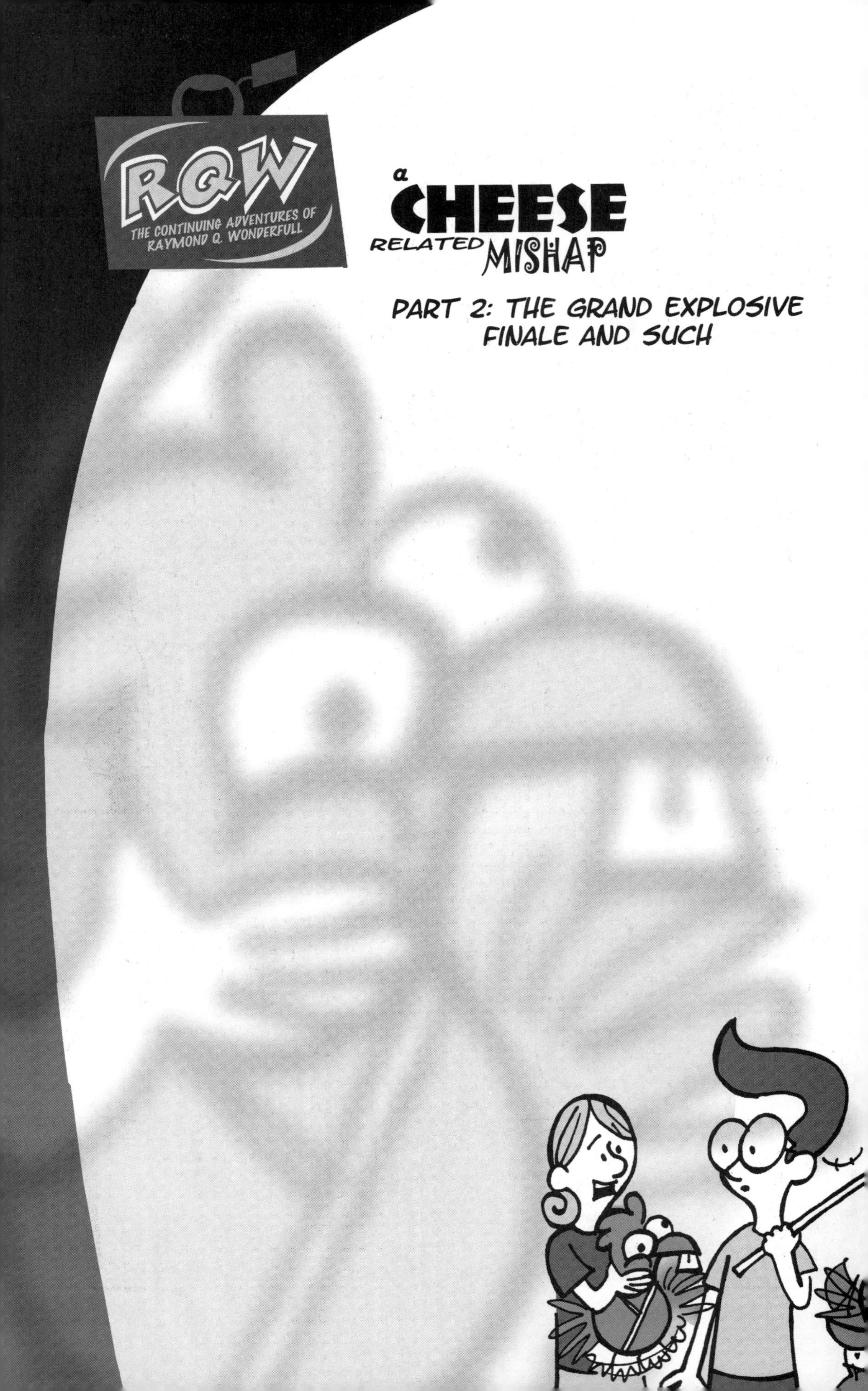
RQW
THE CONTINUING ADVENTURES OF RAYMOND Q. WONDERFULL
a CHEESE RELATED MISHAP
PART 2: THE GRAND EXPLOSIVE FINALE AND SUCH

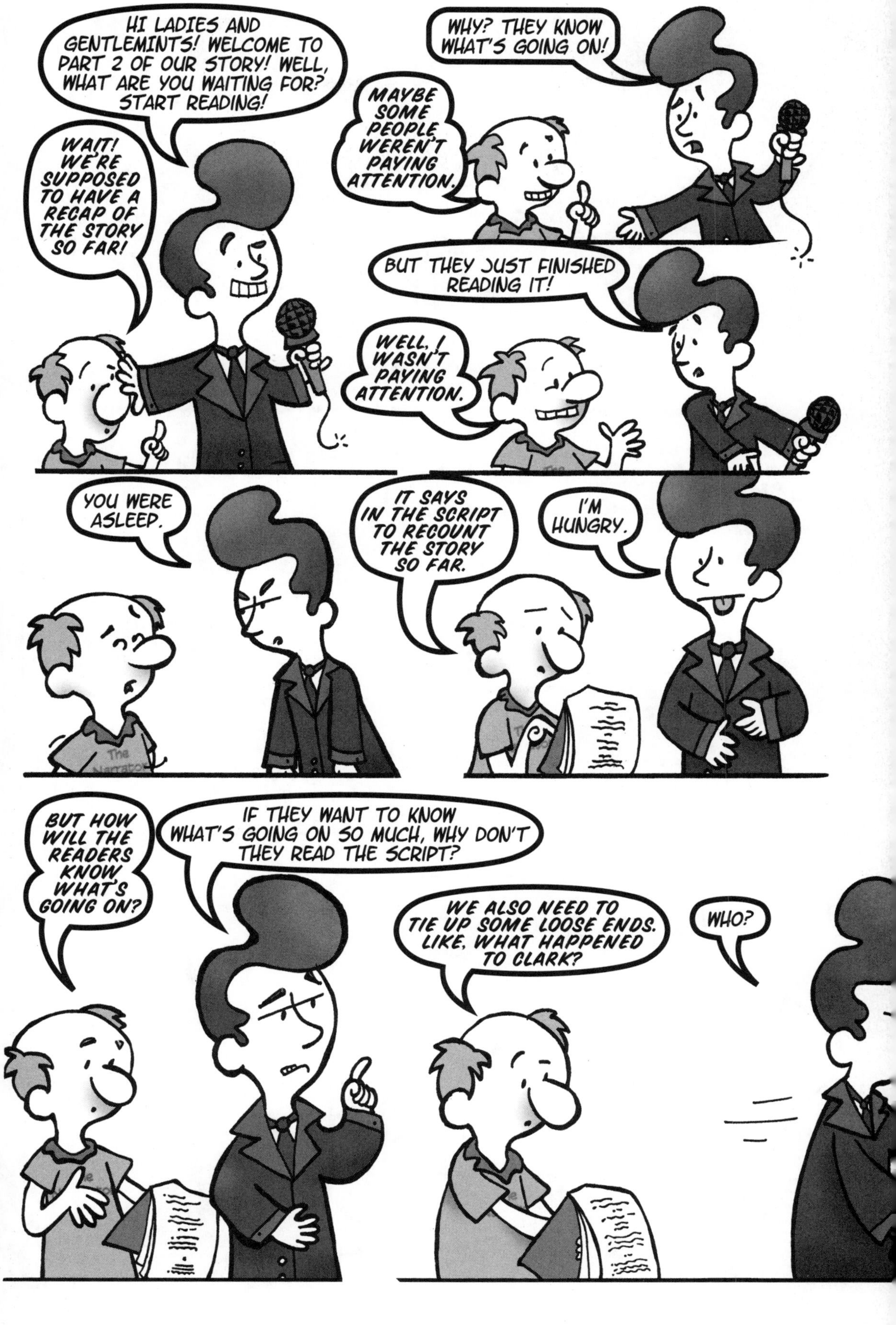
HI LADIES AND GENTLEMINTS! WELCOME TO PART 2 OF OUR STORY! WELL, WHAT ARE YOU WAITING FOR? START READING!
WAIT! WE'RE SUPPOSED TO HAVE A RECAP OF THE STORY SO FAR!
WHY? THEY KNOW WHAT'S GOING ON!
MAYBE SOME PEOPLE WEREN'T PAYING ATTENTION.
BUT THEY JUST FINISHED READING IT!
WELL, I WASN'T PAYING ATTENTION.
YOU WERE ASLEEP.
IT SAYS IN THE SCRIPT TO RECOUNT THE STORY SO FAR.
I'M HUNGRY.
BUT HOW WILL THE READERS KNOW WHAT'S GOING ON?
IF THEY WANT TO KNOW WHAT'S GOING ON SO MUCH, WHY DON'T THEY READ THE SCRIPT?
WE ALSO NEED TO TIE UP SOME LOOSE ENDS. LIKE, WHAT HAPPENED TO CLARK?
WHO?

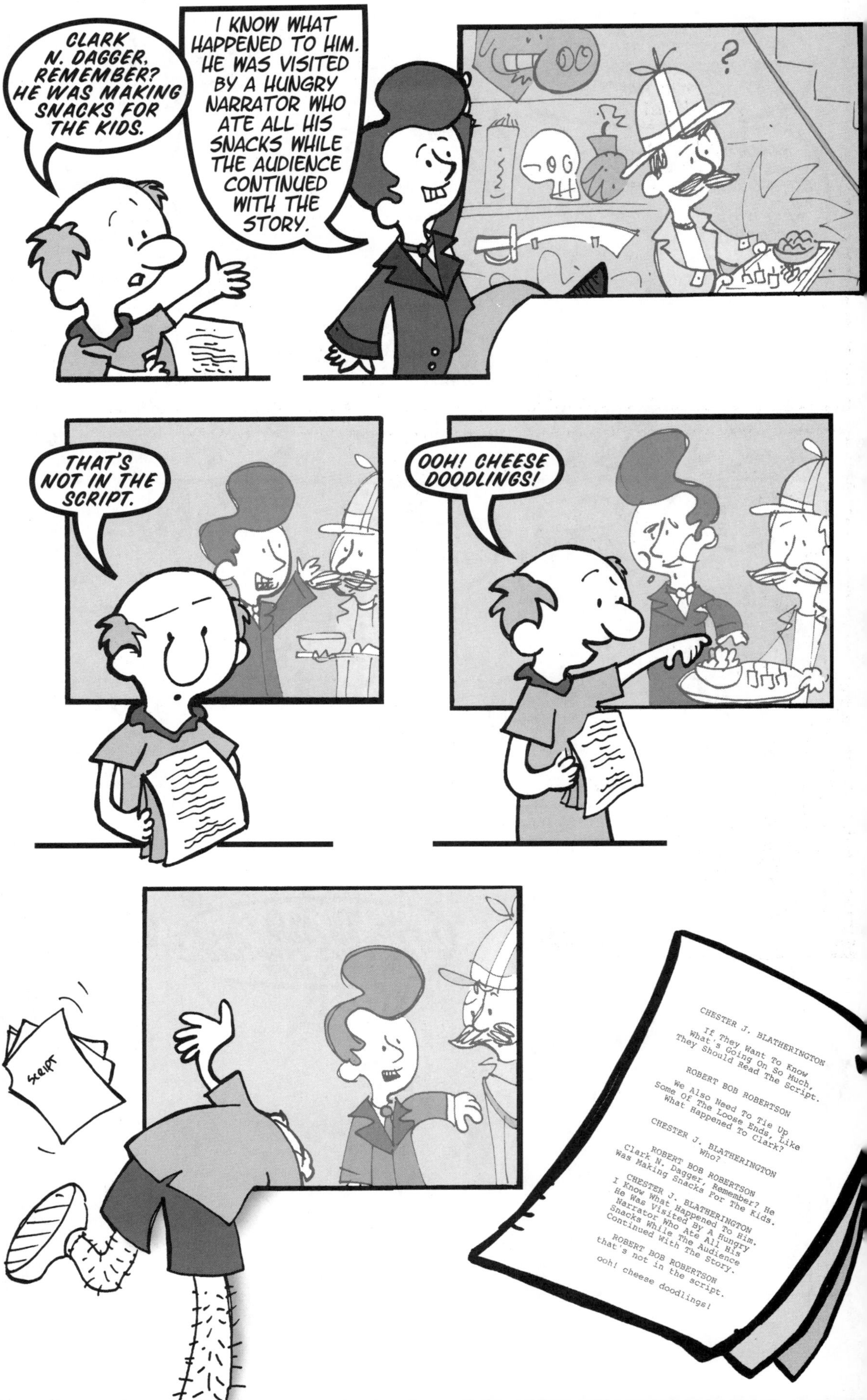
CLARK N. DAGGER, REMEMBER? HE WAS MAKING SNACKS FOR THE KIDS.
I KNOW WHAT HAPPENED TO HIM. HE WAS VISITED BY A HUNGRY NARRATOR WHO ATE ALL HIS SNACKS WHILE THE AUDIENCE CONTINUED WITH THE STORY.
THAT'S NOT IN THE SCRIPT.
OOH! CHEESE DOODLINGS!
SCRIPT
CHESTER J. BLATHERINGTON
If They Want To Know What's Going On So Much, They Should Read The Script.
ROBERT BOB ROBERTSON
We Also Need To Tie Up Some Of The Loose Ends, Like What Happened To Clark?
CHESTER J. BLATHERINGTON
Who?
ROBERT BOB ROBERTSON
Clark N. Dagger, Remember? He Was Making Snacks For The Kids.
CHESTER J. BLATHERINGTON
I Know What Happened To Him. He Was Visited By A Hungry Narrator Who Ate All His Snacks While The Audience Continued With The Story.
ROBERT BOB ROBERTSON
that's not in the script.
ooh! cheese doodlings!

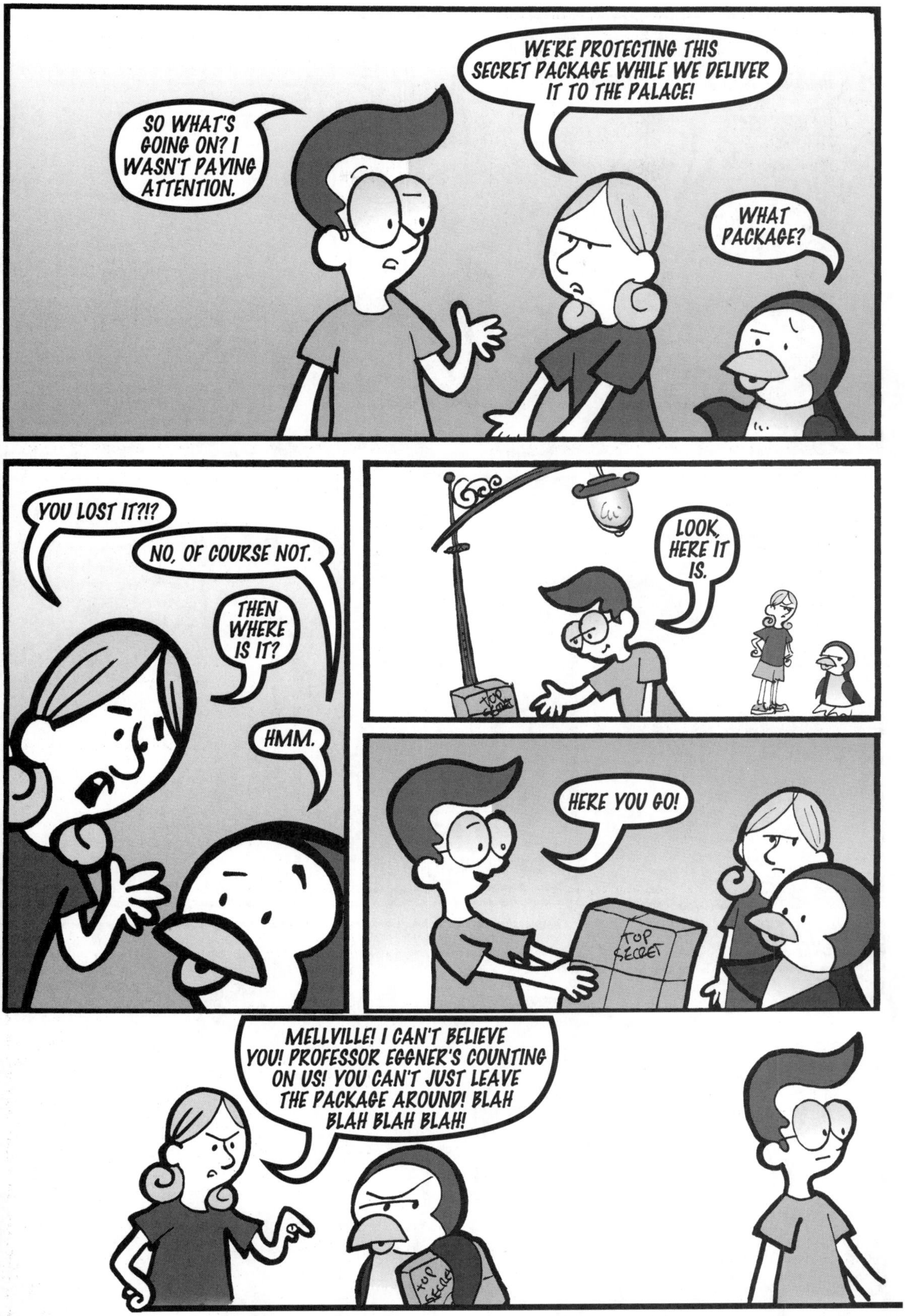
SO WHAT'S GOING ON? I WASN'T PAYING ATTENTION.
WE'RE PROTECTING THIS SECRET PACKAGE WHILE WE DELIVER IT TO THE PALACE!
WHAT PACKAGE?
YOU LOST IT?!?
NO, OF COURSE NOT.
THEN WHERE IS IT?
HMM.
LOOK, HERE IT IS.
TOP SECRET
HERE YOU GO!
TOP SECRET
MELLVILLE! I CAN'T BELIEVE YOU! PROFESSOR EGGNER'S COUNTING ON US! YOU CAN'T JUST LEAVE THE PACKAGE AROUND! BLAH BLAH BLAH BLAH!
TOP SECRET

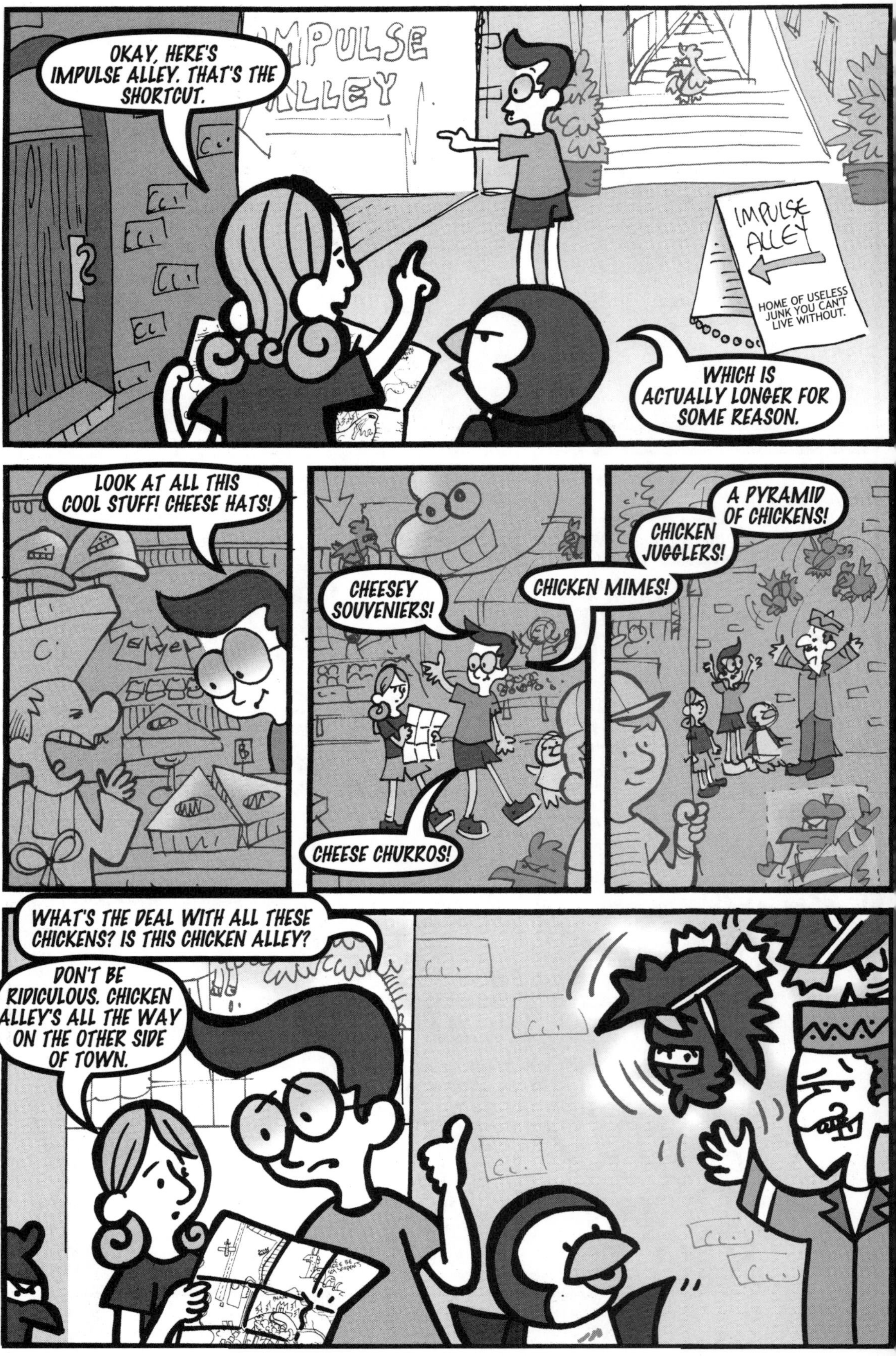
OKAY, HERE'S IMPULSE ALLEY. THAT'S THE SHORTCUT.
IMPULSE ALLEY
IMPULSE ALLEY
HOME OF USELESS JUNK YOU CAN'T LIVE WITHOUT.
WHICH IS ACTUALLY LONGER FOR SOME REASON.
LOOK AT ALL THIS COOL STUFF! CHEESE HATS!
CHEESEY SOUVENIERS!
CHEESE CHURROS!
CHICKEN MIMES!
CHICKEN JUGGLERS!
A PYRAMID OF CHICKENS!
WHAT'S THE DEAL WITH ALL THESE CHICKENS? IS THIS CHICKEN ALLEY?
DON'T BE RIDICULOUS. CHICKEN ALLEY'S ALL THE WAY ON THE OTHER SIDE OF TOWN.

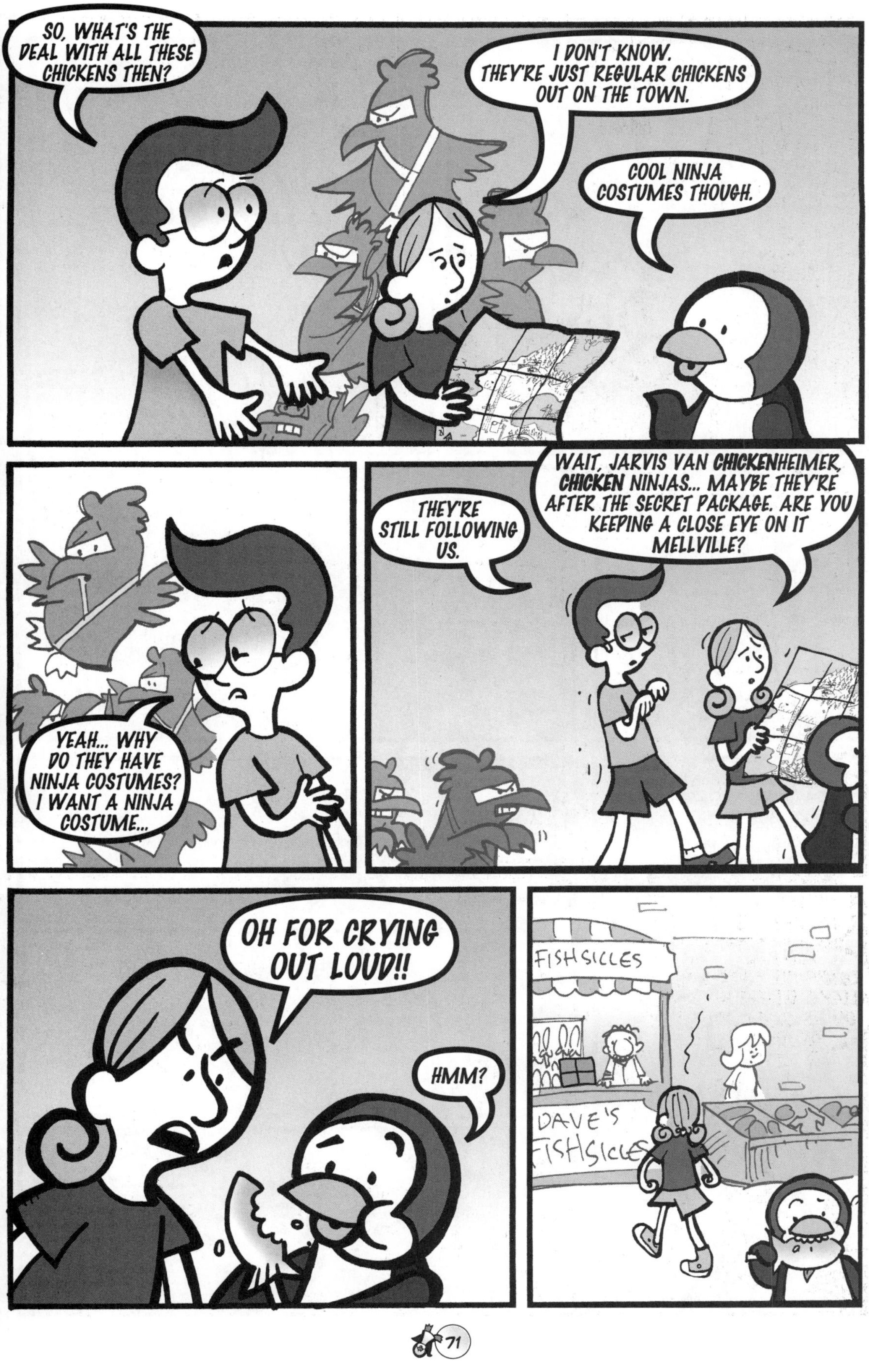
SO, WHAT'S THE DEAL WITH ALL THESE CHICKENS THEN?
I DON'T KNOW. THEY'RE JUST REGULAR CHICKENS OUT ON THE TOWN.
COOL NINJA COSTUMES THOUGH.
YEAH... WHY DO THEY HAVE NINJA COSTUMES? I WANT A NINJA COSTUME...
THEY'RE STILL FOLLOWING US.
WAIT, JARVIS VAN CHICKENHEIMER, CHICKEN NINJAS... MAYBE THEY'RE AFTER THE SECRET PACKAGE. ARE YOU KEEPING A CLOSE EYE ON IT MELLVILLE?
OH FOR CRYING OUT LOUD!!
HMM?
FISHSICLES
DAVE'S FISHSICLES

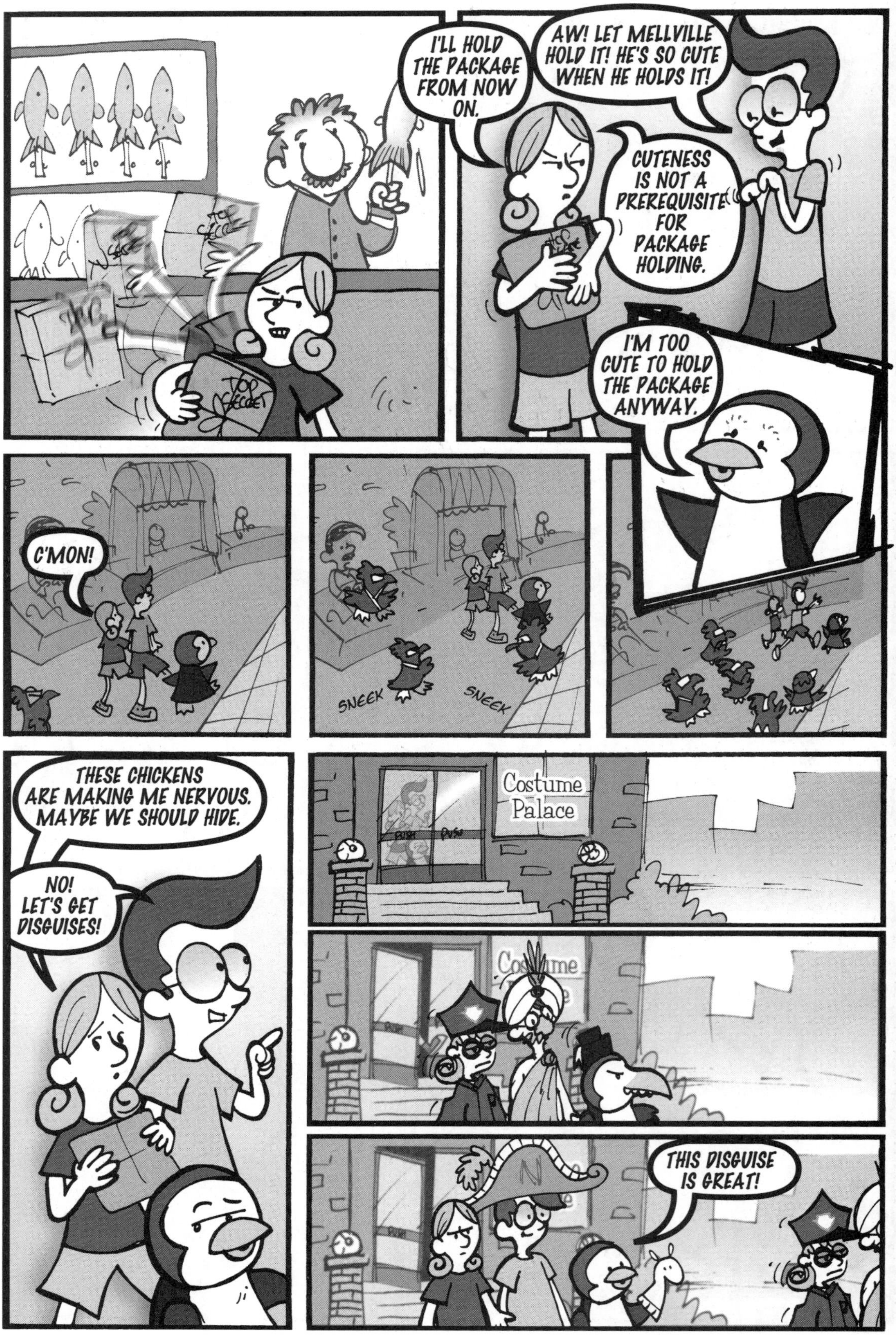
I'LL HOLD THE PACKAGE FROM NOW ON.
AW! LET MELLVILLE HOLD IT! HE'S SO CUTE WHEN HE HOLDS IT!
CUTENESS IS NOT A PREREQUISITE FOR PACKAGE HOLDING.
I'M TOO CUTE TO HOLD THE PACKAGE ANYWAY.
C'MON!
SNEEK
SNEEK
THESE CHICKENS ARE MAKING ME NERVOUS. MAYBE WE SHOULD HIDE.
NO! LET'S GET DISGUISES!
Costume Palace
THIS DISGUISE IS GREAT!

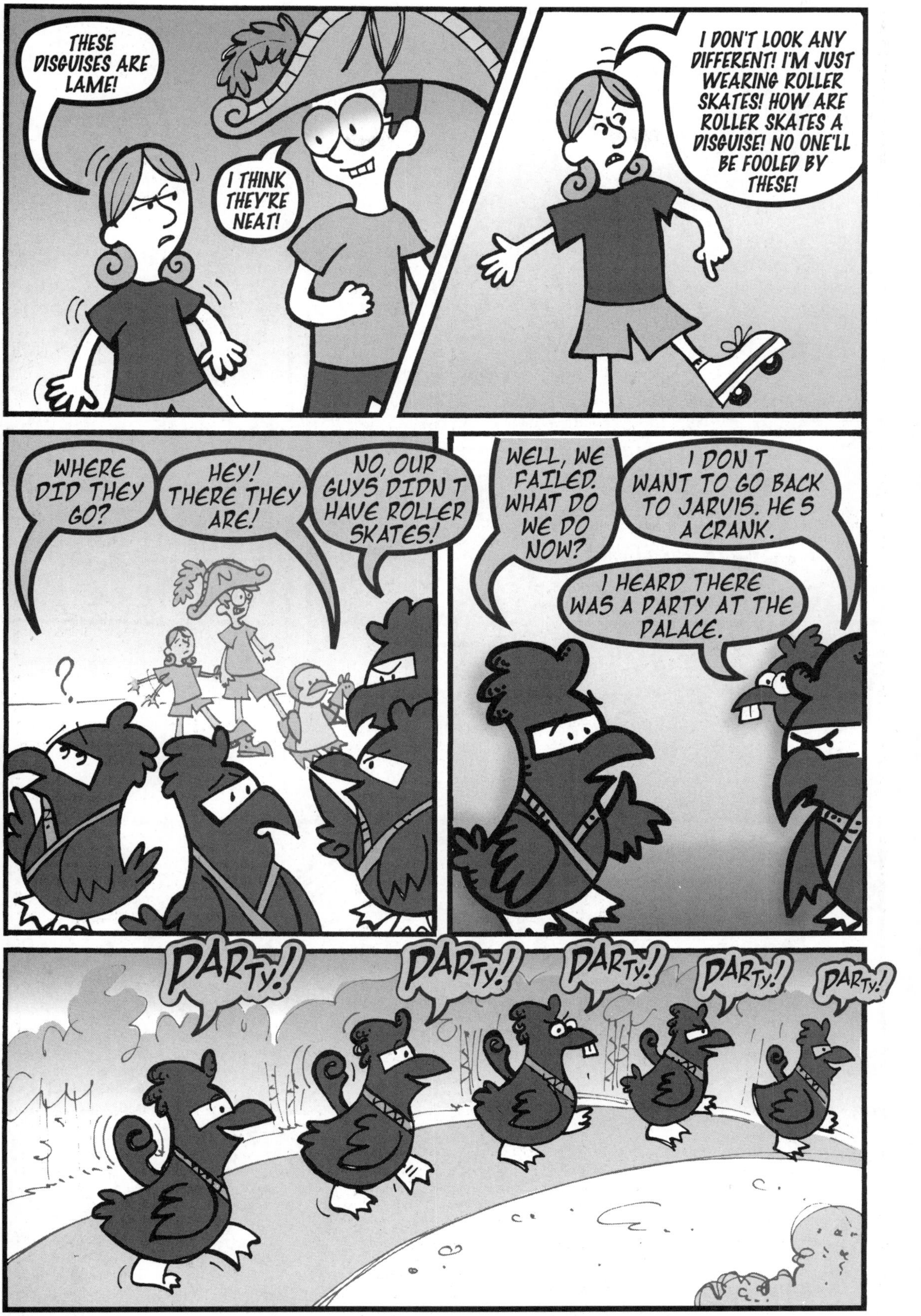
THESE DISGUISES ARE LAME!
I THINK THEY'RE NEAT!
I DON'T LOOK ANY DIFFERENT! I'M JUST WEARING ROLLER SKATES! HOW ARE ROLLER SKATES A DISGUISE! NO ONE'LL BE FOOLED BY THESE!
WHERE DID THEY GO?
HEY! THERE THEY ARE!
NO, OUR GUYS DIDN T HAVE ROLLER SKATES!
WELL, WE FAILED. WHAT DO WE DO NOW?
I DON T WANT TO GO BACK TO JARVIS. HE S A CRANK.
I HEARD THERE WAS A PARTY AT THE PALACE.
PARTy!
PARTy!
PARTy!
PARTy!
PARTy!

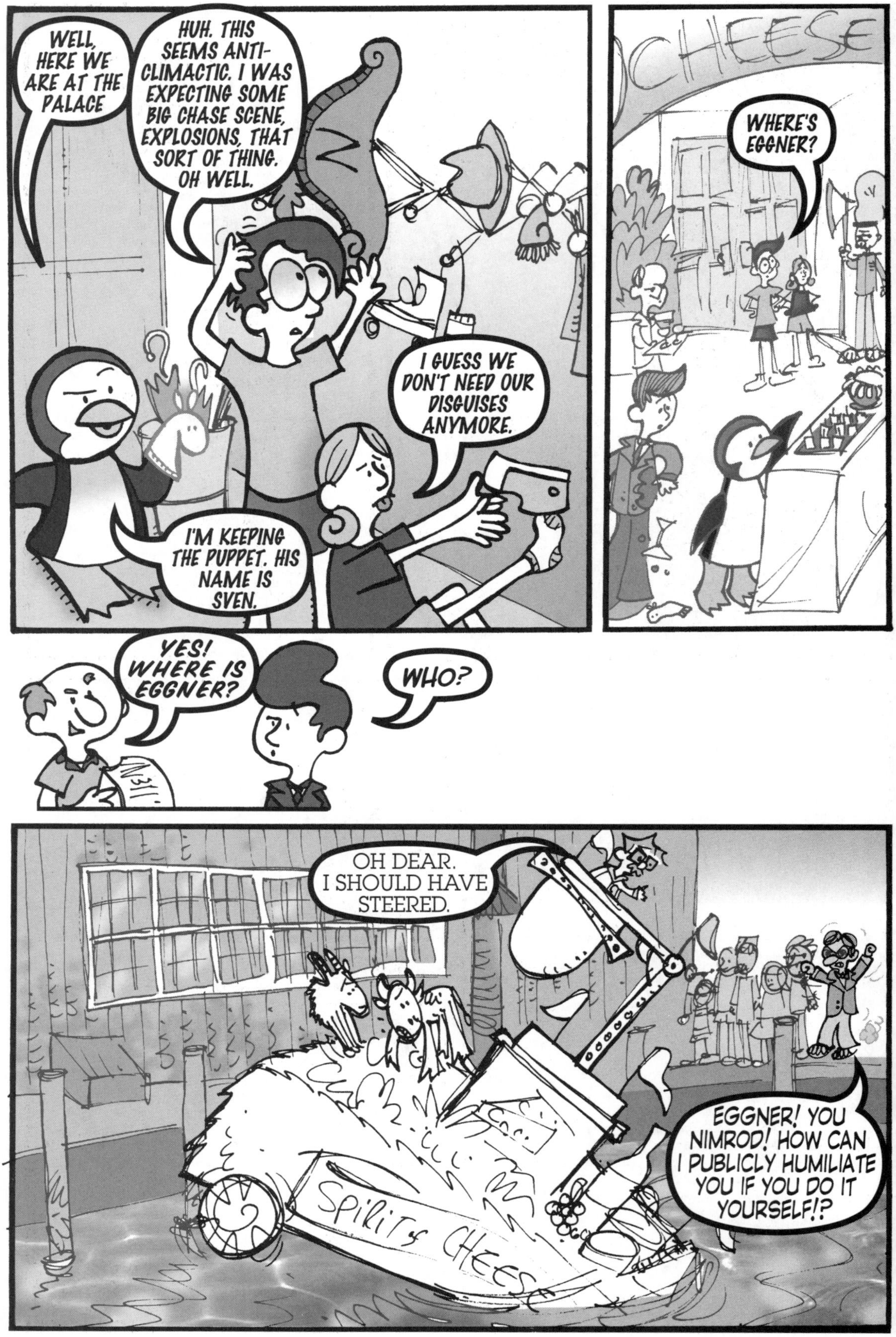
WELL, HERE WE ARE AT THE PALACE
HUH. THIS SEEMS ANTI-CLIMACTIC. I WAS EXPECTING SOME BIG CHASE SCENE, EXPLOSIONS, THAT SORT OF THING. OH WELL.
I GUESS WE DON'T NEED OUR DISGUISES ANYMORE.
I'M KEEPING THE PUPPET. HIS NAME IS SVEN.
CHEESE
WHERE'S EGGNER?
YES! WHERE IS EGGNER?
WHO?
OH DEAR. I SHOULD HAVE STEERED.
EGGNER! YOU NIMROD! HOW CAN I PUBLICLY HUMILIATE YOU IF YOU DO IT YOURSELF!?
SPIRIT of CHEES

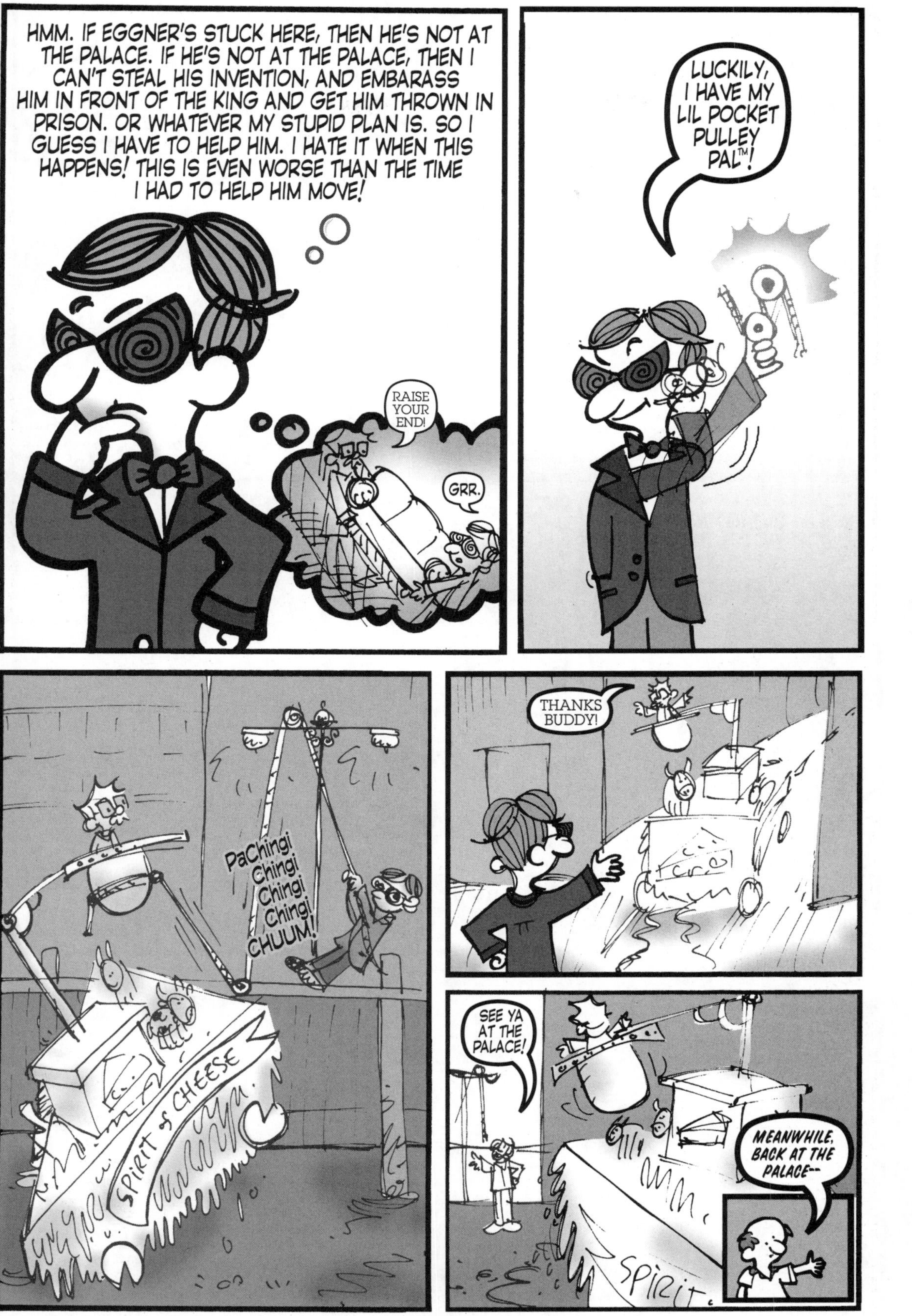
HMM. IF EGGNER'S STUCK HERE, THEN HE'S NOT AT THE PALACE. IF HE'S NOT AT THE PALACE, THEN I CAN'T STEAL HIS INVENTION, AND EMBARASS HIM IN FRONT OF THE KING AND GET HIM THROWN IN PRISON. OR WHATEVER MY STUPID PLAN IS. SO I GUESS I HAVE TO HELP HIM. I HATE IT WHEN THIS HAPPENS! THIS IS EVEN WORSE THAN THE TIME I HAD TO HELP HIM MOVE!
RAISE YOUR END!
GRR.
LUCKILY, I HAVE MY LIL POCKET PULLEY PAL™!
PaChingi Chingi Chingi Chingi CHUUM!
SPIRIT of CHEESE
THANKS BUDDY!
SEE YA AT THE PALACE!
SPIRIT
MEANWHILE, BACK AT THE PALACE--

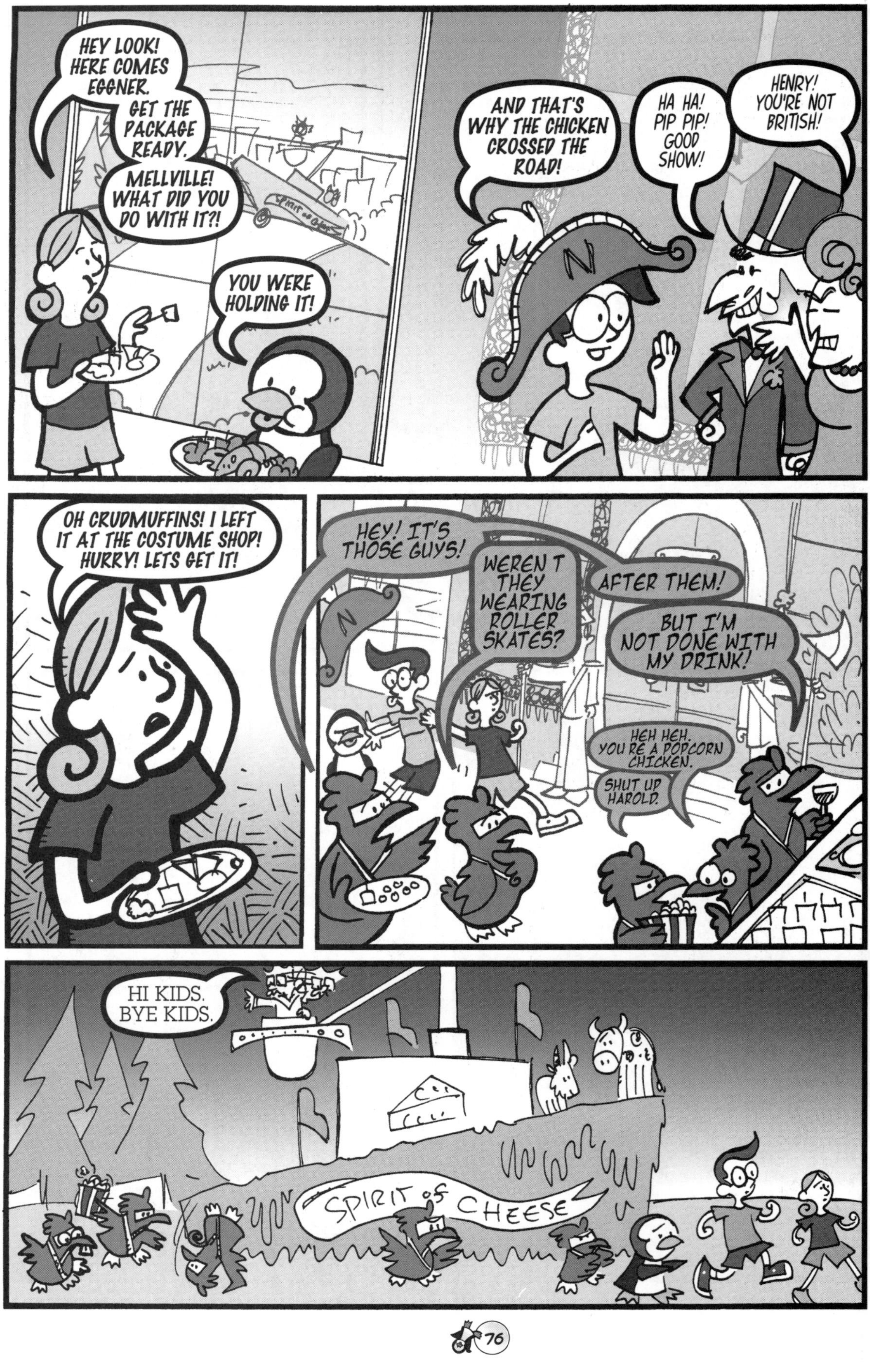
HEY LOOK! HERE COMES EGGNER.
GET THE PACKAGE READY.
MELLVILLE! WHAT DID YOU DO WITH IT?!
YOU WERE HOLDING IT!
AND THAT'S WHY THE CHICKEN CROSSED THE ROAD!
HA HA! PIP PIP! GOOD SHOW!
HENRY! YOU'RE NOT BRITISH!
OH CRUDMUFFINS! I LEFT IT AT THE COSTUME SHOP! HURRY! LETS GET IT!
HEY! IT'S THOSE GUYS!
WEREN T THEY WEARING ROLLER SKATES?
AFTER THEM!
BUT I'M NOT DONE WITH MY DRINK!
HEH HEH. YOU'RE A POPCORN CHICKEN.
SHUT UP HAROLD.
HI KIDS. BYE KIDS.
SPIRIT of CHEESE

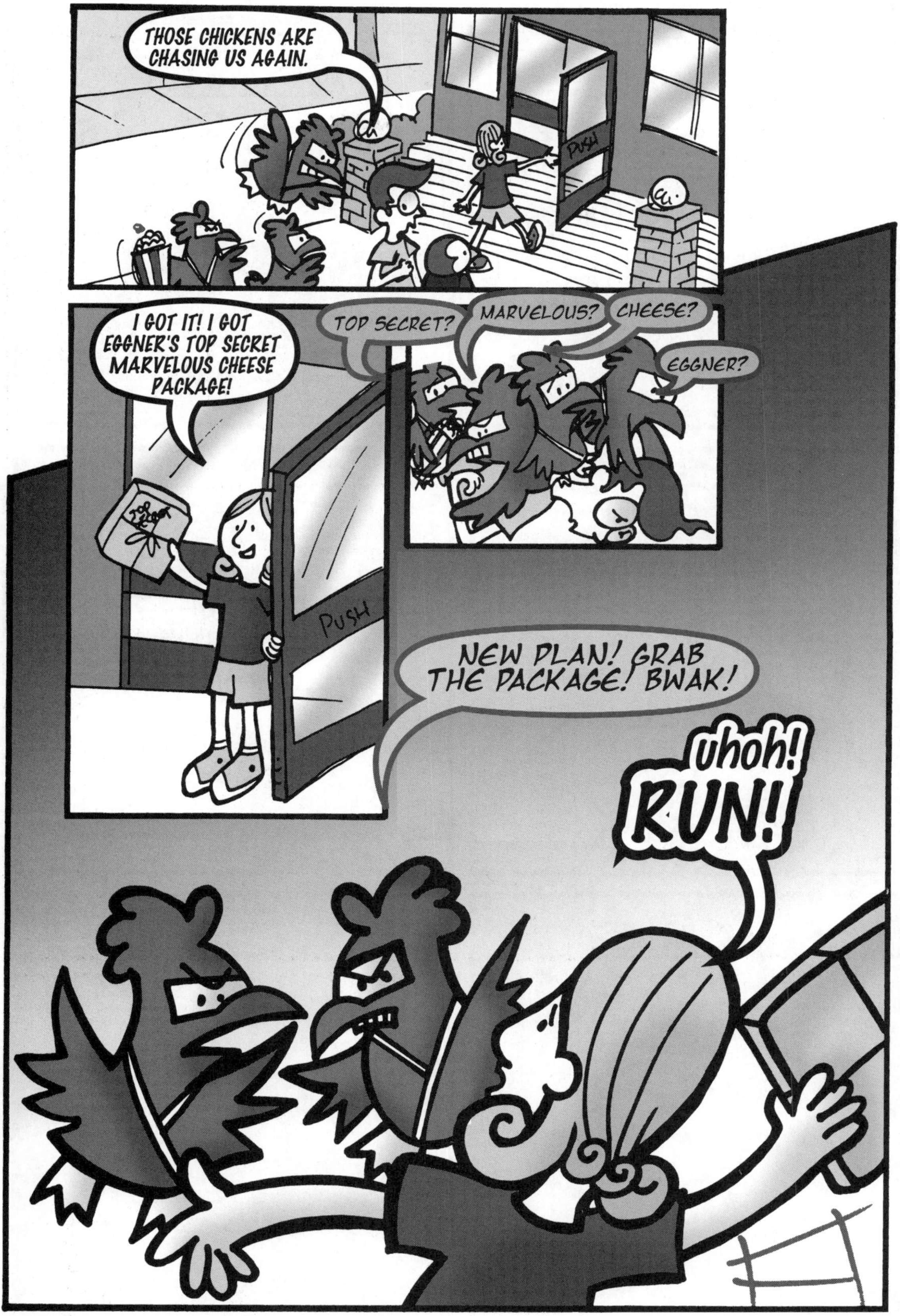
THOSE CHICKENS ARE CHASING US AGAIN.
PUSH
I GOT IT! I GOT EGGNER'S TOP SECRET MARVELOUS CHEESE PACKAGE!
PUSH
TOP SECRET?
MARVELOUS?
CHEESE?
EGGNER?
NEW PLAN! GRAB THE PACKAGE! BWAK!
uhoh!
RUN!

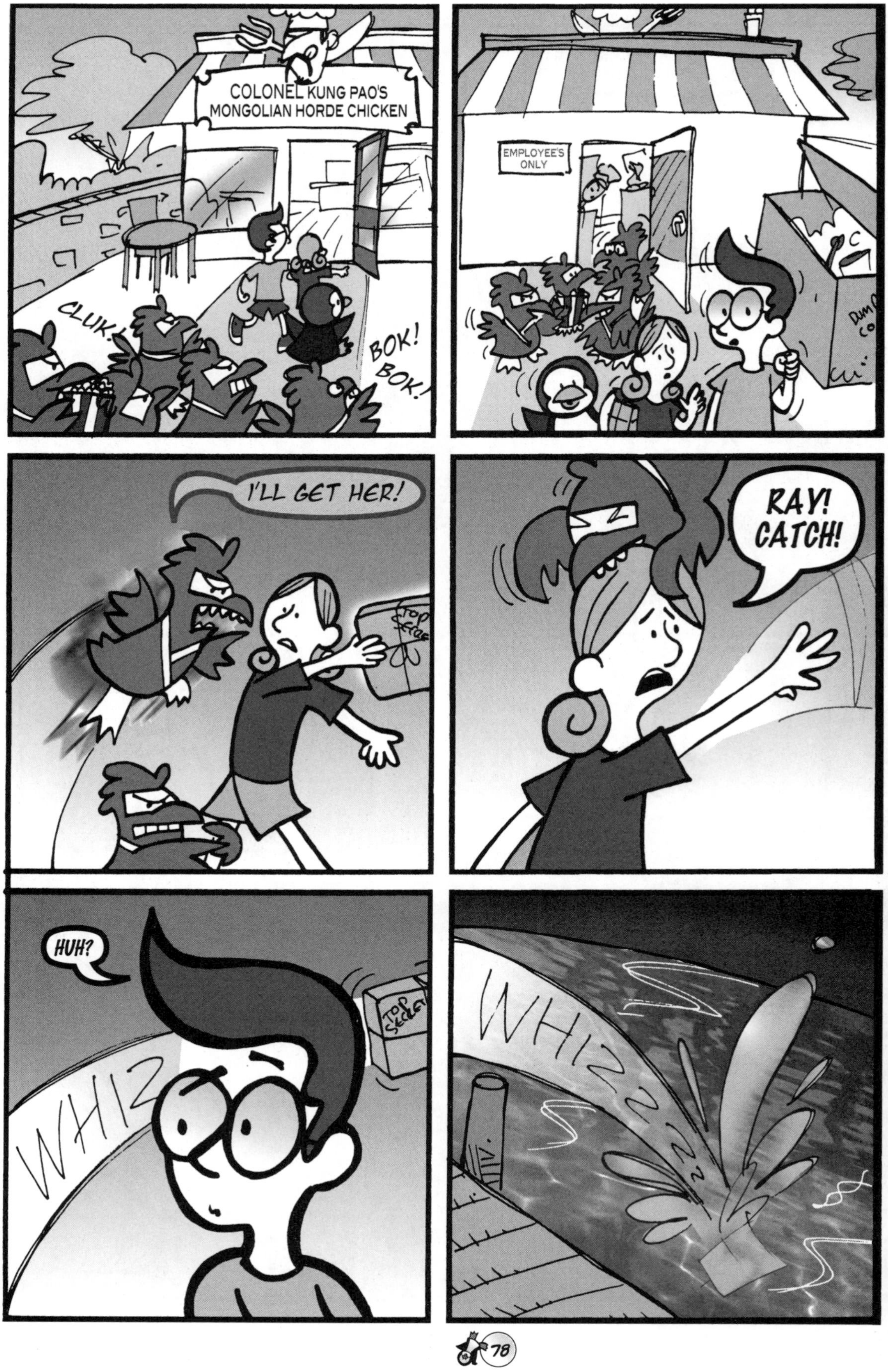
COLONEL KUNG PAO'S
MONGOLIAN HORDE CHICKEN
CLUK!
BOK!
BOK!
EMPLOYEE'S ONLY
I'LL GET HER!
TOP SECRET
RAY! CATCH!
HUH?
TOP SECRET
WHIZ
WHIZZZZ

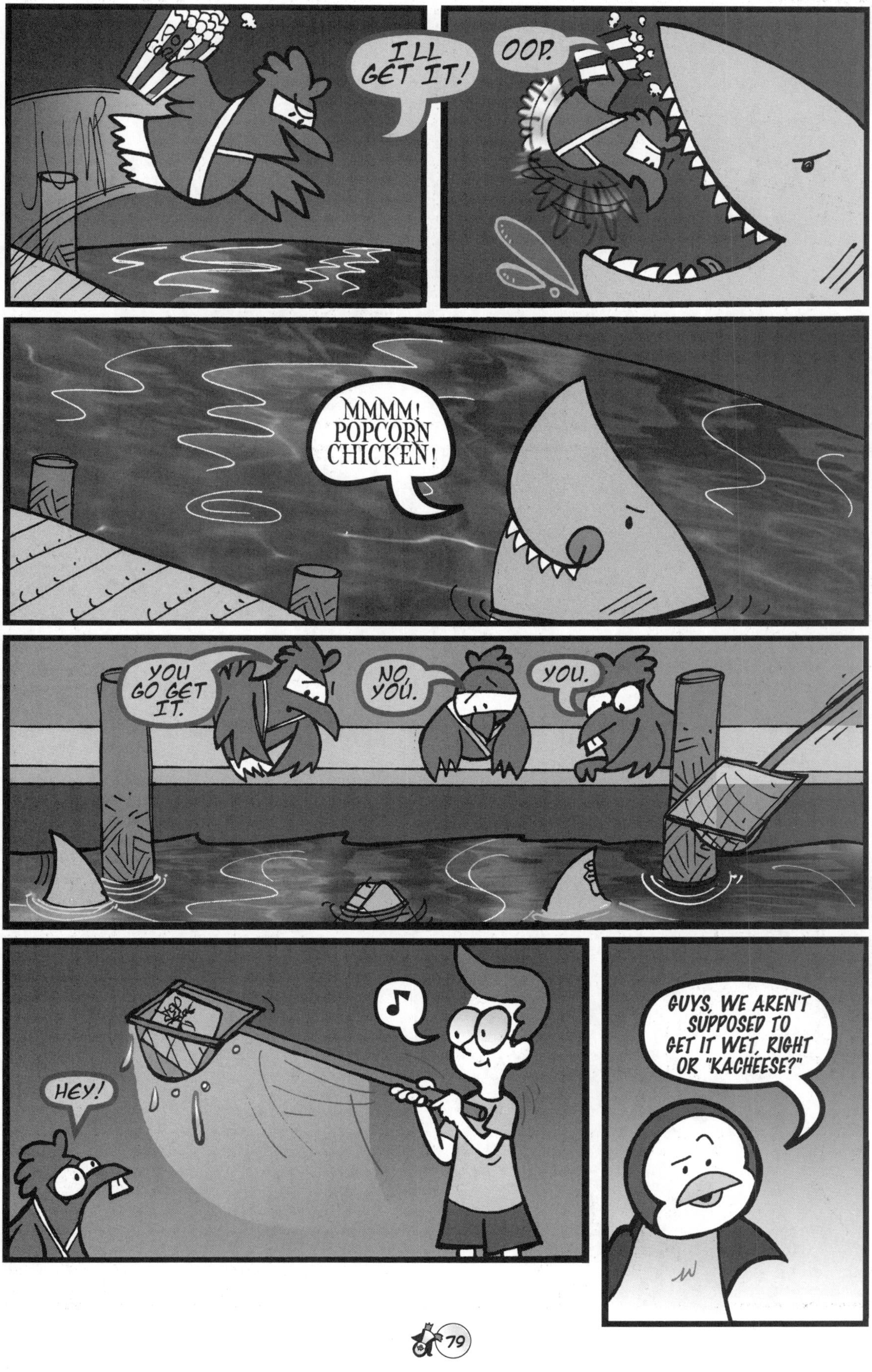
I'LL GET IT!
OOP.
MMMM! POPCORN CHICKEN!
YOU GO GET IT.
NO, YOU.
YOU.
HEY!
GUYS, WE AREN'T SUPPOSED TO GET IT WET, RIGHT OR "KACHEESE?"

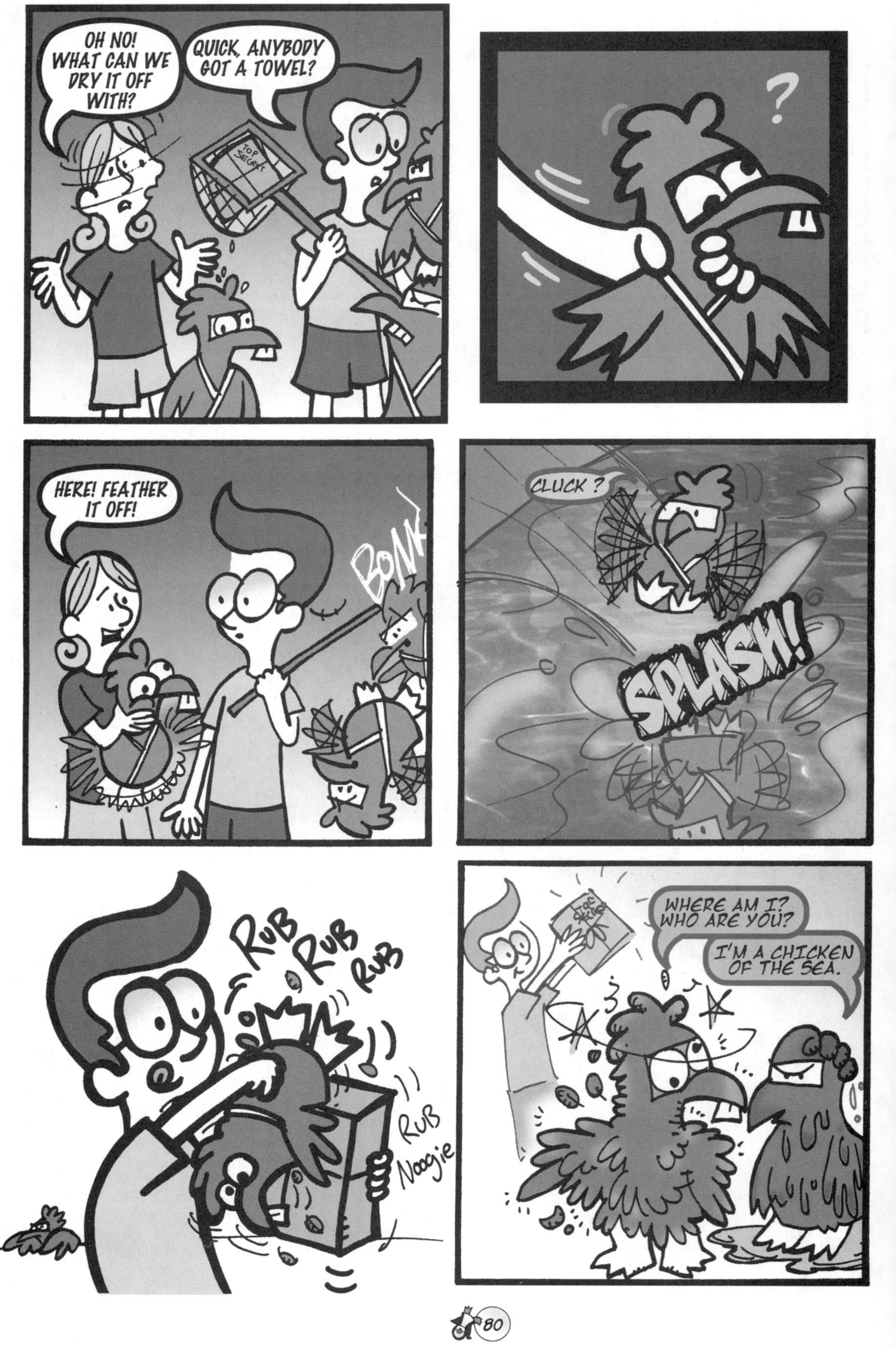
OH NO! WHAT CAN WE DRY IT OFF WITH?
QUICK, ANYBODY GOT A TOWEL?
TOP SECRET
?
HERE! FEATHER IT OFF!
BONK
CLUCK ?
SPLASH!
RUB RUB RUB
RUB Noogie
WHERE AM I? WHO ARE YOU?
I'M A CHICKEN OF THE SEA.

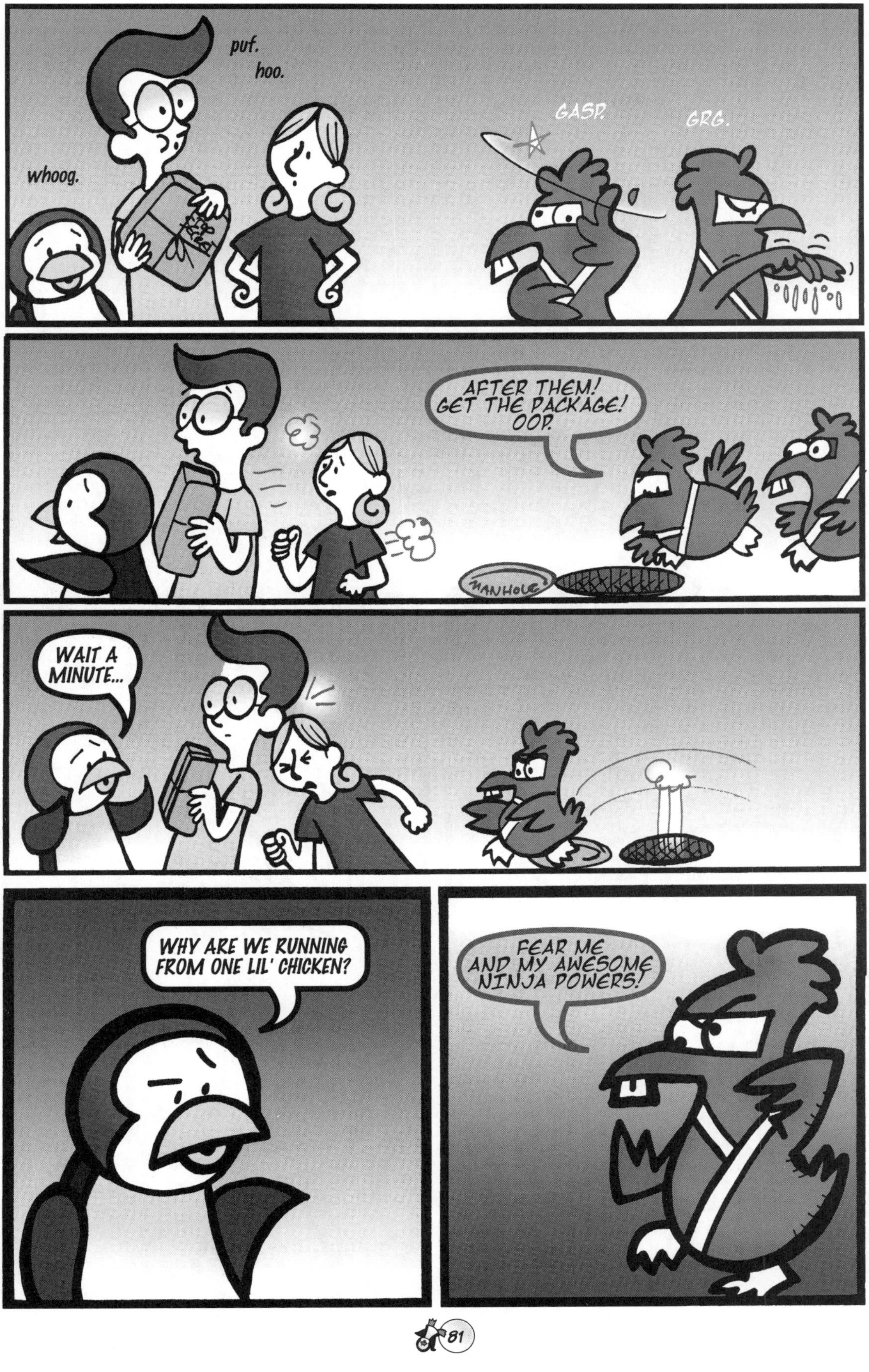
puf.
hoo.
whoog.
GASP.
GRG.
AFTER THEM! GET THE PACKAGE! OOP.
MANHOLE
WAIT A MINUTE...
WHY ARE WE RUNNING FROM ONE LIL' CHICKEN?
FEAR ME AND MY AWESOME NINJA POWERS!

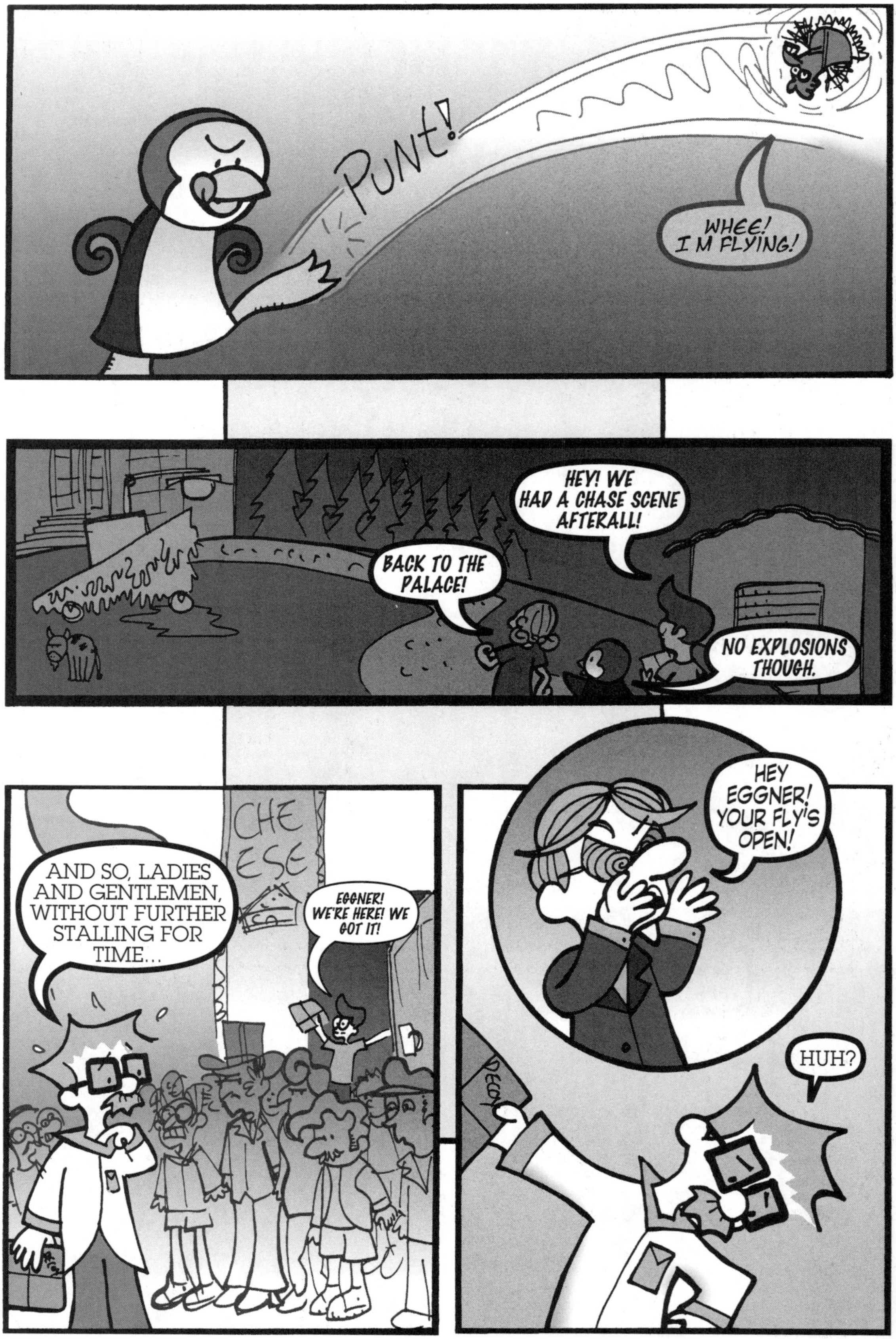
PUNT!
WHEE! I M FLYING!
BACK TO THE PALACE!
HEY! WE HAD A CHASE SCENE AFTERALL!
NO EXPLOSIONS THOUGH.
AND SO, LADIES AND GENTLEMEN, WITHOUT FURTHER STALLING FOR TIME...
CHE ESE
EGGNER! WE'RE HERE! WE GOT IT!
HEY EGGNER! YOUR FLY'S OPEN!
HUH?

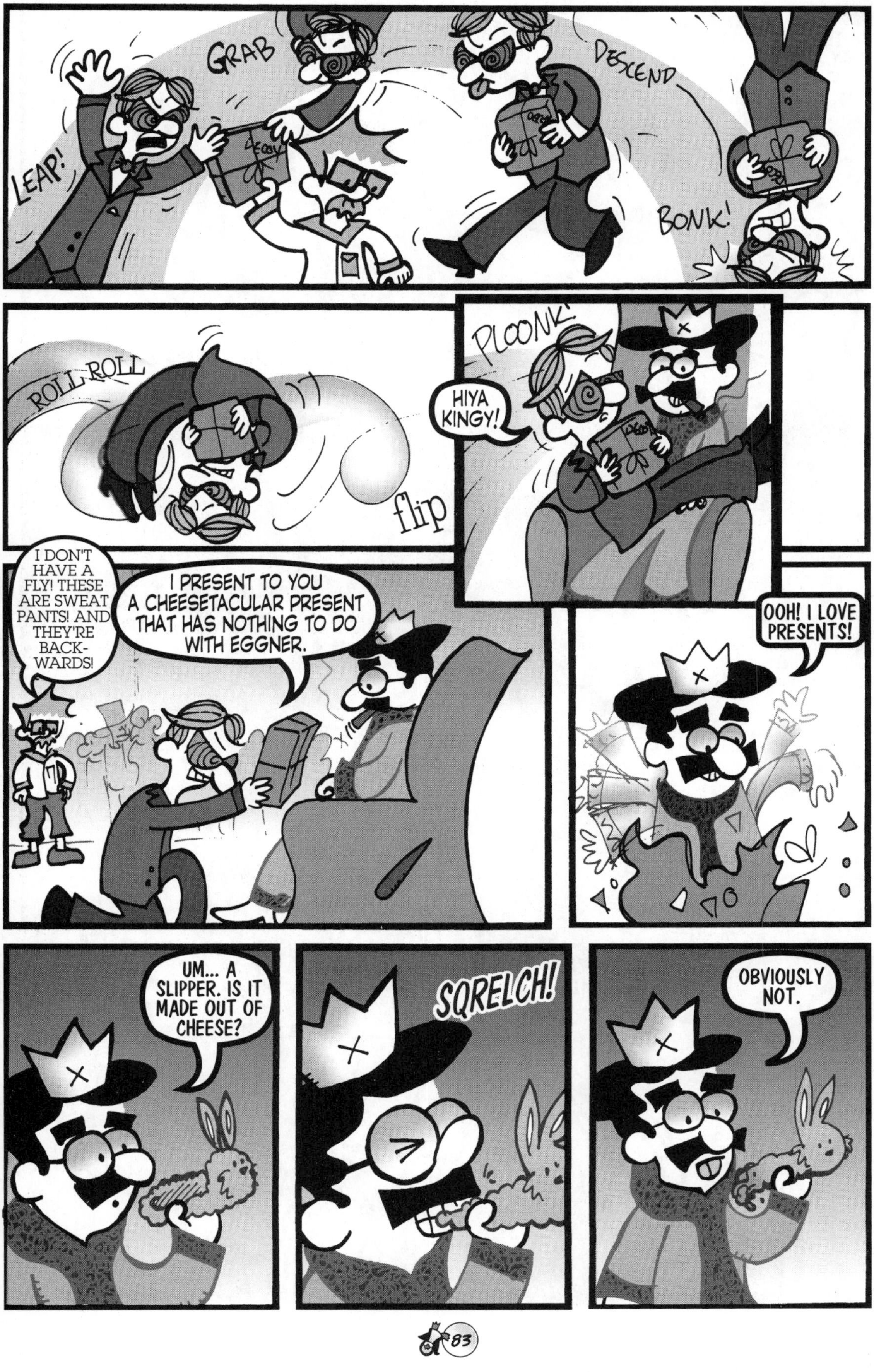
LEAP!
GRAB
DESCEND
BONK!
ROLL ROLL
flip
PLOONK!
HIYA KINGY!
I DON'T HAVE A FLY! THESE ARE SWEAT PANTS! AND THEY'RE BACK-WARDS!
I PRESENT TO YOU A CHEESETACULAR PRESENT THAT HAS NOTHING TO DO WITH EGGNER.
OOH! I LOVE PRESENTS!
UM... A SLIPPER. IS IT MADE OUT OF CHEESE?
SQRELCH!
OBVIOUSLY NOT.

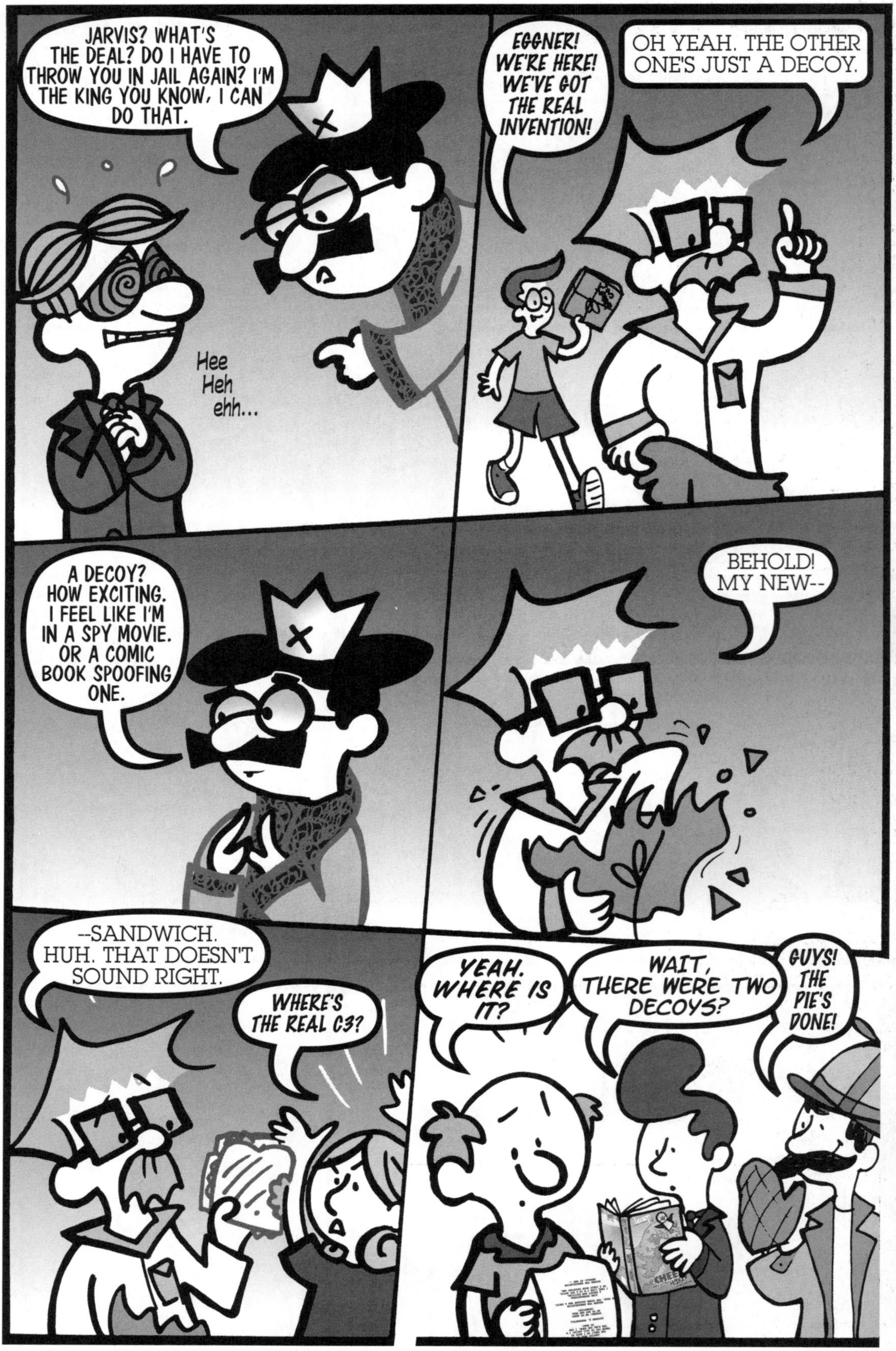
JARVIS? WHAT'S THE DEAL? DO I HAVE TO THROW YOU IN JAIL AGAIN? I'M THE KING YOU KNOW, I CAN DO THAT.
Hee Heh ehh...
EGGNER! WE'RE HERE! WE'VE GOT THE REAL INVENTION!
OH YEAH. THE OTHER ONE'S JUST A DECOY.
A DECOY? HOW EXCITING. I FEEL LIKE I'M IN A SPY MOVIE. OR A COMIC BOOK SPOOFING ONE.
BEHOLD! MY NEW--
--SANDWICH. HUH. THAT DOESN'T SOUND RIGHT.
WHERE'S THE REAL C3?
YEAH. WHERE IS IT?
WAIT, THERE WERE TWO DECOYS?
GUYS! THE PIE'S DONE!

YES. WHERE IS THE REAL C3?

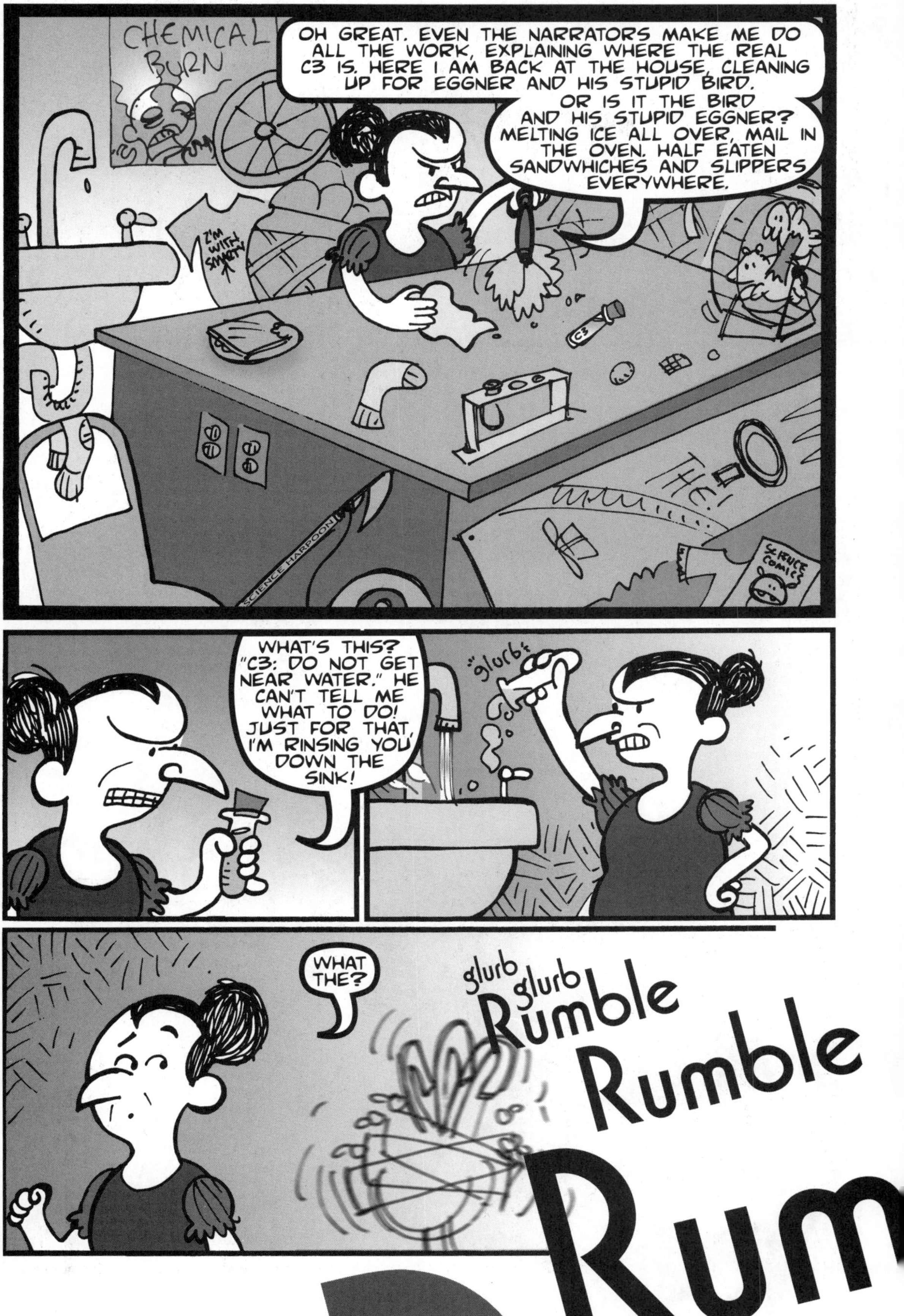
CHEMICAL BURN
OH GREAT. EVEN THE NARRATORS MAKE ME DO ALL THE WORK, EXPLAINING WHERE THE REAL C3 IS. HERE I AM BACK AT THE HOUSE, CLEANING UP FOR EGGNER AND HIS STUPID BIRD.
OR IS IT THE BIRD AND HIS STUPID EGGNER? MELTING ICE ALL OVER, MAIL IN THE OVEN. HALF EATEN SANDWHICHES AND SLIPPERS EVERYWHERE.
I'M WITH SMARTY
C3
SCIENCE HARPOON
SCIENCE COMICS
WHAT'S THIS? "C3: DO NOT GET NEAR WATER." HE CAN'T TELL ME WHAT TO DO! JUST FOR THAT, I'M RINSING YOU DOWN THE SINK!
glurb
WHAT THE?
glurb glurb
Rumble
Rumble
Rum

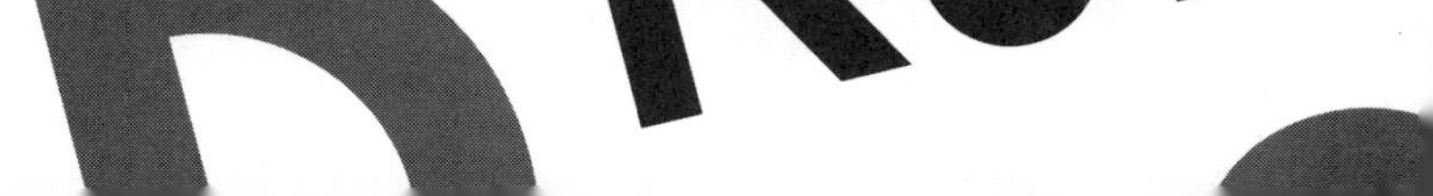
R

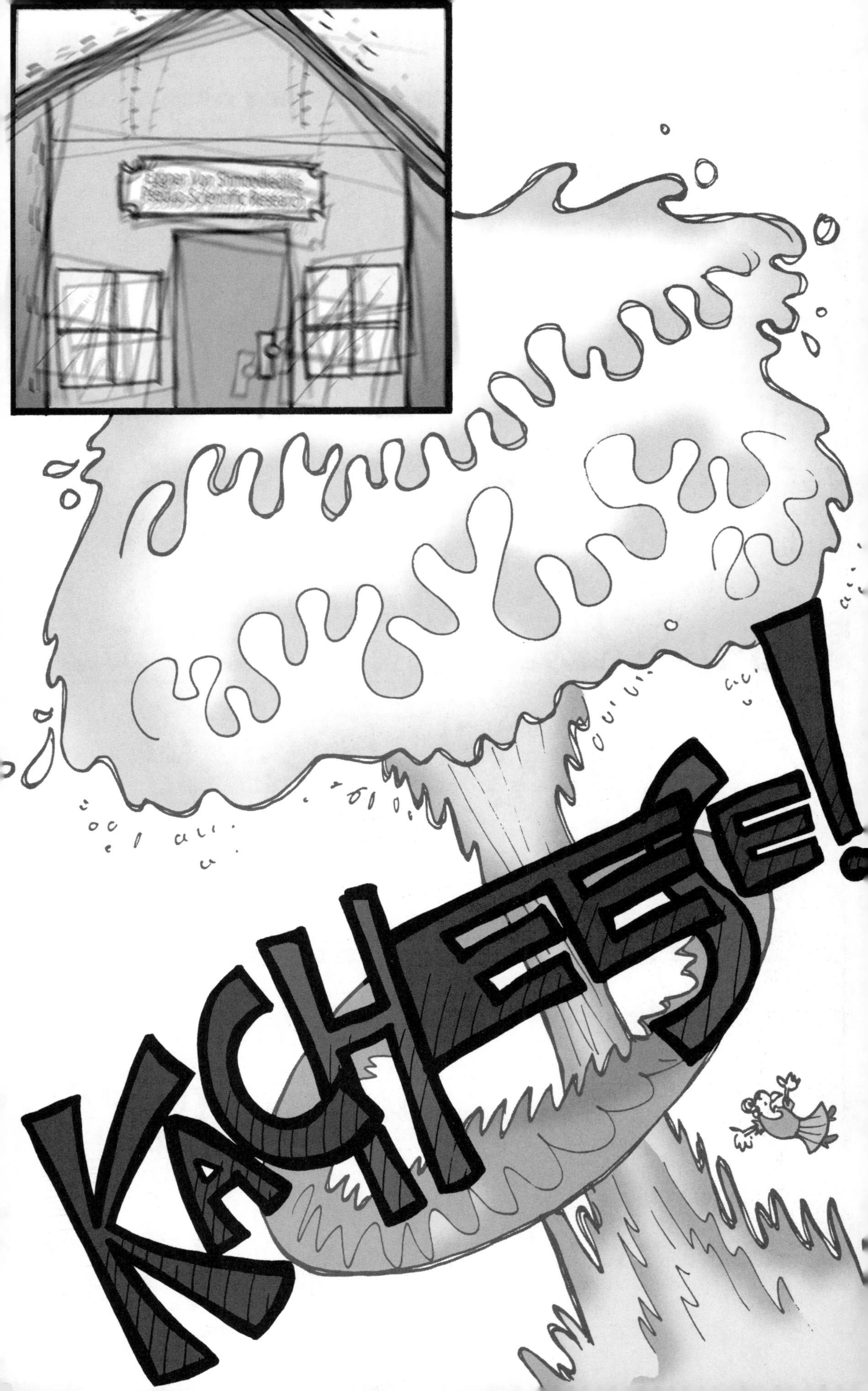
KACHEESE!

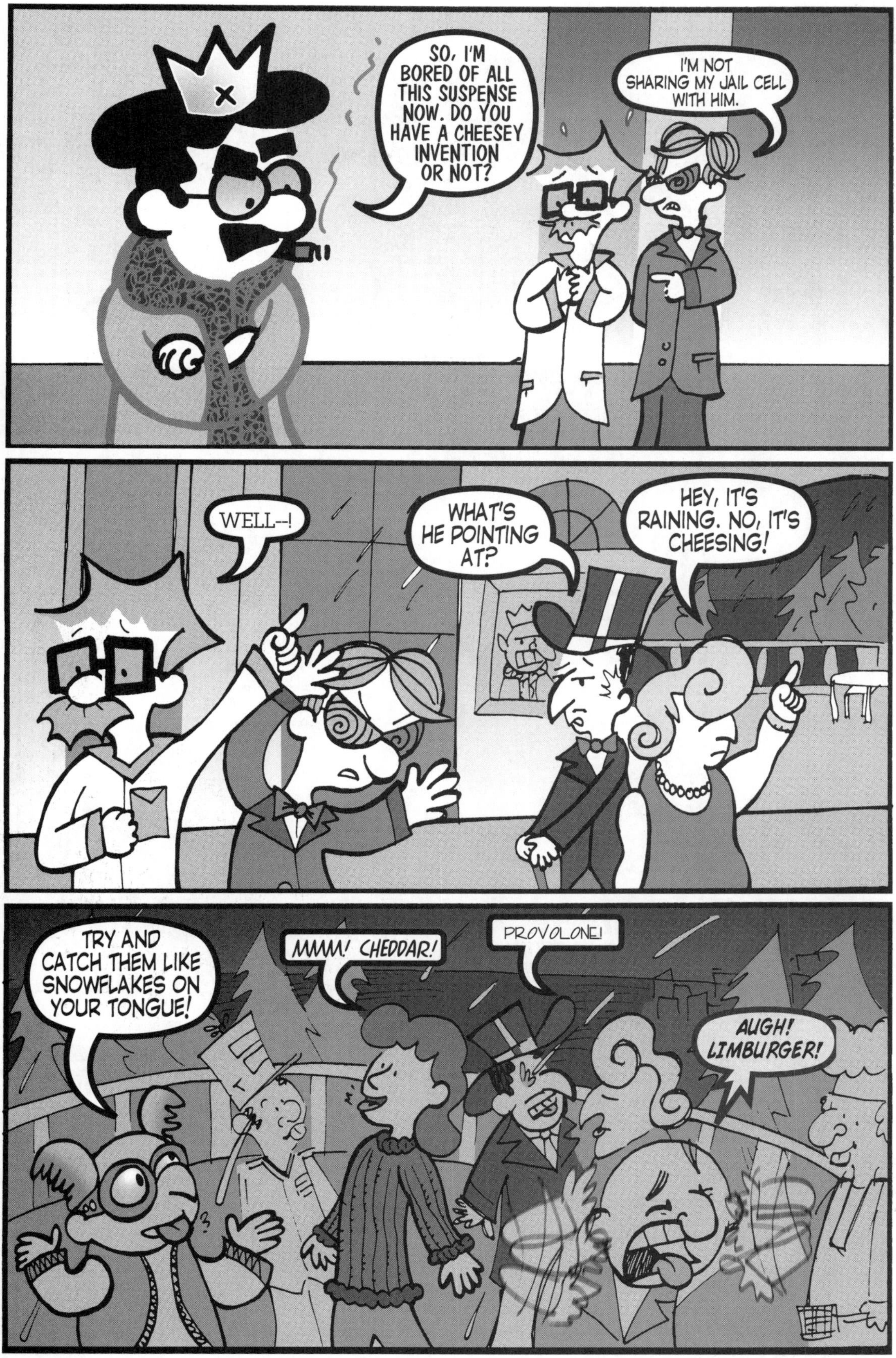
SO, I'M BORED OF ALL THIS SUSPENSE NOW. DO YOU HAVE A CHEESEY INVENTION OR NOT?
I'M NOT SHARING MY JAIL CELL WITH HIM.
WELL--!
WHAT'S HE POINTING AT?
HEY, IT'S RAINING. NO, IT'S CHEESING!
TRY AND CATCH THEM LIKE SNOWFLAKES ON YOUR TONGUE!
MMM! CHEDDAR!
PROVOLONE!
AUGH! LIMBURGER!

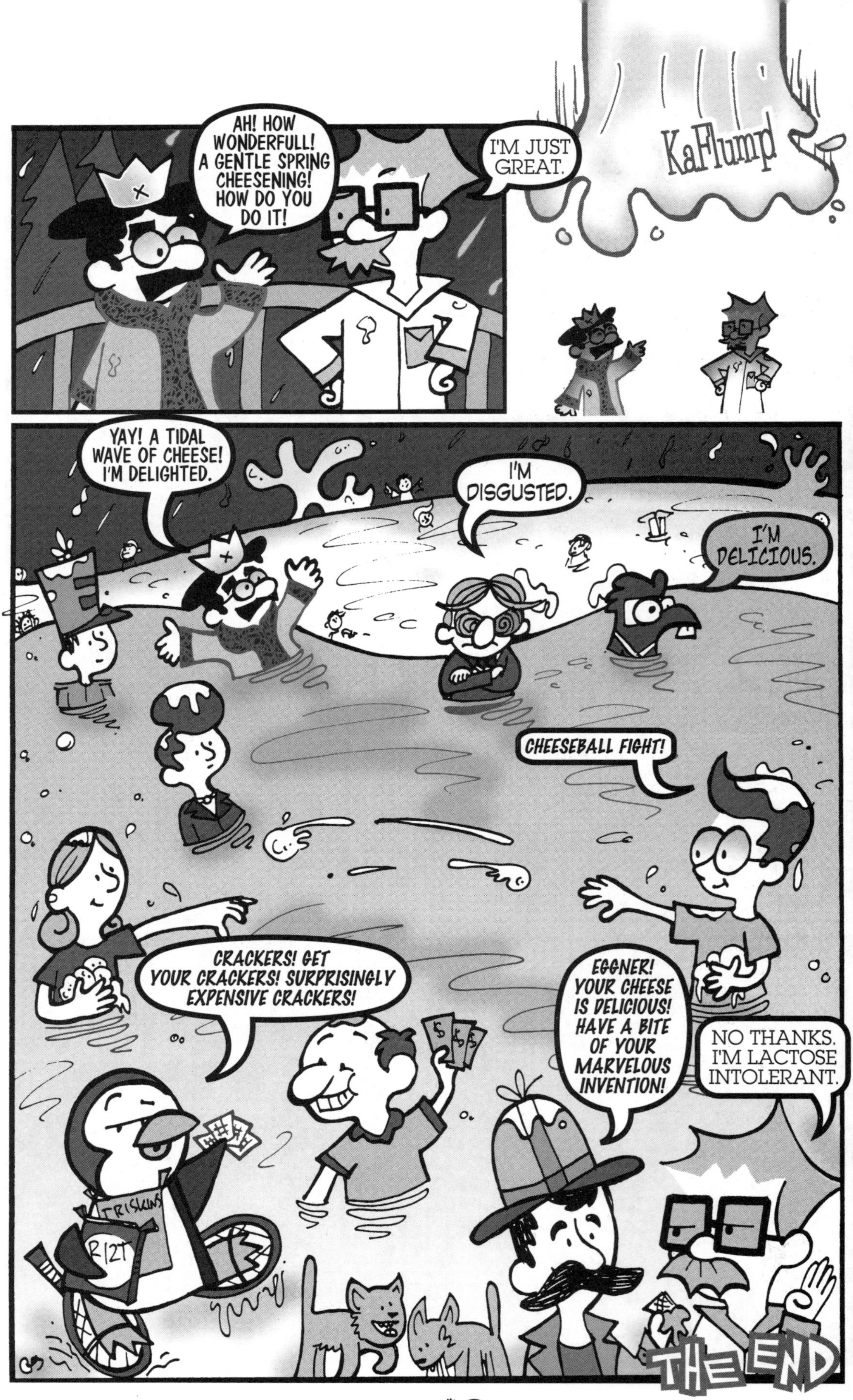
AH! HOW WONDERFULL! A GENTLE SPRING CHEESENING! HOW DO YOU DO IT!
I'M JUST GREAT.
KaFlump
YAY! A TIDAL WAVE OF CHEESE! I'M DELIGHTED.
I'M DISGUSTED.
I'M DELICIOUS.
CHEESEBALL FIGHT!
CRACKERS! GET YOUR CRACKERS! SURPRISINGLY EXPENSIVE CRACKERS!
EGGNER! YOUR CHEESE IS DELICIOUS! HAVE A BITE OF YOUR MARVELOUS INVENTION!
NO THANKS. I'M LACTOSE INTOLERANT.
THE END

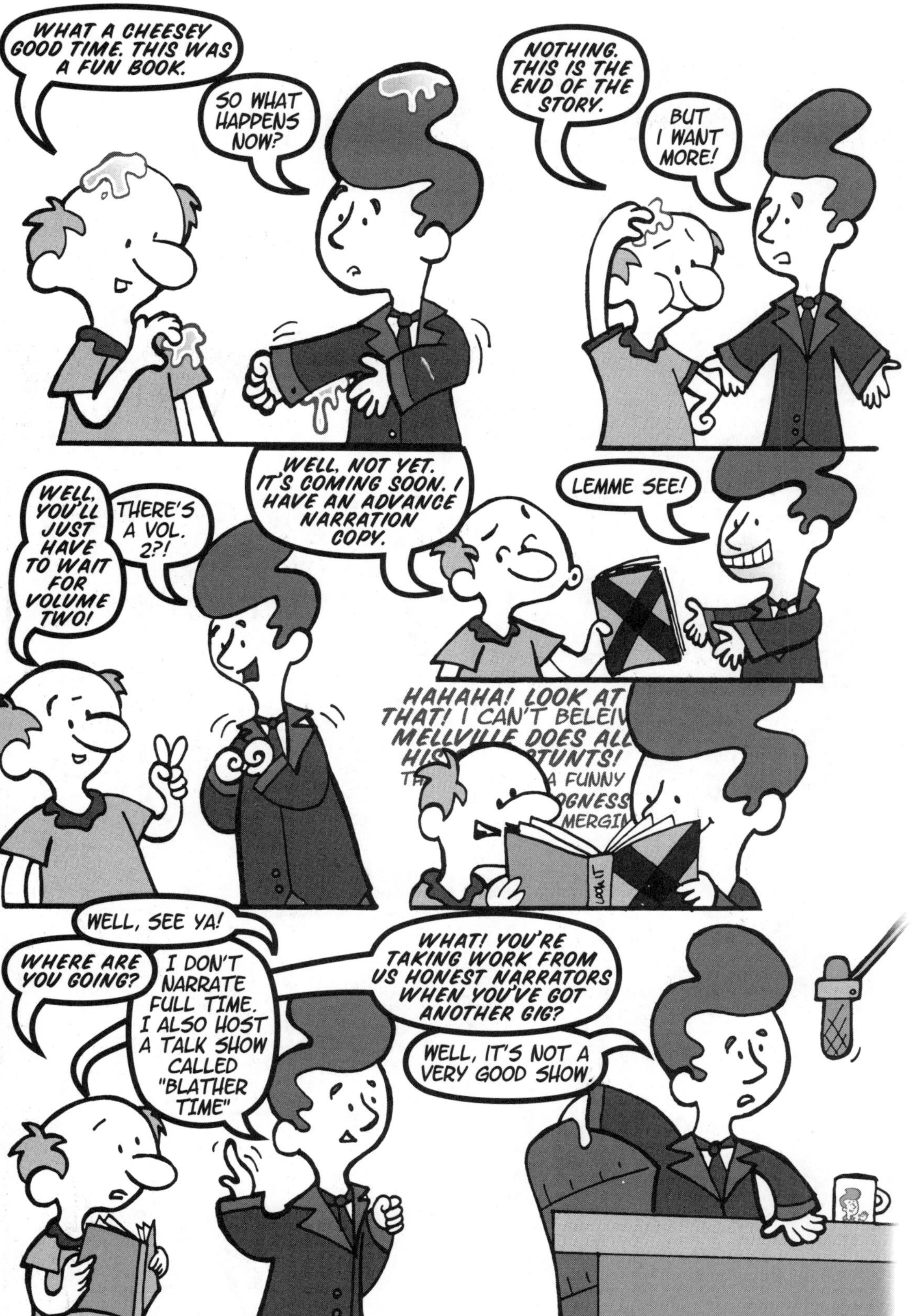

WHAT A CHEESEY GOOD TIME. THIS WAS A FUN BOOK.
SO WHAT HAPPENS NOW?
NOTHING. THIS IS THE END OF THE STORY.
BUT I WANT MORE!
WELL, YOU'LL JUST HAVE TO WAIT FOR VOLUME TWO!
THERE'S A VOL. 2?!
WELL, NOT YET. IT'S COMING SOON. I HAVE AN ADVANCE NARRATION COPY.
LEMME SEE!
HAHAHA! LOOK AT THAT! I CAN'T BELEIV
MELLVILLE DOES ALL
STUNTS!
A FUNNY
OGNESS
MERGIN
LOOK IT
WELL, SEE YA!
WHERE ARE YOU GOING?
I DON'T NARRATE FULL TIME. I ALSO HOST A TALK SHOW CALLED "BLATHER TIME"
WHAT! YOU'RE TAKING WORK FROM US HONEST NARRATORS WHEN YOU'VE GOT ANOTHER GIG?
WELL, IT'S NOT A VERY GOOD SHOW.

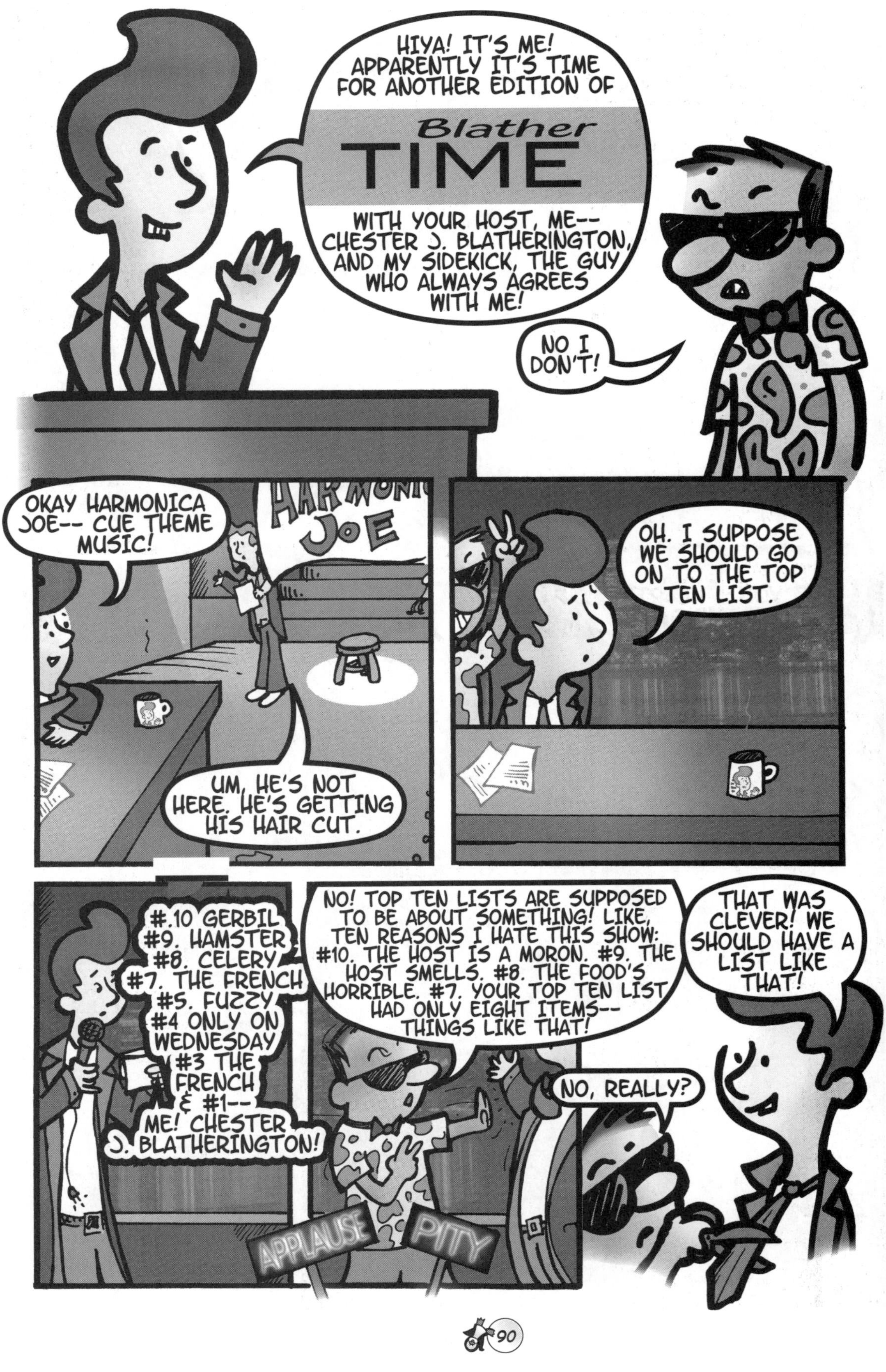
HIYA! IT'S ME! APPARENTLY IT'S TIME FOR ANOTHER EDITION OF
Blather TIME
WITH YOUR HOST, ME-- CHESTER J. BLATHERINGTON, AND MY SIDEKICK, THE GUY WHO ALWAYS AGREES WITH ME!
NO I DON'T!
OKAY HARMONICA JOE-- CUE THEME MUSIC!
HARMONICA JOE
UM, HE'S NOT HERE. HE'S GETTING HIS HAIR CUT.
OH. I SUPPOSE WE SHOULD GO ON TO THE TOP TEN LIST.
#.10 GERBIL #9. HAMSTER #8. CELERY #7. THE FRENCH #5. FUZZY #4 ONLY ON WEDNESDAY #3 THE FRENCH & #1-- ME! CHESTER J. BLATHERINGTON!
NO! TOP TEN LISTS ARE SUPPOSED TO BE ABOUT SOMETHING! LIKE, TEN REASONS I HATE THIS SHOW: #10. THE HOST IS A MORON. #9. THE HOST SMELLS. #8. THE FOOD'S HORRIBLE. #7. YOUR TOP TEN LIST HAD ONLY EIGHT ITEMS-- THINGS LIKE THAT!
APPLAUSE
PITY
THAT WAS CLEVER! WE SHOULD HAVE A LIST LIKE THAT!
NO, REALLY?

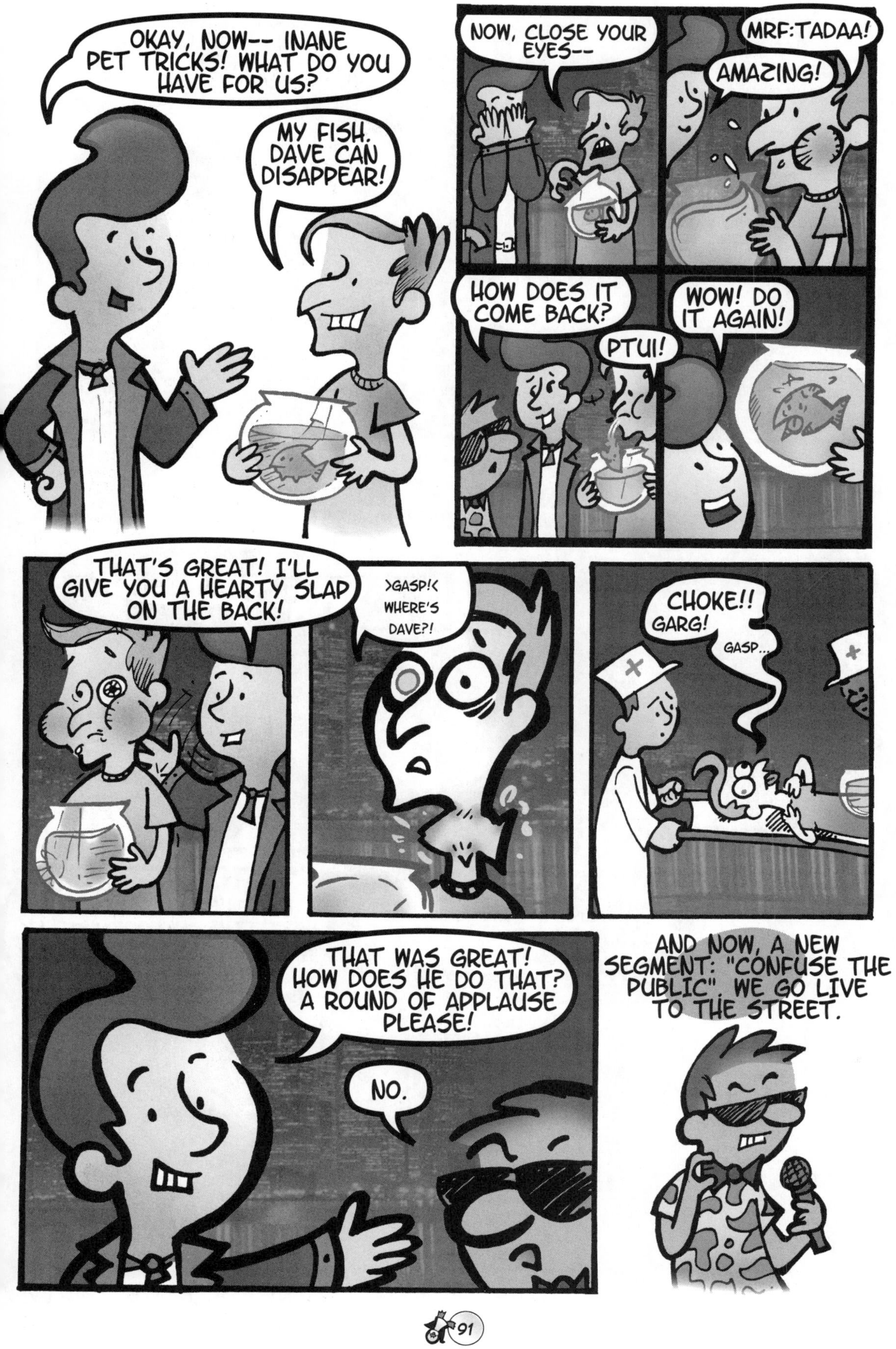
OKAY, NOW-- INANE PET TRICKS! WHAT DO YOU HAVE FOR US?
MY FISH. DAVE CAN DISAPPEAR!
NOW, CLOSE YOUR EYES--
MRF:TADAA!
AMAZING!
HOW DOES IT COME BACK?
PTUI!
WOW! DO IT AGAIN!
THAT'S GREAT! I'LL GIVE YOU A HEARTY SLAP ON THE BACK!
>GASP!< WHERE'S DAVE?!
CHOKE!! GARG!
GASP...
THAT WAS GREAT! HOW DOES HE DO THAT? A ROUND OF APPLAUSE PLEASE!
NO.
AND NOW, A NEW SEGMENT: "CONFUSE THE PUBLIC". WE GO LIVE TO THE STREET.

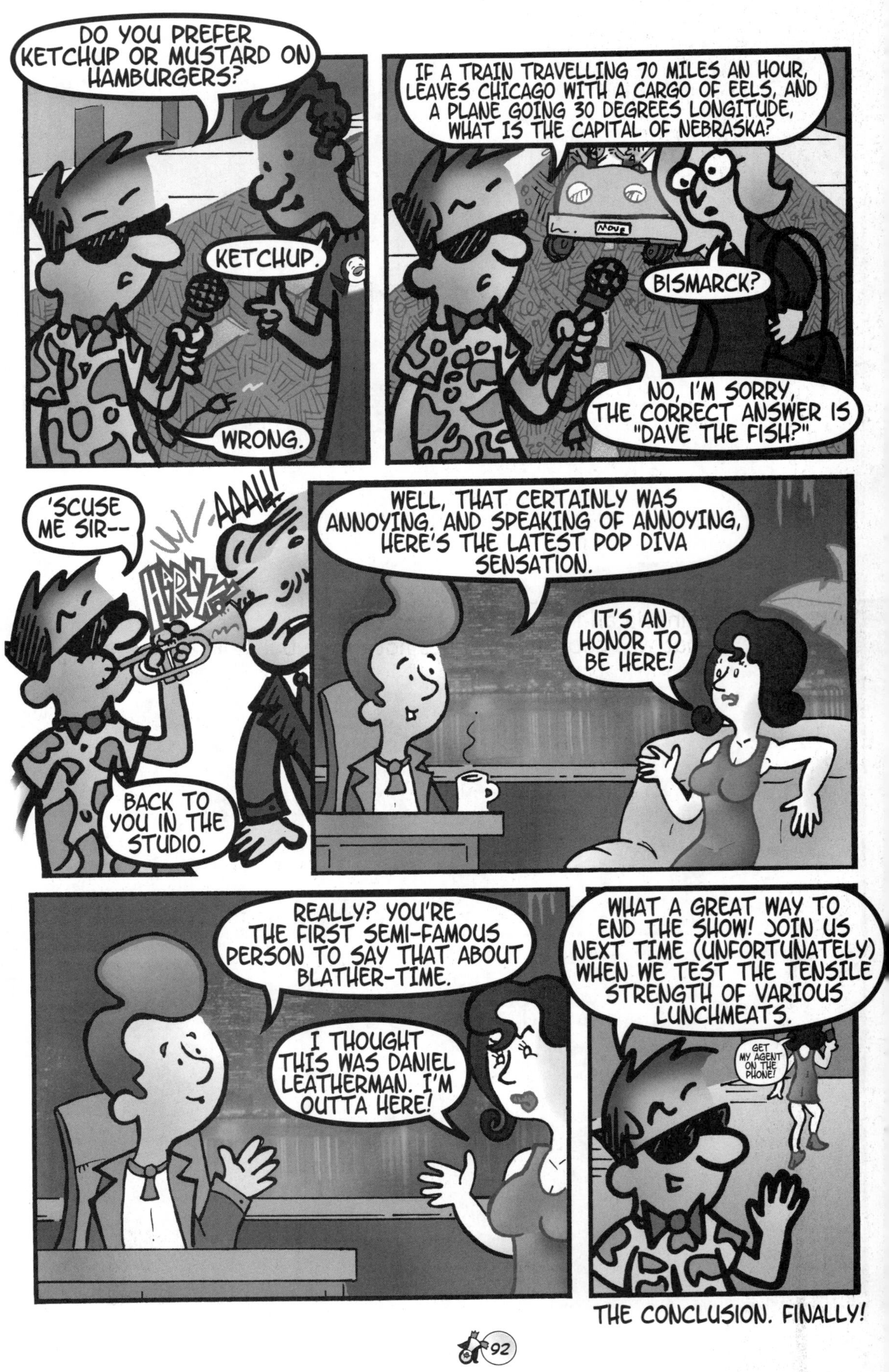
DO YOU PREFER KETCHUP OR MUSTARD ON HAMBURGERS?
KETCHUP.
WRONG.
IF A TRAIN TRAVELLING 70 MILES AN HOUR, LEAVES CHICAGO WITH A CARGO OF EELS, AND A PLANE GOING 30 DEGREES LONGITUDE, WHAT IS THE CAPITAL OF NEBRASKA?
BISMARCK?
NO, I'M SORRY, THE CORRECT ANSWER IS "DAVE THE FISH?"
'SCUSE ME SIR--
AAAH!
BACK TO YOU IN THE STUDIO.
WELL, THAT CERTAINLY WAS ANNOYING. AND SPEAKING OF ANNOYING, HERE'S THE LATEST POP DIVA SENSATION.
IT'S AN HONOR TO BE HERE!
REALLY? YOU'RE THE FIRST SEMI-FAMOUS PERSON TO SAY THAT ABOUT BLATHER-TIME.
I THOUGHT THIS WAS DANIEL LEATHERMAN. I'M OUTTA HERE!
WHAT A GREAT WAY TO END THE SHOW! JOIN US NEXT TIME (UNFORTUNATELY) WHEN WE TEST THE TENSILE STRENGTH OF VARIOUS LUNCHMEATS.
GET MY AGENT ON THE PHONE!

THE CONCLUSION. FINALLY!

Outroduction

You thought I was kidding about the short quiz, huh? Take out your # 2 pencils and let's begin. No cheating.

#1. RQW was named after:
- A. Raymond Q. Wonderfull
- B. Really Questionable Wackiness
- D. Mellville

#2. You know that part in the book where Mellville has amnesia and all those turtles throw him in the volcano? That was cool. Wait, that's not in the book. That's a free story on our website. You should check it out.

#3. True or Not So True: The website where you can see that cool story is www.DontEatAnyBugs.com ?

#4. This really isn't a quiz, is it? More of a shameless plug for the really cool website, www.DontEatAnyBugs.com.

#5. No, this isn't a shameless plug, but the next page is.

#6. Number 5 wasn't really a question, was it?

#7. 2X +53 = 370924.7. Solve for X. Or don't. Whatever.

ANSWERS:
#1. Yes
#2. No
#3. Maybe
#4. 42
#5. I don't know
#6. Yellow

If you got all the answers correct, you've won a free tuna fish sandwich! Send $27 to Po Box 291, Tehachapi, CA 93581 for shipping and or handling.

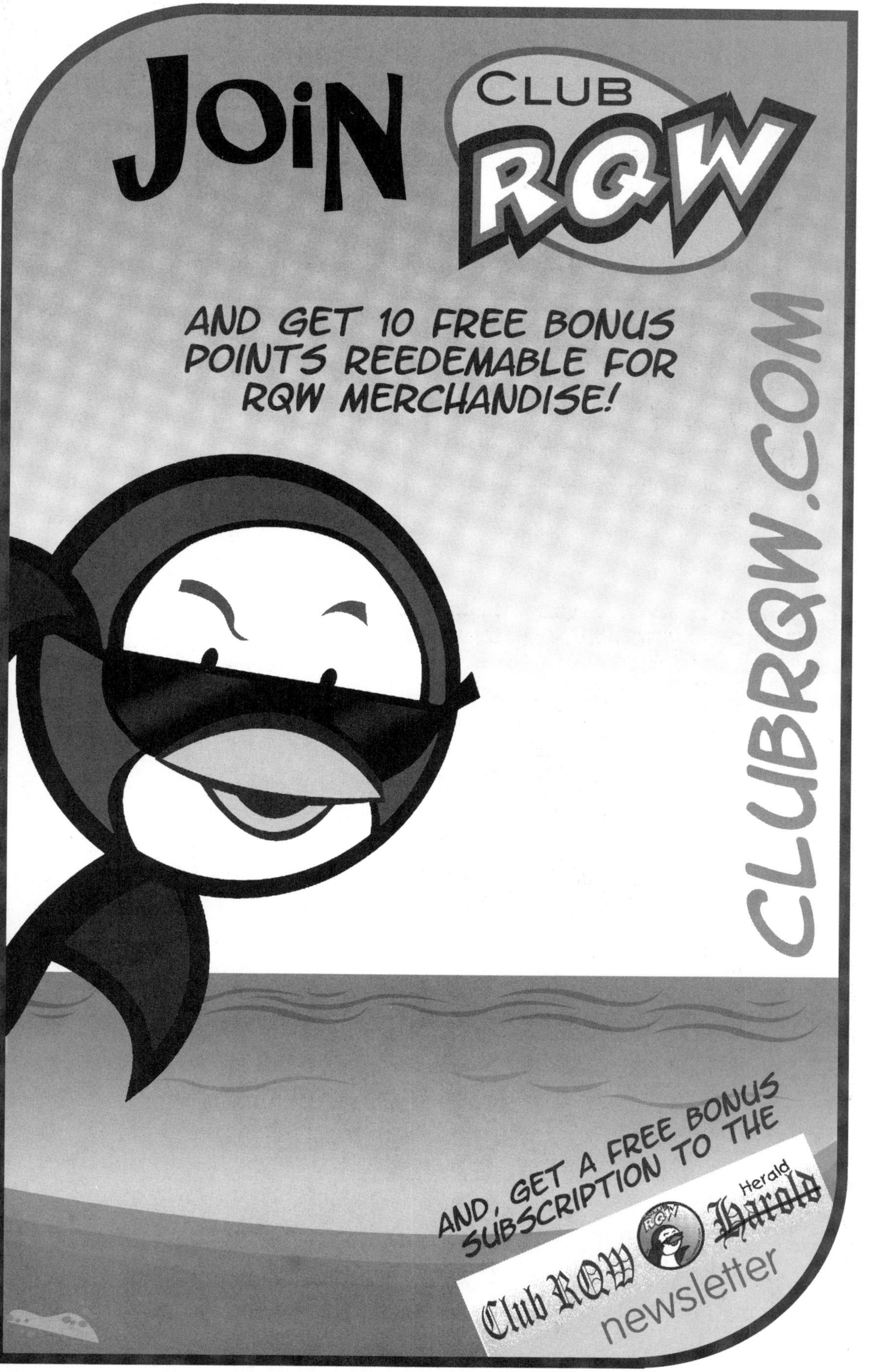
JOIN
CLUB RQW
AND GET 10 FREE BONUS POINTS REEDEMABLE FOR RQW MERCHANDISE!
CLUBRQW.COM
AND, GET A FREE BONUS SUBSCRIPTION TO THE
Club RQW ~~Harold~~ Herald
newsletter

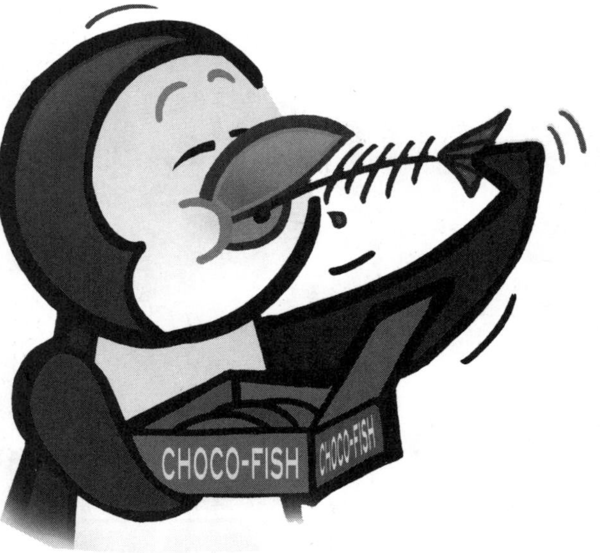
CHOCO-FISH
CHOCO-FISH